YOUNG PEOPLE
READING

Open University Press

English, Language, and Education series

General Editor: Anthony Adams
Lecturer in Education, University of Cambridge

TITLES IN THE SERIES

YOUNG PEOPLE READING
Culture and Response

Charles Sarland

Open University Press
Milton Keynes · Philadelphia

Open University Press
Celtic Court
22 Ballmoor
Buckingham
MK18 1XW

and
1900 Frost Road, Suite 101
Bristol, PA 19007, USA

First Published 1991

British Library Cataloguing-in-Publication Data

Young people reading: Culture and response.
– (English, language, and education series)
 I. Sarland, Charles II. Series
 028.5

 ISBN 0–335–09879–7

Library of Congress Cataloging-in-Publication Data

Sarland, Charles, 1944–
     Young people reading : culture and response / Charles Sarland.
        p.   cm. – (English, language, and education series)
     Includes bibliographical references and index.
     ISBN 0–335–09879–7
     1. Youth–Books and reading.   2. Popular literature–Appreciation.
  3. Fiction–Appreciation. I. Title. II. Series.
  Z1037.A1S24   1991
  0.28.5′5–dc20   91–17908
                                                                CIP

Typeset by Graphicraft Typesetters Ltd., Hong Kong
Printed in Great Britain by St Edmundsbury Press Limited, Bury St Edmunds, Suffolk

Fictions have to match the minds of their readers, and to be written in such a way that, by tempering the impossibilities, moderating excesses, and keeping judgement in the balance, they may so astonish, hold, excite, and entertain, that wonder and pleasure go hand in hand.

(Cervantes, *Don Quixote*: 1950, p. 425)

Yeh, if they read a book it's got something to do with them in it, cause they fit their own ideas to it.

(Year 10 'non-reading' boy)

Contents

General editor's introduction

One of the earliest titles we published in this series was Donald Fry's book, *Children Talk About Books*. In the present volume Charles Sarland acknowledges his own indebtedness to this book. In many ways his own book is a further contribution to an area of scholarship that is still insufficiently explored. In spite of much recent work in the area of reader-response approaches to literature, there are still too few studies which look directly at what young readers themselves make of the books they read, especially when these occupy the area of voluntary reading, perhaps not explicitly sanctioned by the world of school. One important common element in the work of both Fry and Sarland is their ability to get young people talking and to demonstrate their sympathetic response to what they have to say about the books they are reading. Too often, in other work of this kind, our information about school student responses is based upon their written accounts and this inevitably introduces an extra dimension through which their responses have to be filtered.

Sarland's concern is with a whole area of reading which is generally much neglected in school. There will still be few schools where the reading of James Herbert is sanctioned by the English Department. Yet in his study here of student responses to *The Fog*, or to such other works as *First Blood* and *Carrie*, Charles Sarland shows the importance of such popular literature in the experience of the young people he so vividly presents to us. What emerges is a powerful picture of a sub-culture from which many teachers have been excluded, or from which they have excluded themselves. I have recently been working with an English teacher from further education and he has opened my eyes to the all-pervasive influence of the work of Virginia Andrews in the experience of many of the students that he teaches. From my work with him and my reading of Charles Sarland's work, I now look at railway station book stalls in a quite different light. I had read some James Herbert earlier but many of the other works that Sarland discusses were new to me before I read the manuscript of the present volume.

This seems to me indicative of the position of many English teachers, including myself, in our lack of awareness of many aspects of popular culture, especially popular literature. The research on which Sarland's book is based provides ample evidence for the existence of such a culture and for the subtlety of the responses of many young people to what it provides in their experience. There are many fascinating insights here as seen, for example, in the very different reactions of male and female readers to *The Fog*.

Predominant in this book is the question of 'voice'. Almost all of the authors discussed have their own very clearly identifiable authorial voice (undoubtedly one reason for their popularity); so, too, do the school students that Sarland interviewed and whose voices he records in his written text with considerable skill. The other voice is Sarland's own. He discusses in some detail the problems involved in the transformation of thesis into a book – something of which the editor of a series such as this is necessarily well aware. In this book we hear Charles Sarland's own voice responding to the texts, engaging in a dialogue, alongside those of the young people whose culture is the major concern of the work.

In order to enable his analysis of this culture Sarland draws upon an eclectic range of theoretical work ranging from sociology to literary criticism. Indeed, one of the major theoretical contributions of the book is the way in which it builds bridges between different disciplines, some of which may be less than familiar to many teachers of English. It is an area that has been charted earlier by the work of such key figures as Richard Hoggart and Raymond Williams but which has been, as yet, too little explored at classroom level. In his own contribution, in the present volume, to contemporary cultural studies Charles Sarland enlarges our horizons and expands our awareness of the literature that can, and should, find a place in our classrooms.

Anthony Adams

Preface

If this book has a direct precursor it is surely Donald Fry's *Children Talk About Books: Seeing Themselves as Readers*. In that book Fry looks at 'response' from the perspective of the children themselves. He devotes a large amount of space and time to their perspectives, and he is thus led to discuss popular material, notably Enid Blyton and James Herbert. For Fry, reading development is not some step-by-step progress through progressive mastery of mechanical skills. Rather it is a process of taking experience of the world, as well as knowledge and expectations about how stories work, and finding a book that offers enough promise of emotional satisfaction in the light of those expectations and that experience to make it worthwhile to persist with reading it. He argues that the delights of fiction that are often claimed only for 'educated' readers reading 'great literature' are actually just as great for kids reading books that are all too often regarded as 'just kids' books'.

Fry keyed into two of my major concerns. I, too, doubted that reading development was some step-by-step mastery of technical skills, and I, too, was convinced that the emotional satisfaction that children and young people gained from reading material that was not highly regarded was none the less just as 'genuine' as that supposedly offered to the few by 'literature'. My interests had dated from 1974, when I was lucky enough to take a course on children's literature that was run by Aidan Chambers. He impressed on me, then, the importance of taking seriously the literature that was read by children, and of recognizing that any consideration of that literature had to take into account the particular nature of its readers. As he wrote in 1980:

> We need a critical method which will take account of the child-as-reader; which
> will include him rather that exclude him; which will help us to understand a book
> better and to discover the reader it seeks. We need a critical method which will tell
> us about the reader in the book.
>
> (p. 215)

The idea of a critical method that allowed analysis of books in such a way as to take account of their readership became increasingly important for me, and later, when I was equally fortunate in becoming a student of Margaret Spencer/ Meek's, she confirmed such perspectives. This is what she wrote, also in 1980:

> We have reached the point where we must look at the prospects for research into a literary theory that can encompass literature written with children as part of the acknowledged audience, so that developmental considerations can be included, so that judgements relevant to adult literature need not be excluded, and the historical progression can be enlightening.
>
> (Meek 1980, p. 30)

and here, in 1987, she calls for an academic study of children's literature that takes into account

> culture, history, language, literature, psychology, sociology ... to say nothing of the children's and the teacher's reading autobiographies ...
>
> (Meek 1987, p. 106)

I take very seriously her injunction that if we are to understand what happens when children read, then we have to raid all the relevant theory about how fiction works, and all the relevant research about how children work. That is what I have tried to do in writing this book.

The following symbols are used in transcriptions of interviews throughout the text:

* * * Transcript omitted because of asides or repetitions that obscure the argument.

– – – Tape indecipherable.

(??) Transcript uncertain.

... Speaker trails off or is interrupted.

Acknowledgements

I must offer thanks to the head, teachers and pupils of 'Hill Hall' comprehensive school, specifically the following – whom I have to represent in their aliases, but they will, I hope, recognize themselves should they come to read this book. So, from year 7 (though they thought of themselves as first year), Victoria, Lakshmi, Donna (who left half-way through), Paul, Dave, Wayne, Lena, Louisa, Judy, Alan, Barry, Henry, Anthony, Belinda, Cleo and Angel; and from year 10 (who thought of themselves as fourth year), Tricia, Caroline, Pippa, Roland, Kenneth, Peter, Carole, Nina, Iris, Mary, Tracey, Deborah, Rosie, Ken, Nemesh, Jagdish, Sara, Tina, Carol, Ted, Gavin, Damon, Jenny, Toni, Eleanor, John, Tony, Terry and Matthew. This is their work, and without them it would never have happened. I also need particularly to thank the three teachers who gave me continuous support throughout the project, Jane Frenbridge, Paul Whitemarsh and Gail Rodes. They allowed their classes to be disrupted, they reorganized their curriculum, and generally lent their support in innumerable ways, and I shall always be grateful to them.

Some of the material in this book has appeared in other forms in 'Pearl of Wisdom, or How the Swine Discriminate', *The Cambridge Journal of Education*, vol. 15, no. 2 (1985), pp. 92–7; and in 'Re-reading Pulp: Seeing the Response Through the Fog', *English in Education*, vol. 22, no. 2 (1988), pp. 42–53.

1 Setting the frame

Introductory

Educational research is problematic from a number of perspectives. Governments suspect it, the academic world looks askance at it, it is seen to be 'inadequately theorized'. Teachers, we are told, are notoriously dismissive of it as irrelevant. Education is under the same attack as the other human 'soft' sciences, unsure whether it is even a science at all. Lacking a substantial theoretical history of its own it has to draw upon neighbouring theoretical fields – sociology, psychology, economics, history, politics, linguistics, and so on – and, like those disciplines, when under attack it tends to revert to the measurable in order sustain its credibility with a few incontrovertible statistical facts. This book has few 'facts' of that sort. It has, rather, a considerable amount of data and a considerable amount of analysis. That analysis does not occur in a vacuum, and in this first chapter I explore some of the frames within which it occurs.

In the first place I shall outline some of the factors that led to the inception of the book. Then I shall take some of the evidence I gathered in the pilot study about why teachers chose to read or study the books they did with classes, and analyse it in a particular way. Then I shall attempt to analyse the researcher, i.e. myself, in the same way. This is particularly necessary, it seems to me, since so much of my data was gathered in free-flowing interview discussion. If I offer an analysis of my self, the reader can at least make some allowance for that self in deciding for herself or himself how to read this book.

A note about terms

You will rapidly become aware of a certain shiftiness on my part about the term 'literature' and a tendency to use terms such as 'narrative fictions'. 'Literature', of course, is a highly problematic term, carrying with it connotations of the good and the true. For that reason I tend to avoid it, only using it in such combinations as 'popular literature' where my usage will, I hope, conform to the general. Otherwise I tend to use terms like 'story', 'book', 'fiction' somewhat interchangeably as seems appropriate at the time.

My use of the word 'culture' will also seem loose to some, as I talk of 'girls culture', 'male culture', 'adolescent culture' and so on. Others may enter into the debate about whether what I am referring to is a culture, a sub-culture, or whatever. What I am concerned with is the making of meaning and value, the sharing of knowledge, opinion and prejudice, and the delineation of a shared emotional response to the world and its artefacts. It is this that I assume culture to be and I shall use the word as and when seems appropriate. When others use it differently I shall indicate the fact.

General beginnings

Seeing fish: A river passes by the end of what used to be our garden before we moved – one of those sluggish Fenland rivers whose flow is directed by the artificial banks that have been constructed over the years to protect the surrounding agricultural land from flooding, and whose pace is controlled by recently automated sluice gates, presumably for the same purpose. The river, for me, was a facility for recreational walking, an economic history to speculate upon, a geography to wonder about, a place for bird life, an enjoyment of boating. When I looked at the water I saw ripples, or weed, or reflections of trees and cows, or the play of the wind, or ducks and moorhens. My next door neighbour, however, fished, and when he looked at the river he saw fish. Occasionally he tried to teach me to see fish. He would point to a brownish colouration, that I had taken for an effect of the light, and say, 'Look at that lovely chub!' – or he would indicate an angularity and exclaim, 'See that pike sitting on the bottom there, dead still he is!'

... and I began to learn to look differently.

Firstly

Books, like rivers, have histories, and the one that you are reading is no exception. So let me say, to start with, that it is a report on an investigation that has its roots in my experience as a middle school English teacher in the late 1970s and early 1980s. As such, and in line with the Bullock Report (DES 1975), I then had a belief in the educative role of 'good literature', and, with younger pupils, of 'good' children's literature. I worked in a school that moved from being a mixed-ability school to being a streamed school, and I became interested in the fact that books like Nina Bawden's *Carrie's War* that had always been successful with mixed-ability classes were not successful with lower streams, though they remained successful with top-stream classes. A mundane enough experience in all conscience, to which the standard response was then, and still is, that less able classes obviously couldn't manage the texts that more able classes could. Suspicious as I was, even then, of explanations of 'ability', such an explanation in any case failed to explain why those same 'less able' children could manage the texts that the 'more able' children could when both lots of children were mixed up in one class.

At around the same time a top-stream 12-year-old boy offered me James Herbert's *The Fog* to read. It would be accurate to say that I was appalled by the book (though not by the fact that a 12-year-old was reading it, given that such a book existed). I thought it was exploitative and degrading, that it was 'trash'. I was also totally gripped by it and read it from cover to cover at a sitting! Somewhat later, another boy, a middle-stream 13-year-old, who by all accounts had not voluntarily read a single piece of fiction since he was nine, picked up *The Rats*, James Herbert again, and read it with considerable enjoyment. When I last spoke to him he was looking for more. So I was left with some questions. What was it about the work of popular authors like Herbert, or at a younger age, Blyton and Dahl, that could unite young readers across the ability levels where more 'respectable' authors of supposedly greater literary worth succeeded in dividing them? And what was the nature of 'reading development' when a child who had not read fiction for four crucial years could pick up and enthusiastically read a 188-page adult novel of some considerable narrative complexity?

At this point I was fortunate enough to have the opportunity to explore some of these issues in an MA thesis, doubtless even now lurking unread in the bowels of the Institute library in London (Sarland 1982a). (And it needs to be said, in parenthesis, that such an opportunity for wider reflection should be the right of all teachers, not just the lucky few, and it further needs to be said that the education of our children would benefit enormously from such reflection. It is a measure of the political threat that such wider reflection would pose that it does not happen.)

That said, in my own case it was the reading that I was enabled to do in structuralism and semiotics that started to open up new ways of reading texts that, in turn, offered the promise of some explanations of what I had observed. I was particularly interested in Roland Barthes' suggestion in *S/Z* that texts generated meaning in terms of five codes that ran through them, and my initial investigations demonstrated, in a somewhat mechanical way, that all those codes could be seen in operation when some 12- and 13-year-olds read and responded to fiction by such authors as Enid Blyton and Nina Bawden. It rapidly became clear to me, however, that the investigation of the mechanical operation of codes was not going to be a sufficient explanation of response, and that it was necessary to proceed with a wider cultural investigation. This book is that investigation.

My subject, then, is fiction, mostly written fiction, but including some video. My subject is also the young people who read that fiction, what they have to say about it, and what they have to say about the world in general in relation to that fiction. My subject is thus also not simply 'response', but that social meaning making which is known as culture. I shall report the findings of my research into the response of the young people to the books that they read and the videos that they watched, but in the chapters that follow you will find that I detail elements of culture of these young people that apparently have nothing whatsoever to do with the books at all. The young people in question were 16 first-years (year 7, 11–12-year-olds) and 30 fourth-years (year 10, 14–15-year-olds)[1] in an 11–16 comprehensive school, Hill Hall, in a large town in the South East of England that I have characterized with startling unoriginality as 'Bigton'.

Secondly

I also need to say that this book appears in a series devoted to 'English, Language, and Education', and at a time when the National Curriculum is just beginning to bite in our schools. As such it willl be looking to find particular audiences who will, incidentally, be in the throes of educational change that is not of their making. The thesis that I propound may therefore strike some of you as useful, but others may feel impatient. So let me offer both a warning and a promise.

Briefly, I suggest two things:

1 That the nature of what we have hitherto called 'response' is an altogether wider concept than we familiarly imagine. I shall argue that the books are but a part of the wider social meaning making that is culture, hoping thus to reposition 'response' in a wider cultural framework. What I am offering, in other words, is a study of the cultural, ideological and experiential factors in the interaction between young people and fictional texts. The book is in this sense more a study in culture (in the anthropological sense rather than the traditional 'lit. crit.' sense) than a study in response, and I shall offer a series of 'snapshots of culture', a series of vignettes in which cultural meaning making and fiction are interrelated. I am, to pick up the metaphor, attempting to look below the surface ripples of 'response' to see if I can catch the broader movement of the fish of culture.

2 I know that another part of that educational change is the changing role of coursework in the examination years. In the early 1990s in Britian there are already signs of a backlash here, though it seems clear that wider reading is always going to be encouraged. So long as that is the case, teachers are having to find ways of dealing with reviews and responses to popular literature. The other strand of this book will be concerned with ways of approaching such literature to discover what it means and how it means it, and I shall be suggesting that popular literature, both popular children's literature and popular adult literature – pulp horror, romance and so on – can provide just as 'valuable' a reading experience as we have traditionally ascribed to 'quality' fiction.

Thirdly

I also need to say that this report is the product of research done for a doctoral degree. The doctoral thesis tends to have a bad press when it is turned into a book. Ostensibly, the writer has two choices. He or she can leave it as it is, making for some pretty indigestible reading, hence the bad press. Or she or he can disguise its origins. I shall be attempting to do the latter, in the hope that I will make it more readable. But I offer the initial information in order that the reader can place the text immediately in one of its political and historical frameworks, i.e. as a product of an academic hoop-jumping exercise in a British university in the mid-1980s.

This, then, is a brief account of how this book came to be written, and what sort of thing it is. In the next section I want to change the focus completely and look specifically at teachers' ideas about the process of teaching fiction in school.

Teachers' book choice

As well as the main study in one school, the research consisted of a pilot study, in which I visited five schools, and in the course of which I asked teachers about the reasons that underlay their choice of texts to use with children and young people in school. The schools in question were a rural primary school, an urban 9–13 middle school, an urban 13–18 comprehensive school, a 13–18 comprehensive school serving a small market town, and Hill Hall itself. I want to discuss the teachers' comments within a framework drawn from a particular theoretical perspective.

Malcolm Yorke in 1977 examined teachers' objectives in teaching literature. Generally he found that teachers saw literature as fostering understanding, toleration, moral standards, love of the beautiful, and as offering insight into the relationship between humankind and nature. They saw it as relaxing, and yet also cathartic. While he concentrated on teachers of the 9–13 age group he also talked with primary and secondary teachers. Yorke's teachers effectively present a developmental model of children's reading, with enjoyment of reading as the central concern that unites primary, middle and secondary teachers. As the age of the children taught got higher, so other objectives were included. Literature for older pupils should include themes such as death and loss, the understanding of self and society, and should involve considerations of moral concern. Older pupils should be concerned with critical consideration of character, event and theme, and the evaluation of literary merit, and the study of literature should foster the development of awareness of the use of language.

Yorke's work suggests the influence of the Leavisite tradition. In so far as things are changing, and in my investigation in the pilot study I would argue that in the case of the teachers I talked with, they have not changed that far, one of the ways in which that change can be understood is against the background of that Leavisite framework.

The work of Douglas and Dorothy Barnes, with Stephen Clark, in 1984, investigates all aspects of the English curriculum: the 'selection from culture' as they define it. They confirm some of Yorke's findings, particularly the central concern that literature shall be enjoyed, and they also confirm that the purpose of studying literature relates to wider issues of pupils' views of themselves and the world. With many a cautionary word that no teacher exemplifies one version uniquely, they identify five 'versions of English' at 15+:

1 *The cultural tradition*. The exam syllabuses constrict the choice of texts considerably to what might be considered as high culture, or to respectable attempts at it in more modern texts. The teachers in their study never justified the choice of texts in these terms, however, they always rather spoke of finding something suitable for the class.
2 *Personal growth*. Applied particularly to lower sets, this version seeks to change pupils' views of the world by giving them experiences of alternatives by means of personal involvement in literature, though, as they point out, 'many are resistant to any such invasion of their privacy' (Barnes *et al.* 1984, p. 247).
3 *Belles lettres*. This approach eschews the personal involvement of the pupil: literature is treated as a body of knowledge to be written about in answers to examination questions.
4 *Basic skills*. For bottom sets, literature is used only as a source for comprehension exercises, or for relaxation.
5 *Public rationality*. This version moves away from the personal experience of literature to discussion of public issues. Literature may be introduced to examine point of view, bias, style of address, and considerations of audience.

There is nothing in my own pilot study that would essentially contradict the findings of either Malcolm Yorke or of Barnes, Barnes and Clark. However, it will become clear as the book develops that I am particularly interested in the notions of contradiction, of schism, of conflict: notions that are useful in the analysis of some literature, particularly when we are considering young readers. It is to this notion of contradiction that I wish to address myself.

In my own pilot study I asked teachers why they chose the books that they did to use with children. I had no follow-up procedure except to ask them to explain or expand terms if I was not clear what they meant. I took notes rather than taping the interviews. In their discussions with me I was often aware that what they said was contradictory. Like Barnes and his colleagues, I, too, tried to list all their comments, and relate them thematically. I succeeded – I was able to get the teachers' reasons for choosing books to 'fall into' six categories:

1 Practical availability and usefulness of the text.
2 Teachers' personal predilections.
3 Audience directed – texts chosen to appeal to the pupils.
4 Development of the pupil and/or his or her reading.
5 Books chosen because of their quality.
6 Books chosen because they furthered the transmission of high culture.

The objections to such a classification can easily be raised 'quality' and 'high culture' seem to be related. All teaching in school is directed towards children, so in that sense is aware of audience. The notion that reading should develop can imply some sort of high-culture goal. The books that appear on the exam syllabuses or that are to be found in the stock cupboards are also there because of some view about high culture and what ought to be taught.

My own objection to my classification is that it obscures the contradictions that I noticed in the teachers' comments, and it is that element of contradiction that I wish to explore here. In what follows, the evidence I present is impressionistic, and the argument is polemical. I offer it none the less as a starting point, an alternative perspective for further study. I shall examine first contradiction, then cultural capital. To do so I must ask the reader to bear with me in some theoretical discussion, predominantly Marxist in its thrust.

Contradiction

Theory

Marx himself, in a pamphlet on *Historical Materialism* suggests that material change in the economic base is fought out in the ideological superstructure. In other words, economic change is always going to be a battle of one sort and another, with different interests struggling for power. But that battle will also be fought out at an ideological level in such state institutions as education, or the law, or in religion, or in culture itself. At the end of Thatcher's eighties we are undergoing economic change at a pretty rapid rate. Old industries are contracting, new ones starting up. In 1984, when I was actually talking with the young people, the consumer boom was on the horizon, now it is already apparently over. Against such a background, it has been a decade of bitter political fighting between the Tories and the trades unions, with law after law passed restricting union power, and with teachers themselves losing negotiating rights despite their own struggle in the earlier part of the decade. All of which is by way of saying that we live in a changing world, characterized for the most part by struggle. Such struggle, and the contradictions and schisms that are its constituent parts, will be writ both large and small in ideological terms within culture in some form or another. Such is part of my subject.

Althusser in 1971 identifies the education system as the most important 'ideological state apparatus', along with the family, of the present century. He suggests that ideology is manifest in practice, in this case educational practice. He suggests, too, that ideological state apparatuses are the 'site of class struggle' (p. 140). He argues further that individuals have ideas which in one way or another affect their practice and it is in their practice that their ideology will become manifest. The practice of an individual within the ideological state apparatus will be part of ideology and will constitute a contribution to ideology. Individuals are both constituted by and constitutive of ideology. If this is the case, then we may look to individuals to be also sites of struggle, and it is such an analysis that seems useful here.

To move away from the abstraction of that paragraph, and to put it another way, in the next few sections I am going to be characterizing individual teachers, and myself, as contradictory. This does not mean that I think that we are hopelessly incapable of making up our minds. It means rather that teachers find

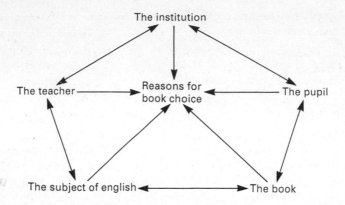

Figure 1   Teachers' reasons for book choice

themselves acting in a social world which is itself full of contradiction and struggle, in which they have to make day by day decisions about the best course of action in the classroom and in the school. Thus they are at one and the same time acting according to the social constraints of the world, and acting upon those social constraints in one way or another – to change them, or to reinforce them, or whatever.

Teachers gave me reasons for choosing books to use in the classroom. I shall be suggesting that these reasons inevitably sit within a conflictual framing, and are inevitably part of a divided culture. Thus, for instance, some of the reasons for a choice of book might be seen to fit in with the administrative convenience of the school, or with the prevailing structures of authority and power, while other reasons for the same choice might be seen as offering pupils opportunities for critical reflection on those same structures of authority, power and administrative convenience.

Framing the choice

The reasons given by teachers for the choice of books to use with children in school can be set, I would argue, within a framework of five elements, shown in Figure 1. Each element offers guidelines and imposes constraints, and some of these will be contradictory. The framework thus places the teacher in a position of conflict of which he or she can be explicitly aware. Alternatively, teachers can seem to be less aware of the conflict, but none the less make statements which seem to be contradictory, and which can be understood as exemplifying contradictory emphases within the framework.

The institution
The institution places curricular, financial, organizational, and what I might call

socio-political constraints upon the teacher. I will give an example of each category of constraint.

1 *Curricular*. Teachers choose books because, say, they are related to work being done in Humanities, or because they fit in with a primary topic.
2 *Financial*. Most obviously in this category the constraints of the stock cupboard are frequently mentioned.
3 *Organizational*. Books are chosen, for example, because they serialize well in 30-minute chunks.
4 *Socio-political*. In this category books are chosen, for example, because they are on the exam syllabus. Or, to take another example, teachers in secondary schools feel they need to monitor the private reading of their pupils. What is allowed in the classroom or what can be offered in coursework folders is always an issue. In one school, for instance, the national press had got hold of a story about a book of dubious content – it contained swearwords – in the school library. As a result teachers became somewhat cautious about what got into the library.

The teacher
The teachers may choose books in order to fulfil some personal agenda, because they like them, or because they want a change in what they are teaching. This requirement can be openly or covertly in conflict with institutional constraints, teachers being forced to teach books they do not like, for instance, because that is all there is in the stock cupboard.

The pupil
Though the pupil is implicitly the referent of all activity in school, teachers make explicit comments that place the pupil as a central focus. Reading is for the enjoyment, the pleasure, of the pupil. Sometimes books are read to a class because the children have requested them; one primary teacher, for instance, had read Blyton to her class on that basis, a requirement that is for her in conflict with her personal enjoyment. Alternatively, books are chosen because they are deemed to be suitable for the age/ability range of the class. A different view of the pupil is expressed by teachers who want to stretch them, to develop their language, to broaden their experience, to make them think more deeply. As one teacher put it: 'Jane Austen is good for their souls.' Such a view might be seen as in conflict with: 'The teacher has to convince the punters, Dickens won't do that,' – those two comments came from the same English department in a comprehensive school.

It will be seen that as children move from school to school, or even from teacher to teacher, they will find conflicting views of what it is they are supposed to get from books. Furthermore, teachers can emphasize the importance of the child perspective at the same time as recognizing the institutional constraints or at the same time as insisting upon their personal preferences as teachers. Thus the teacher who thought Jane Austen was good for the pupils also wanted to tackle *Pride and Prejudice* because he wanted a personal challenge; while the teacher who recognized the need to please the punters also wanted to exclude pulp horror and romance from his classroom. The teacher in the main study, Gail Rodes, who read John Steinbeck's *The Pearl* with her year 10 middle-stream class, recognized that it was not liked, but was forced to use it because it was all that there was in the stock cupboard that was suitable for the ability range – suitability, availability and enjoyment all in conflict.

Within the enculturation process of the child's engagement with fiction in school we already see some of the elements of conflict outlined by Althusser above. The children can find that their perspectives are variously recognized and denied; the teachers can find that their aims are variously furthered or thwarted. And I am further suggesting that these conflictual aims will be found *within* the practice of individual teachers.

The discussion of the book and the subject of English is predicated upon some analysis of the notion of cultural capital, and is therefore reserved until the end of the next section.

Cultural capital

In a major international survey undertaken by Purves in 1973, he suggested that the literature taught in the schools in all the countries surveyed was drawn from the elite culture. We need, here, to explore questions of elitism. It is Q. D. Leavis in 1932 in *Fiction and the Reading Public* who traces the historical development from what she sees to be a unitary culture where the masses had their tastes dictated 'from above' (p. 78) to a culture divided between the highbrow, the middlebrow and the lowbrow of the time in which she was writing. In Elizabethan times, she argues, Shakespeare wrote for all; by the 1920s a small number of authors wrote for a small educated elite. She laments the decline of popular taste, as do many more recent writers, Richard Hoggart in 1957, Ken Worpole in 1984 and Robert Leeson in 1985 among them. She calls for the 'training of a picked few who would go out into the world equipped for the work of forming and organising a conscious minority [to perform] educational work in schools and universities' (p. 214).

English teachers will be familiar with this missionary tradition, inherited from Arnold and pursued by the Leavises. T. S. Eliot in 1948 also explicitly argues for the place of a cultural elite in a civilized society whose function is to enrich the cultural life, at all levels, of the whole society. The education system should be organized, Eliot suggests, in such a way that the minority elite culture can be sustained.

As Margaret Mathieson points out in *The Preachers of Culture*, the claim that the elite culture constitutes a central strand of a liberal humanist education, and the subsequent promotion of that elite culture, has influenced the teaching of English for the whole of this century. The Bullock Report (DES 1975, p. 124), for instance, quotes the Newsom Report: 'all pupils, including those of very limited attainments, need the civilising experience of contact with great literature and can respond to its universality'.

In *Bluebeard's Castle* George Steiner raises objections to Eliot's work and the Arnoldian tradition which promotes the civilizing influence of culture, by reminding us that the perpetrators of some of the worst horrors of the Second World War were also men of culture. But Steiner shares Eliot's pessimism about the decline of culture, and for an alternative perspective that attempts to explain the function of this devotion to high culture, and its persistence in the exam syllabus and the English curriculum, it is necessary to go elsewhere.

It is Gramsci in his *Prison Notebooks* who suggests that the creation of an intellectual elite, who regard themselves as an autonomous group within society, acts hegemonically in the interests of the state. The role of the school is central in the creation of the intellectual elite. Each aspect of social life needs its own intellectuals, and some will be more valued than others. For schooling itself, Bourdieu argues in 1973, the intellectual elite is enshrined in the academic institution. The intellectuals in the academic institutions do not wield power directly, he suggests, nor are they so highly rewarded as those who do, i.e. the heads of industry and commerce. But they are necessary to the state because of the hegemonic function that Gramsci has suggested they fulfil. They are therefore granted a degree of autonomy and are able to generate their own alternative systems of symbolic capital that will then have a real exchange value in the academic marketplace. Central here is the notion of *cultural capital.* Certain selections are made from the culture and awarded cultural value. Acquisition of cultural capital gains the bearer access to the academic marketplace. The family, Bourdieu suggests, is the main agent of transmission of cultural capital. The school and the academic institution act as the main agents that determine the exchange value of the cultural capital in the academic marketplace.

Cultural capital may be gained by the mastery of codes deemed to be necessary for the appropriation of the work of art, Bourdieu argues. This mastery is granted to the few in specially designed institutions of higher education, in our case university English departments, access to which is controlled, through the exam system, by the universities themselves. Central are questions of moral value. Decipherment of the codes depends in part upon recognizing and sharing moral values, and access will only be allowed to those who have been enculturated into sharing such values. The codes themselves tend to remain implicit. If the codes become explicit, Bourdieu argues, then too many will be able to gain access to the cultural capital and it will lose its value.

My account of Bourdieu's work may seem somewhat reductive, and he perhaps more clearly refers to the French situation, but it seems to have application to Leavisite practice, and thus throws light on the major influence on the teaching of literature in our schools up to the present day. What it does not describe, however, is the complexity, the contradictoriness even, of the views of the teachers that I talked with, and the ways in which, on the one hand, some of their views could be seen as supporting the value system that validated the cultural capital, and thus the prevailing hegemony, and, on the other, some of their views could be seen as undermining it. Indeed, most of the teachers I talked with would have been highly indignant at the implied suggestion that they were merely cogs in the hegemonic wheel, operating to select that small minority worthy of purchasing a share in the cultural capital.

Giroux, in *Ideology, Culture, and the Process of Schooling*, suggests that because the intellectual establishment has to be given relative autonomy by the state, there is therefore room within that establishment for counter-hegemonic initiatives. He insists upon the possibility of radical intervention in the world, based on critical analysis and reflection. He gives as an example the work of Freire who, Giroux argues, allows people to generate their own meanings through critical reflection upon their own reality, and thus to intervene and act upon that reality in new and radical ways. (For an example have a look at *Pedagogy of the Oppressed* by Paulo Freire himself.)

Within school there can always be an option that allows pupils to reflect critically upon the world. If this happens, so the argument would run, they are then able to intervene critically upon the world when the opportunity arises. The teachers I talked with varied according to how explicit they were about the contradictions in their situation, and varied, too, in the explicitness of their values. None expressed to me the need for *radical* intervention, but they all, to a greater or lesser extent, were hoping to prepare their pupils for a *critical* intervention in the world. When teachers explain that the views of the pupils are important, and choose books that they think the pupils will be able to relate to, then I would suggest that such approaches are designed to act in the interests of the emancipation of the pupils. When those same teachers explain that, despite their views, the availability of texts restricts their choice, I would suggest that such constraints act in limiting the autonomy of pupils.

I should emphasize here that I only asked teachers for their views. I did not, except coincidentally, observe their practice, and that would be essential to sustain my argument with any degree of conviction. But among the reasons for book choice already discussed there are some which would seem to reinforce the prevailing hegemony within society, and within school itself, and some that run counter to it.

We are now in a position to return to the two remaining elements in the analysis I started in the previous section – 'the book' and 'the subject of English'.

The book

The teachers make a number of statements about the quality of the books they choose. Often they use the word 'good' and assume shared values as to what a good book is. Asked to expand, they suggest that the plot is 'good' – 'well constructed', one teacher said – or that the characterization is 'good'. Some teachers suggest that better-quality books can only be done with top streams. Almost all the secondary teachers talk about the need to do 'reasonable' literature. One or two teachers find it difficult to elaborate on questions of quality at all. One said: 'It's just an instinctual reaction.' The difficulty that many teachers have in explaining what 'good' means in relation to books, or in relation to characterization, or to plotting, would seem to bear out Bourdieu's suggestion that the codes of decipherment of the cultural capital often remain implicit.

Some teachers, however, were more explicit. Books with strong themes are chosen, or books with plenty of action and not too much description – these for younger or less able classes. Other teachers take a clear Leavisite line. They are protecting the culture against 'instantaneity and superficiality', against the 'excitement and economy of the video revolution'. They are teaching literature to broaden children's minds, to foster an interest in the arts, to prepare future audiences for the Royal Shakespeare Company, to develop the sensibilities. Popular literature is to be rejected because it is badly written, has a limited vocabulary and is ungrammatical. Again it is possible to see such views in Bourdieu's terms. The arts, the Royal Shakespeare Company, are part of the cultural capital, and access to them through the development of the sensibilities is access by means of learning to share the underlying ground of moral value, as Terry Eagleton has shown in *Criticism and Ideology*. We are now into issues of high culture, and here choices of title, and the relationship of those choices to the canon of great literature, are important.

At Hill Hall, the main study school, the titles on offer from the exam board at 16+ were *Macbeth, The Nun's Priest's Tale, Jane Eyre*, a selection of poems by Wordsworth, Keats, Hopkins, Edward Thomas and Auden, *The Tempest, The Woodlanders* (Hardy), *The Devil's Disciple*, a collection of short stories, and *The History of Mr Polly*. This list is not exceptional, as Barnes and Seed in 1984 confirm. The teacher of the top-stream class had chosen the first four of those. By Frank Kermode's rule of thumb of canonicity – that a confession that one had not read the book in question would be humiliating (!) (*The Genesis of Secrecy*, p. 5) – virtually all those titles are well established in the canon. In other words, they are an established part of the cultural capital.

With younger children the canon of great literature is not directly at issue, but there have been attempts to establish a canon of children's literature. Fred Inglis in 1981 initially lists Carroll, Kipling, Burnett, Ransome, Mayne and Pearce, and later adds recent authors such as Sutcliffe, Peyton, Avery, Lively, Garner, Gardam, Bawden and Aiken. In terms of that list, the texts chosen for younger classes would seem to have a less certain claim.

Two texts stand out in both the pilot and the main studies as the most often read in the primary school, and they are *Charlie and the Chocolate Factory* by Roald Dahl, and *The Lion, the Witch and the Wardrobe* by C. S. Lewis. Despite various attempts to defrock Lewis – by, for instance, David Holbrook in 1973 – he remains of abiding interest, and by Kermode's rule of thumb he would perhaps be in the canon. Dahl is much more controversial: highly regarded when he first emerged on the scene for his inventiveness and use of language, he is now under fire. Among other titles read to classes in the school of the main study were *The Last Battle* by C. S. Lewis, *The Weathermonger* by Peter Dickinson, *Exeter Blitz* by David Rees, *The Silver Sword* by Ian Serraillier, and *Mrs. Frisby and the Rats of NIMH* by Robert C. O'Brien. Margery Fisher in her *Classics for Children and Young People* has canonized the Lewis and the Serraillier, and Dickinson and Rees are both 'taken seriously' as children's authors. If one of the hopes in introducing children to books is that they will grow up to read the adult canon – and such hopes are expressed by many, including Aidan Chambers in both 1973 and 1983, and Fred Inglis in 1981 among others – then the creation of a mini-canon that apes the adult one is germane. Such a mini-canon can then be seen, in Bourdieu's terms, as the training ground for mini-capitalists. But the canon can be fired in more than one direction (to metaphorically double the *n* for a moment), and to consider that possibility I will move to my final element in the framework within which teachers choosing books to use with children find themselves.

The subject of English

John Dixon's report on the Dartmouth Conference, *Growth through English* (1967), established three models of English teaching: the skills model, the cultural transmission model, and the personal growth model. The Bullock Report (DES 1975) linked the last two models together, seeing personal growth as being established through the reading of good literature (i.e. the transmission of the high culture). And we have seen, above, in the study of Douglas Barnes and his colleagues, that these ideas are still alive and well. These divisions emerged again when teachers related their choice of books to wider consider-ations of English studies.

Teachers at all levels talk about using the books to service language skills. Comprehension, vocabulary and grammar are all mentioned. In two of the schools I visited, an explicit language-deficit model was applied to the children, and the reading of books was seen as a vital tool in compensating for that deficit. Reading is for learning, for communication. Such promotion of functional liter-acy has one clear purpose: in the words of HMI (*English from 5 to 16*, 1986, p. 8), to be able to 'Follow a series of written instructions or directions'. But the promotion of literacy, even from a deficit model basis, is also seen by the teachers as the fostering of the ability to 'read critically'.

In contrast to such utilitarian views, teachers also talk about using literature to spark off creative writing by the pupils themselves (i.e. the personal growth model). Such much more clearly counter-hegemonic reasons often sit side by side with utilitarian reasons for choosing books. Teachers of older pupils, even when taking an overtly Leavisite stance, sometimes place that within a political framework. One teacher makes it plain to me that the demands of great literature are needed to fit students for critical appraisal of the demands of a Thatcherite world. Otherwise texts are selected from the canon but with an eye on their accessibility to the pupils, and the opportunities that they will offer pupils for discussion, or for written work.

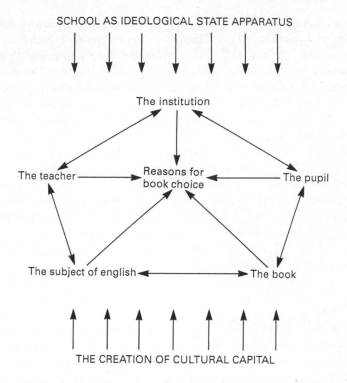

SCHOOL AS IDEOLOGICAL STATE APPARATUS

The institution

The teacher — Reasons for book choice ← The pupil

The subject of english ← → The book

THE CREATION OF CULTURAL CAPITAL

Figure 2   Teachers' reasons for book choice set within political frameworks

Interim conclusion

I have suggested that the reasons that English teachers offer for their choice of books can be set within a framework of five elements. I have suggested that these elements are often in conflict, and that conflict can be seen to be written into the very rationale of the teachers, whether overtly acknowledged or not. I have set that five pointed model within two other related political frameworks: that of the school as an ideological state apparatus, and that of the function of academic English studies as the creation of cultural capital (see Figure 2).

Within those frameworks there are also contradictions and conflicts, and I have tried to suggest that the conflicts within the English framing are also conflicts within the political framings. For instance, I would suggest that those initiatives that teachers take to foster the autonomy and critical reflection of the pupils they teach can be seen as counter-hegemonic within the political framings. But I would also suggest that the various constraints of stock, exam syllabus, utilitarian models of language use, and other elements detailed above, can be seen as promoting the prevailing political hegemony. What I wish to emphasize is that the teachers have all sorts of contradictory impulses, constraints and reasons when it comes to book choice. If teachers are, in Althusser's terms, constituted by and at the same time constitutive of ideology, then it should not be surprising that they exemplify some of the contradictions of that ideology in a changing world. But I would also wish to suggest, along with Giroux and Freire, that teachers are not mindless cogs in a machine, but individuals struggling to make sense of of a complex world, and to do the best by the children they teach.

Framing the researcher

If the teachers are riven by contradiction, what about the researcher? In this section I am going to offer some autobiographical detail in order that the reader may have some idea of where I am coming from. Although I shall present different aspects of my self under the headings of teacher/reader, politics, and interest in narrative, you will, I think, find that these interpenetrate and interweave.

English teacher/reader

Any researcher carries into the field what is sometimes known as a second record: a body of experience and knowledge that inevitably affects the observations and assumptions that he or she makes and the conclusions he or she draws. In my case I have already suggested something of mine in the first part of this chapter. I was a middle school teacher for some 12 or 13 years, but I trained as a secondary teacher, having before that taken a multi-subject degree. English was one of those subjects. The English was Leavisite in assumption – and it was an assumption I heartily embraced. I firmly believed that if only the mass of the population would read English literature then their sensibilities would be suitably trained and the world would be a better place. I always, too, had an interest in children's literature – I loved reading it and have even attempted to write it. I applied all those Leavisite principles to children's literature – and came to admire authors like William Mayne, Phillipa Pearce, Nina Bawden, and from an earlier generation, Nesbit and Ransome. Teaching, as I did for a while, in the independent sector, it was possible to hold such admiration in conjunction with the daily experience of the classroom – even if the match was a little uneasy. In the state sector that uneasy congruence was more penetratingly challenged. In particular, I found it impossible to write off the lower streams as in some sort of way intellectually impoverished simply because they didn't appreciate the richness of Rosemary Sutcliffe or the subtleties of *Tom's Midnight Garden*. At the core of my unease was an inchoate notion that pupils in the lower streams had as much to offer as the more academic. I did not believe there was anything wrong with their language. They seemed just as witty and just as creative as their more academic contemporaries. They seemed just as bright and a good deal more critical than their more academic contemporaries. Furthermore, I believed that they were just as finely discriminatory in their judgements, it was just that they weren't discriminatory in the way that I wanted them to be. It wasn't that they didn't discriminate between Bawden and Blyton: they jolly well did, but they came to the 'wrong' conclusion. Not surprisingly, such views tended to put me at odds with some of my headmasters (they were all male) and fellow professionals.

As I say, all of this was recognized at a fairly inchoate level. I had read no sociolinguists at this stage. I hadn't even heard the term 'deficit model' though as soon as I did I recognized that it informed the rationale offered for streaming, and the pedagogy of the remedial departments with whom I had by and large co-operated. And it was with nothing less than joy that I finally came upon Harold Rosen's vigorous rebuttals of that deficit model, and his related wider insistence upon the political nature of English teaching. As far as the actual texts were concerned, structuralism, semiotics, and the Marxist approaches of critics like Eagleton were a great help in allowing me to deconstruct my own Leavisite views, and led me to ways of reading popular texts that seemed to be helpful when it came to talking about them with children and young people.

It will be seen, then, that my research was not by any stretch of the imagination disinterested. I wanted to explore the ways in which those non-academic pupils did read and, by extension, which texts. I wanted to explore the discriminations that I firmly believed they made, and to see how these might relate to the discriminations more academic pupils made, or that I made myself. In other words, I firmly believed that non-academic pupils had plenty to say, but that very often their views did not count, or that quite simply they were not even given the opportunity to offer them. I wanted to give them a say, too.

But in addition, by pursuing this work as a doctoral thesis, I, too, was buying into the cultural capital. And by teaching, as I now do, in a university department of Education. I, too, am engaged in the transmission of cultural capital – at least in the form of 'educational knowledge', whatever that might be. And I know full well that access to that cultural capital is delimited by our admission procedures. I justify this by saying that the university is *the* place for critical reflection on the world, but I know full well that we all of us critically reflect upon the world in our day-to-day struggle in our work, and in our social lives. So there are contradictions here. I shall pick up on the political ones in the next sub-section. Here let me draw attention to some within my own readings.

I still want to insist upon the 'quality' of what I read. There are some books that give me a great deal of pleasure, but I now know that what I am engaged in is the formation of a club. I want to say to people – as I have been recently – 'Isn't Rumer Godden great?' and I want them to say 'Yeh!' And I know why it is that I am enthusiastic about her work: I know that it is about the dependency of action on character, and also about the coolness and the penetration of her depiction of children. And I know that these are old-fashioned Leavisite virtues. What I have learned is that my pleasure sits within a particular social context: that I come from a class background that aspired to the paternalism of *The*

Diddakoi; that I have a culturally shared sympathy for the plight of the decaying middle class depicted in *Greengage Summer*. All of which is at vigorous odds with my political opposition to paternalism, and my political rejection of any pleas for sympathy from that now decayed middle class.

Rumer Godden is an example from my current reading; and she has led me inevitably to politics despite myself.

Political

When I trained as a teacher there was a shared belief in the values of a liberal education. In his way Leavis was an important figure in the establishment and maintenance of those values in the area of English. But they go wider and have a longer provenance. Indeed, it is often argued that Thatcher's legacy of free-market individualism, and the Tories' promotion of popular capitalism, are but an extension of the Victorian liberal tradition. From the left, which was my position, we, too, justified the social changes we wanted to see in terms of greater individual freedom and autonomy. In the 1960s that liberal assumption of the necessity for individual freedom was the ground of all our debate. Comprehensive schools were espoused because they gave a whole area of society opportunities for self-realization that had previously been denied to it, and mixed-ability teaching had the same rationale. Furthermore, it was good for the classes to mix. All children would learn to be tolerant, and the utopia of an undivided society was a very real light in some of our eyes. We firmly believed that the only real problem with the world was misunderstanding, and the mixed-ability class in the comprehensive school would solve all that. These ideas are not yet dead. They informed the Humanities Curriculum Project in the 1970s, and the later work of Lawrence Stenhouse in promoting action research and the teacher as researcher. In 1988 John Elliott, in his address to the British Educational Research Association conference, insisted that they were needed now more than ever to fight the increasing consumerization of education. They still inform my own teaching of students on a PGCE course. Such values were then, and still are, known as 'educational values'.

So there's me entering the profession, an idealistic young teacher, all bushy-eyed and starry-tailed, believing both in the lovability of kids, and in the profound rationality of the teaching enterprise based upon implicit shared educational values about the value of the individual and the sacredness of his or her learning. I had one wonderful experience for six weeks in ILEA, working in Walworth Comprehensive School with the then English department. They, too, believed that education was a rational enterprise built upon shared values. That experience informed my teaching career. I had seen that education could work, and for ever after I carried that hope that I would be in a situation where it could work again. All in all I worked for seven heads, and two of them more or less did share those values.

However my larger experience ran contrary to that. I discovered that rational argument was limited or even ignored in the decision-making processes of schooling. I found that decisions were made by those in power with little or no reference to the views of staffs, either individually or collectively. I learned that it didn't matter how much evidence there was about the inadequacy of testing, about the effects of labelling, about the advantages of mixed-ability teaching, about the importance of starting from where the child was, about the need for learning to be real learning and not divorced from content in mindless exercises – such evidence was totally ignored. I found myself teaching kids who moved from a mixed-ability class in one term to a semi-remedial bottom stream in the next, and who simply laid down their pens as they discovered what had happened to them. They had no say, their parents had no say, I, their teacher, had no say, I, as head of an English department, had no say. I began to have a more and more sour view of the operation of schools and schooling. I increasingly recognized that educational explanations for decisions were simply inadequate – and that any explanation that made any sense had to be a political explanation: a political explanation in so far as it was to do with the exercise of authority and power within the school, and political in so far as that exercise of authority and power seemed to be directly related to the exercise of authority and power in society at large. Only political explanations helped me to identify whose interests were being served by what was actually happening in school, and only thus was I able to start to formulate some coherent analysis of my experience. The only thing that kept me going was the kids themselves. But I recognized that many of their lives were being violated by the schooling they were experiencing. And I observed my tired and increasingly cynical colleagues and my tired and increasingly cynical self, and recognized that our lives, too, were being violated by our involvement in schools and schooling. I noted that we continuously had our creativity thwarted, that any attempt to contribute to the thinking that informs school policy could be ignored and rejected, and I noted thus how either destructive anger or cynicism is nurtured, or as often as not, one after the other.

The reader will detect some passion, or at the very least some passionate rhetoric, in the previous paragraph. Such passion is often thought of as inappropriate in a book such as this. Instead, it should contain dispassionate analysis written either in an anonymous third person, or by a restrained 'I' who presents the front of detached academic. By choosing, as I have done, to offer some analysis of that 'I' it seems to me only right that some of my passion should be revealed. To continue, then, perhaps somewhat more dispassionately ...

It was only when I came across Althusser's work, discussed above, that at last I had an analysis of how schools operate in a capitalist society that actually related to and explained my own experience. Before that, as you will have gathered, my experience had politicized me to a degree. Change, I realized, would be brought about by collective action fought out in the political arena, and I came to recognize the futility of individual action, though it didn't stop me from making futile individual gestures. It was some time, however, before I realized that there was a clash between my increasingly Marxist views and my adherence to liberal educational values.

From all of this a number of things follow – apart from a fairly jaundiced view of many of the people who tend to become head teachers. First, in order to understand how schools and schooling work, and thus how the teaching of English operates within school, I have to resort to Marxist explanations of one sort and another. As you will, I hope, have recognized, I resist more determinist Marxist analysis that allows individuals no control over their own lives, not least because ...

Second, I have a fellow feeling for all ordinary classroom teachers. That is why I laboured hard, above, *not* to represent them as mindless cogs in the hegemonic wheel, nor as incapable of making up their minds.

And third, my experience has increased my sympathy for the kids who find themselves at the bottom of the pile in this process. So once again I am back at one of the central aims of the research, which was to give kids like that a say.

But thereby hangs the contradiction. For still I am adhering to the principles of liberal education – hoping that my work will lead to individual pupils having greater autonomy, greater opportunities for maximizing their individual potential – at the same time as recognizing that the only real change will come with collective action. Within a comparatively stable capitalist country I have no option. The moment I cross the school threshold I am enmeshed in the contradictions of schooling. My only options are how I enter into the struggle. So I, too, am riven with contradiction, but I too wish to refute the view of my self as a mere cog within the hegemonic wheel. I am caught, in other words, in the age-old philosophical opposition between free will and determinism.

I have painted a picture of my self in order to show you what sort of animal it was that engaged in the research. Into that research I took my passions, my commitment, my beliefs, my politics and my contradictions. No matter how hard I tried to ensure that my manner was laid back – that I was some sort of neutral receptor – I was inevitably doomed to failure. To illustrate my point, when I asked the interviewees about their perceptions of my role they variously suggested:

- that I was not like a teacher because I did not exert enough control (year 7 boys);
- that I was like a teacher because I had to have the head's approval to be in school (year 10 bottom-stream boys);
- that they could tell me things because, unlike teachers, I would listen (year 10 middle-stream girls);
- that they knew when they had said something interesting because I would lean forward and look enthusiastic (year 10 top-stream boys);
- and that they were enabled to express opinions that they otherwise would have kept quiet because they had an idea from what I had said that I would not disapprove, in contrast to their teachers (year 10 top-stream boys).

That is another way, perhaps, of outlining the contradictory nature of natural-istic social research. In order to gain as much information as possible the researcher must take a neutral stand, yet such a stand is inherently impossible. The researcher has a history, and an agenda. She or he can pretend as much as they like, but that is incontrovertible. That history and that agenda cannot be left back at the office, and will inevitably affect the nature of the results. And I do not suggest such an analysis in order to disarm criticism, rather to arm it. The reader can then say, not that Sarland went in with an agenda and thus his research is invalid, but rather that Sarland's agenda was such and such, and that affected his findings in such and such a way.

Stories

In this subsection I want to account for a concentration on narrative. Once again I shall take a personal perspective.

I remember studying *Gulliver's Travels* at university, and being struck that none of the critical accounts of the book made any mention of one of the major *pleasures* that I had in reading the book, and that was my pleasure in it at the level of an adventure story. I wanted to know, for most of the book, what was going to happen next. I was able to pursue that pleasure in story in my readings of children's books, but more important was the seminal interest of a couple of friends in Hollywood cinema of the 1940s, 1950s and early 1960s. They taught me how to be enthusiastic about Hitchcock, and Nicholas Ray, and Sammuel Fuller, and Howard Hawks, and John Ford, and Anthony Mann, and latterly, Blake Edwards. And I learned from them, and from scattered readings among the *auteur* theorists, how to read the narrative of a popular action movie, and find in it moral complexity, subtlety of characterization, plus the more abstract, quasi-musical pleasures of pacing and emotional variety in an unfolding story-line. Interestingly enough, as if to give our enthusiasm respectability, we looked, along with, for example, Robin Wood in his book on Howard Hawks, to find Leavisite virtues in the films of these men: there were no women directors in our pantheon. But most particularly, in distinction from the film critics of quality newspapers, we did not think that a film, in order to be good, had to have a liter-ate dialogue, nor did we think it had to look like an animated Van Gogh – though I must confess *Lust for Life* didn't do badly in that respect. We knew that the narrative itself could be rich and complex and that the behaviour of characters on screen could reveal hidden depths and ambiguities, for all that their dialogue might consist of nothing more riveting than 'She makes good biscuits.'

Of course, subsequent reading of subsequently translated work from continen-tal Europe serves to give that enthusiasm for narrative a new respectability, but again I include this autobiographical information to suggest that I already had available to me ways of reading popular texts that might reveal their interest, and thus that in some ways it seemed 'only natural' to me to go in and talk to young readers about the storyline.

Conclusion

I have suggested in this chapter that the engagement with English teaching, and the wider engagement with schools and schooling, is an engagement within a conflict-ridden social nexus. This is just as true for the researcher as it is for the teacher. I have further suggested that these conflicts will be written into the actions and views of the individuals concerned, and this, too, is just as true for the researcher as it is for the teacher. In my portrayal of my self, however, I hope I have given you a picture not only of the contradictions that frame me, but also a feel for the experience and consequent motivation that led me to undertake the research in the first place. Next I want to try and give you a picture of the circumstances of the research and the details of my methods – these are the subject matter of Chapter 2.

Note

1 Throughout this book I shall use the nomenclature of the National Curriculum in England and Wales for the year groups. Thus 11–12-year-old pupils are year 7, and 14–15-year-old pupils are year 10. The children and the staff refer to each other in terms of the traditional secondary first year, fourth year, etc., and where this occurs in transcript I have let is stand.

2 Doing the research

Introductory

As I have indicated, my central thesis is that response is but an aspect of wider cultural meaning making. The thorough investigation of such an assertion would be a major undertaking. At school age it would involve comparing inner-city children with rural children; it would involve comparing children from the ethnic minorities with each other, and with children from the dominant culture; it would involve comparing children of different academic attainment; it would involve comparing children from different class backgrounds; it would involve comparing girls with boys; it would involve comparing children of different ages. Such a study would also need a sophisticated system of checks and balances to ensure that differences due to ethnic group could not be explained, say, in terms of class difference. This is not such a study! It is a much more modest affair. However, I did hope to compare girls with boys, and I did hope to compare different ages. I also hoped to compare children of different academic attainment. Other variables I hoped to keep constant by working within one catchment area, and ideally within one school. Within those constraints Hill Hall Comprehensive School proved to be a promising site for the research.

The school

The school was an 11–16 comprehensive school of some 1400 pupils and served a large council estate, Fen Common, and some smaller private estates. The council estate had a small proportion of high-rise dwellings, dating from the late 1960s, and a large proportion of newer semi-detached and low-rise terraced development that had been built progressively through the 1970s. The school dated from the second half of the 1970s, and also doubled as a community centre, with a sports hall and a well-patronized adult education programme in the evenings.

The estate had a reputation for being rough, a reputation I had gathered through rumour and, doubtless, prejudice, when I had worked not so far away some two or three years previously. That this was not entirely unfounded was confirmed by the head of the school:

> It's known that, certainly before my time at the school, problem families were moved into Fen Common * * * it is certainly known by certain officials that many problem families were in this area, and it is regarded by the other services, like social services, probation and police, as being a noted region for children, families, people at risk.

He felt, however, that the estate was now maturing and that the problem families were producing fewer and fewer problems for the school. Two-thirds of the pupils, it was estimated by the head, came from the council estate, one-third from private houses. There were small numbers of Black, Asian, Turkish and Chinese pupils.

The school had a fairly elaborate streaming system. In English this worked as follows. The pupils were mixed-ability in year 7. In year 10 there were two top-stream sets, ten middle-stream sets, and a bottom set. The impression that I got during the pilot study was that the top-stream sets, both year 10 and year 11, were very self-confident, positive in their attitude to work and to the school – perhaps not surprisingly, since, as I was to discover later, many of the prefects were drawn from this small elite group. By contrast, it was my impression that the bulk of year 10 and 11 were disaffected, and working their time until they left. This impression was only somewhat modified in the main study.

Design and administration of the study

The central focus of the study was the relationship between the meanings young people generate in their reading of fictional texts and the meanings they bring to those texts. The perspective of the study was always social and cultural rather than psychological. The study was designed so that differences in response between say, girls and boys, or between say 'high-ability' and 'low-ability' pupils should emerge. Previous work, particularly that of Squire in 1964, suggests that pupils talk best about the books that they are enthusiastic about, and to that end the pupils themselves chose the books.

It was clear to me that to get the fullest response I needed to give the pupils time to talk at length and in depth, and also to digress and anecdotalize away from the text. Working in groups would assist this, as well as allowing shared social and cultural aspects of response to emerge. My previous work, and that of people in the field who have worked with groups on communication and learning (for example, Barnes and Todd 1977), suggest that a group size of three or four is ideal. I was present at virtually all the discussions, and audio-taped them. I generated discussion initially by using a loose interview technique.

I worked with five groups of children from one year 7 mixed-ability class, and with three groups of pupils from a year 10 top-stream class, four groups from a year 10 middle-stream class, and two groups from a year 10 bottom-stream class.

All the groups were volunteers, but I tried to get a spread of ability from group to group. This was easier in the setted year 10 where I was able to choose groups from a top, a middle and a bottom stream. In the year 7 groups I was dependent to a certain extent upon nudges from the teacher, since the class was unstreamed. Luckily I also ended up with a substantial spread of academic achievement in the year 7 class.

The study was also designed to see if there was a contrast between the responses of girls and boys. This was not a major problem, as the self-selected groups tended to be single-sex anyway. I ended up with a total of 25 girls and 21 boys. As indicated, the school had a sprinkling of ethnic minorities, but not enough in any one class for a specifically Black or Asian or Turkish group to emerge. The ethnic minorities were thus represented at random in the groups I talked with. The head's estimate, already mentioned, was that two-thirds of the pupils came from the council estate and one-third from the private estate. In my groups this ratio was reversed – so clearly I did not get a representative cross-section of the school population.

Procedure

The methods of the study arose from its purposes. I shall therefore simply describe the procedure that I went through in order to give an idea of the methods I used.

In order to introduce myself to the classes from which I was going to withdraw groups, and to provide a starting point for initial discussions, I devised a little form for groups to fill in, in which they tried to reach a consensus about books they had enjoyed or hated. Each group had one form only, thus emphasizing the shared nature of response that I was interested in. During the administration of that form the teacher and I, each with a tape-recorder, moved from group to group discussing the titles that the pupils had written down. Subsequent discussion of these forms with the groups cast an interesting sidelight on such questionnaire-type research, for while many of the book titles entered were genuine enough, a proportion of entries were clearly made on grounds other than the actual reading of the book. In some cases a pupil might have heard that a book was good, or liked one out of a series and so assumed that they would like another. This was particularly true for instance of the *Narnia* series by C. S. Lewis where it became clear that many children only really knew the first of the books to be published, *The Lion, the Witch, and the Wardrobe*, through having read it or having had it read to them. On other occasions, if they had seen a film or video, the title would go down even though they hadn't read the book.

On my second visit to classrooms I asked for groups to volunteer to take part in the long-term study. It was made clear that the central interest of the study was the reading of fiction, but that I was as interested in negative response as I was in positive response. It was also made clear that the discussion of video in relation to reading was on the agenda. The pupils were aware that they would 'get out of lessons' to talk with me in a small room somewhere. This incentive proved useful for it threw up groups that were not essentially interested in reading at all.

Once the groups had volunteered, I followed the same procedure at year 7 and at year 10 level. With each group I took in a selection of books, some by popular authors, some titles frequently studied in school, some titles that had emerged in a pilot survey (see below). Each group had to choose a book that they were all prepared to read. I emphasized that they could choose any book they wanted, and that they should not on any account restrict the titles to the selection I had brought in. They could choose a title from the library, or one from elsewhere entirely, that they knew about. Once they had chosen a title I produced three copies and they all read them and came back and talked about them. I was able also to have the pupils out of lessons just so that they could read the book.

The next stage was for each of the other groups to read each title in turn, i.e. group 1 read the title they had chosen, and then read the title that group 2 had chosen, and so on, until each group had read their own title and all the titles chosen by each of the other groups. This research design proved somewhat ambitious! Of the year 7 groups, only one read all five titles, one read four, and the remaining three only read three each. Of the year 10 groups, none came anywhere near reading all possible nine titles. One group read five, one group read four, three groups read three, and the remainder read only two.

The following is a list of the titles chosen and an indication of the source from which they were chosen:

Year 7   Girls: 3 Groups
The BFG (Roald Dahl 1982): from the library.
Iggie's House (Judy Blume 1981): from the library.
Cathy Away (Yvonne Mitchell 1964): from the library.

Year 7   Boys: 2 Groups
Super Gran (Forest Wilson 1978): from among the books I brought in.
Prince Caspian (C. S. Lewis 1951): source unknown – not from among the books
   I brought in.

Year 10   Bottom-Stream Boys
First Blood (David Morrell 1972): they wanted the book of the video. It was the
   first of the *Rambo* movies.

Year 10   Bottom-Stream Girls
Maggie (Lena Kennedy 1979): one of the group had previously read and enjoyed
   it. Not in library or among the books I brought in.
The Dark Crystal (A. C. H. Smith 1982): this was a fantasy video made by Jim
   Henson of 'Muppets' fame. It was chosen by the same group who chose
   Maggie. They changed their minds once they had seen the written text.

Year 10   Top-Stream Boys
John Diamond (Leon Garfield 1980): from the library.

Year 10   Top-Stream Girls: 2 Groups
Sus (Fay Sampson 1982): from the library.
Stranger with My Face (Lois Duncan 1983): from the library.

Year 10   Middle-Stream Girls: 2 Groups
Carrie (Stephen King 1974): from among the books I brought in.
The Fog (James Herbert 1975): from among the books I brought in.

Year 10   Middle-Stream Boys: 2 Groups
Grange Hill Home and Away (Robert Leeson 1982): I had brought in a *Grange Hill* book, though not that one. They wanted the latest *Grange Hill* book.
The Outsiders (S. E. Hinton 1970): from among the books I brought in.

It will be seen that, of the year 7 groups, only one, of boys, chose from among the books I brought in. As for year 10, all the middle-stream groups chose from among the books I had brought in. As well as talking about the books chosen by the pupils themselves we also discussed the books they were reading in class, when the occasion arose:

Year 7: *The Last Battle*
Year 10 top stream: *To Kill a Mockingbird, Cider with Rosie*
Year 10 middle stream: *The Pearl, Of Mice and Men, Kes*

The interviews/discussions

The interviews were carried out from certain assumptions and with certain aims in mind. No one aim had priority over any other aim. They were first of all designed to promote discussion. Second they were conducted in such a way as to allow evidence to emerge from the culture of the young people concerned. Third they were designed to promote discussion about the books. Underlying all the questions that I asked about the books had to be an assumption that the books were worth asking questions about in the first place. Thus, though I always asked the pupils whether they had liked the book, or if they thought it was good, and if so why, I kept my own opinions about the book to myself as far as possible.

I asked three sorts of question (prepared beforehand) about the books. First, I asked general questions. For example: 'Tell me about the book.' This generally elicited a retelling of the main threads of the underlying story or *fabula*, rather than the complexities of plot or *sjuzet*, to use two formalist terms. Or I would ask: 'What are the best bits in the book?' 'Explain to me why they are the best bits.' 'What is it about them that makes them the best bits?' Such an example illustrates my follow-up procedure, a sort of nagging to try to elicit the fullest and most comprehensive response. Such general questions might produce responses that led us into fields that were covered by my specific questions, in which case I would follow up by responding to what they had said, reformulating specific questions in relation to the discussion at that moment.

The second sort of question was about what I perceived to be the theme(s) of the book. Thus for *The Fog* I had questions prepared about the possible symbolism of the fog itself, about the pattern of relationships in the sub-plot episodes, about the nature of Holman's job in relation to corruption in high places. I also wanted to know how they responded to the more notorious sections of the book, the boy's school scene, the lesbian scene, and the mass suicide. I asked if scenes were funny, and what made them funny. On *Iggie's House*, to provide a contrasting example, I had questions about adult secrecy, about racism, about childhood friendship and about men's and women's jobs.

The third sort of question involved closer attention to the text. For instance, I asked about the parallel action/flashback structure of *The Fog* and *Super Gran*. I asked about the multiplicity of narrators in *Carrie*. Using specific examples in each of the books, I asked if they skipped description or if they liked detail. I did not, on the whole, ask detailed questions about the language. If there was a video I asked about the difference between the book and the video. If they didn't like a book I read them extracts – the beginning, a piece of description – to see if they could pinpoint in detail what they disliked overall.

Towards the end of the study I asked general questions, but not about the books. I asked questions about teachers, what their job was, what a pupil's job was, whether a teacher is also an ordinary person. I asked similar questions about parents. I asked what school was for and how it fulfilled its function. I asked about streaming and how they felt about it. I asked if top-stream people were different from bottom-stream people. I asked them about friendship and what it was. I asked questions about wider issues and subjects outside school and family: the police, terrorism, strikes, race and racism, crime and punishment. I asked what the difference was between girls and boys. I asked them what they wanted to be or to do when they left school. I asked them about video nasties. Finally, I asked them about my role as interviewer. If these topics had come up in earlier tapes I skipped them at this stage.

Tom Logan (1984, p. 19) suggests, quoting Zweig, that 'the basic tool of the interviewer is in fact his own personality', and he makes a plea for allowing interviewees to frame their own questions and to set their own agendas. To this end I allowed discussion to meander, to digress. I tried to play a very 'laid back' role. I have given you a taste in the previous chapter of the pupils' views of me. And I have outlined the impossibility that the researcher can be some kind of *tabula rasa*. It can be argued that my research methods lacked rigour, that I should have put the same questions formulated in the same way to each group. Such a procedure is followed, for instance, by Pauline Heather in 1981. I would argue that such an approach would not have allowed digression, and it was digression that I was interested in just as much as direct response to the books. For instance, some of the evidence presented in the following chapters is in the form of stories or anecdotes that the boys and girls tell about their own lives. Such stories and anecdotes would emerge in the flow of conversation, as ideas were sparked off in one member of the group or another, just as they are, I would venture to suggest, in real life. It would be impossible, I would argue, to use more rigorous interview methods and still manage to elicit such material.

The pilot study

In the chapter so far I have mentioned a pilot study a couple of times. In the course of it I did two things. First of all I did a quick survey in five schools, including the school that emerged as the site for the main study, of what was currently being read by children and young people, and second, as you will be aware from Chapter 1, I talked to teachers about their reasons for choosing to use the books they used in class. The survey was intended to provide a background against which to set the choices of individual books in the main study. I surveyed a representative spread of classes in five schools, including the school that was to be the site for the main study.

In the survey I asked pupils to list books, with their authors if they could remember them, in four categories: books that they liked now; books that they liked in the past; books that they disliked now; and books that they disliked in the past. I was particularly concerned with popularity and unpopularity, hoping that such information might be culturally useful. In addition, during the administration of the survey, I deliberately asked the pupils to consult with each other, to jog each other's memories and so on, in the hope of again including some of the social aspects of taste. Whether they did so, or how much they did so, depended a great deal on the teaching style of the teachers of the particular classes I surveyed. In some there was a lot of talk, in others the minimum. As a 'toe in the water' exercise the actual titles that emerged as popular reflected the comparatively recent findings of others. Pauline Heather, in particular, in 1981, had conducted a much more rigorous survey, and all my results simply reflected her work, as well as similar work from Jennie Ingham, also in 1981, and Shirley Crowther in 1986.

In retrospect the survey was useful only to the person who did it, giving me a feel for the current situation. It seems to me that such is almost always the case. By far the most useful surveys are those done by teachers in their own classes. That way you can pick up on fascinating local enthusiasms that get lost in the gross figures of larger and more statistically viable work. Thus one class that I surveyed had a craze for Jilly Cooper for reasons that I never fathomed, another for *Summer of the Dinosaur* by Willis Hall because the teacher had just read it to them.

There were two particular findings, however, that I do want to emphasize, and they arose from the way in which I framed the questionnaire in order to get dislikes as well as likes. I shall concentrate on the findings from the school that emerged as the site for the main study. The first finding was a gender-differentiated response. Thus the year 7 boys heartily disliked the *Famous Five* series, a series that was popular with girls. The second finding was often associated with the first, and always concerned books chosen to be read or studied in class. So, in the year 8 middle set, *Siege at Robin's Hill*, a book read to them in class, was well liked by 11 girls and four boys, and hated by eight boys. Virtually all the books that were disliked by a large number of pupils were the set books, and almost always there was a number of pupils who had enjoyed working on, or listening to those same books. Thus titles that feature on up the school all fall into this category: in year 9, *The Guardians, The Red Pony* (liked by girls, disliked by boys), and in year 10, *To Kill a Mockingbird* (liked by boys and girls, disliked by boys), *Shane* (liked by boys, disliked by girls). One or two titles are fairly well disliked by all. *The Pearl* came in for a hammering in year 11, as did *The Nun's Priest's Tale*.

In my survey Roald Dahl and James Herbert emerged as popular authors, along with *Grange Hill* books and the *Narnia* series. Individual titles that were popular included *Super Gran*, and wider survey information confirms the popularity of authors such as Judy Blume and, more recently, Stephen King. All of which is by way of indicating that many of the books chosen by the groups in the main study were popular books, or books by popular authors.

It will be seen that already in the pilot survey differences in taste were emerging, particularly between boys and girls. What might be meant by that term 'difference in taste' is explored in some detail in later chapters, as is the problem with set books.

The results

The research had been designed to produce 'compare and contrast' sorts of result. I hoped that clear-cut distinctions might emerge between boys and girls, between top-stream and middle-stream and bottom sets, or between the age groups. Though it has proved possible to show some distinctions of this sort, much of the evidence suggests alternative approaches and interpretations. Furthermore, the wealth of the material from the year 10 pupils was such that I have concentrated on them, though where there have been links with what the younger pupils have to say I have included their perspectives, too. Only one chapter (Chapter 8) reverses that pattern.

It might have seemed obvious to analyse each book and then pursue each group's response to it. I have not done this. As the evidence accumulated, it became clear that if I worked in that way it would be more difficult to show how books fitted into what I can only describe as strands of culture. The point is that some readers read books in one way, and some in another. One sort of reading might have emerged from the interest of a reader in violence, while another might have emerged from an interest of another reader in ordering the world. My whole point is that books are part of the wider meaning making that is culture, and *not* the other way round. To have had a chapter on, say, *Super Gran* would have been to have placed the book at the centre, which is not where it is for these young people.

In the chapters that follow, then, I look first at violence. This is an issue that is raised – and, indeed, obsessively returned to – by the year 10 bottom-stream boys, and is echoed in the only book they read in the course of the study. It is, furthermore, male violence that they discuss, violence of boys towards boys, of men towards men.

Next I look at female concerns with violence and the role that the paranormal plays here. These issues are raised most particularly by one of the middle-stream girls' groups and I shall suggest, *inter alia*, that they offer readings of texts that can be identified perhaps as specifically female readings.

Third, I look at the ways in which horror explores the boundaries of cultural order; fourth, I look at the ways in which books offer elements that readers recognize as reflecting their own interests and concerns; and fifth, I look at the reasons why pupils reject texts. These three chapters are linked by discussion of the more general experiential, cultural and ideological interrelationships between readers and texts. It is in the first of these chapters that I address the problems of pulp horror, and the mechanisms by which it operates. And in the third I discuss 'boredom'. The great cry that pupils find books 'boring' very often conceals a good understanding of those books, and a rejection of them on the basis of that understanding.

Finally, I look at issues of futurity, to coin an ugly word: a notion that links planning the future, and cognitive process. It is here that the younger readers provide most of the evidence.

A footnote on 'reading skills: skimming ...' and videos

In the course of the research one or two texts were read that also existed as films or videos. *Carrie* and *First Blood* are the clearest examples. The year 10 bottom-stream boys that chose the latter did not know whether there was a book or not – no more did I – but they had seen the video, or saw it in the course of the study. Two questions arise. The first is whether they actually read the book at all and, if they did not, instead succeeded in 'bluffing' their way through the interviews. The second is, if they did read the book, what was the nature of that reading?

To take the questions in turn: the bottom-stream year 10 group certainly did read *First Blood*, because they complained about some of the differences between the book and the film. Another group, Ken, Nemesh, and Jagdish, who discussed *Carrie* with me, clearly kept the discussion going on the basis of their knowledge of just the film. Indeed, that particular group, at the end of the project, admitted that they had not read a single title, that they had only volunteered for the project to get out of lessons.

Turning to the second question, there seemed to be a variety of techniques used. Some said that they imagined the film as they read the book. Others read the book with the sort of attention that alerted them to differences, which they then pursued rather than skipping, and they were then, in turn, quite capable of imagining the book differently from the film. This was how Rosie accounted for her reading of *First Blood*, for instance.

I specifically questioned the bottom-stream boys about their reading of *First Blood*. They said that they imagined the film as they read the book, and were annoyed at the digressions, particularly into the background of the character of the sheriff. When I asked them about how they dealt with such digressions they said they skipped them. When I asked them how they knew which bits to skip, and how they went about the skipping, Matthew produced an analogy with playing football:

> *CS:*   So what happens when you come across a piece of detail like that that's not particularly important, do you sort of half skip it or what, or do you make the picture in your mind or what.
> *Matthew:* You just skim it, or read parts of it.
> *CS:*   And, how do you know whether you should skim it or whether you shouldn't.
> *Matthew:* I don't know, I just do.

and he continues:

> *Matthew:* Sort of when you're playing football you can see the person, you've about a hundredth of a second to see him, the ball goes straight to him. I don't know how you do it but you do. That's like reading the book.

Later in the same exchange, John suggests:

> *John:*   I read it, but if I don't find it interesting I just sort of right, as if it's being chucked away.
> *CS:*   Yes.
> *John:*   I read it, and collect it, and dispose of it, don't want it.

There was no doubt in my mind that many of the pupils did read the books when they had seen the video, even when they said that they imagined the film while they were reading the book. Matthew's account of an intuitive sort of skimming process and John's related suggestion of a sort of junking process give some idea of what may be involved. It may well account, too, for 'discrepancies' in the reading of the book. None of the bottom-stream boys were aware of the different endings of the book and the film of *First Blood*. Apart from anything else, the book has a fairly complicated change of narrative perspective at the end, and even Rosie, who was well aware that there was a difference, said that she couldn't understand it.

With this sort of detail we are moving towards the main findings of the research, and since my first focus is on the same bottom-stream boys and on their reading of *First Blood*, this footnote provides a convenient link.

3 Male violence

Introductory

John Schostak in *Maladjusted Schooling*, quotes R. D. Laing as saying that 'Normal men have killed perhaps 100,000,000 of their fellow normal men in the last fifty years' (p. 167). Whatever the accuracy of such a horrific figure, it makes the point that we live in a violent world. In a later book, *Schooling the Violent Imagination*, Schostak further suggests that, 'Violence is a normal part of the culture and therefore the structure of everyday life' (p. 9) and that 'Violence underlies the political order' (p. 10). Within the family and the school this violence is mediated and expressed in a number of subtle and complex ways. In his wide-ranging discussion of such issues, Schostak makes a distinction between institutionally and socially approved violence and violence which is disapproved of. In particular, he suggests that the forms of coercion and control that can be found in the school and the family are underpinned by violence and threats of violence: 'social experience is largely political, that is, concerned with decision, power, threats of violence and actual violence. In the dominant childrearing practices we find varying forms of violence which produce or sustain the familial political ordering' (*Schooling the Violent Imagination*, p. 35). The history of violence within the family and the school, he argues, is one of increasing subtlety and covertness. The family, despite being the most frequent site of interpersonal violence in modern society, has become increasingly democratized, and school has developed a tradition of inculcating values and selected knowledge with less and less resort to open authoritarianism. None the less, he suggests, those at the bottom of the pile in school feel increasingly violated:

> More and more children are feeling dissatisfied, frustrated or bored with schools. Many feel that they are a violation of their dignity, independence, age, sex, race, freedom and intelligence. Many react through disruption, truancy, apathy – the strategies are various. It is not news that schools are failing to meet the needs of large numbers of children, research has been showing this consistently for decades.
> (*Schooling the Violent Imagination*, p. 33)

He argues that the schooling system, by selecting and rejecting, creates a resentful group. This contributes to the nurture of what he calls the 'violent imagination':

> Every felt sense of injustice contributes to an overall resentment which permeates the developing drama between self and other, between those like Me and those like Them. This is the stuff of the violent imagination – the dramas, the myths, the folktales, the personal anecdotes which tell of the many violations against the self perpetrated by others.
>
> (1986, p. 33)

and:

> The violent imagination becomes a way in which people make sense of the world, identifying structures of justice and of injustice, freedom and slavery, creation and destruction, war and peace.
>
> (1986, pp. 33–4)

Finally, he suggests that a central concern for adolescents is the struggle to find an identity for the self in the context of a series of identities given to the individual by society at large: teachers, schools, parents, families, peer groups, social workers and the like.

John Schostak's work provides a framing for what follows, for many of the themes he explores seem to have application to the group of year 10 bottomstream boys, and to their reading of *First Blood*.

First blood: the book/movie

The year 10 boys in question talked to me a lot about the videos they watched. When it came to choosing a book to read, they asked if I could get a book of a video they knew. First of all they wanted *Rocky III* but when that proved not to be available in book form they opted for *First Blood*, a video that was in the top 10 at the time.

First Blood is a movie, directed by Ted Kotcheff in 1982, based on the 1972 book of the same name by David Morrell. It stars Sylvester Stalone and is a precursor to the *Rambo* movies. It tells the story of Vietnam veteran, Rambo, a highly trained 'fighting machine' who is unable to settle as a normal member of American society after he returns from the war. Instead he leads an itinerant, semi-hippy existence on the road. Approaching a small town where he hopes to buy a meal, he is given a lift by the local sheriff, Brian Denehey in the movie, who runs him right the way through and drops him off on the other side – we don't want your type here. Rambo returns to town where he is arrested and manhandled by the police. When they attempt to shave him, Rambo, remembering (flashback) being tortured in Vietnam, can finally take no more. Half naked, in the book totally naked, and unarmed, he manages none the less to break free of the men holding him down in the shower, and, snatching up weapons as he goes, he escapes, first from the cells, then from the police station itself, and, hijacking a passing motorbike, makes off into the hills. Here, from the book, is a particularly gruesome piece of description of the carnage he leaves behind him during his escape (Galt is one of the police officers):

> But Galt continued fumbling for his gun, and awkwardly he had it out. He really must have been new on the job: he looked as though he could not believe he was actually raising the gun, his hand shaking, squeezing the trigger, and Rambo slashed the razor straight across his stomach. Galt peered stupidly down at the neat deep slash across his belly, blood soaking his shirt and pouring down his pants, organs bulging out like a pumped up inner tube through a slit in a tyre. He took a finger and tried poking the organs back in, but they kept bulging out, blood soaking his pants and running out his cuffs on to the floor as he made a funny little noise in his throat and toppled across the chair, upsetting it.
>
> (Morrell 1972, pp. 47–8)

This particular detail does not occur in the film but the general tenor of the scene is similar. In both film and book the unarmed individual, forced into a corner by superior numbers of an armed enemy, is able to win out by the sheer channelling of his fighting skills, his personal bodily strength and individual naked aggression.

This theme of individual as superhero continues through the film; in one scene Rambo jumps from a cliff into some trees, breaks his leg, manufactures a splint, sets his leg, and then sews up a gash in his own arm. There are archetypal images of him in the forest disguised as a deer or a tree – man the hunter – and later, back in the town, machine gun resting on one arm, bandoleros slung across his naked chest – the ultimate urban guerrilla. At the end of the movie he sits inviolate, armed to the teeth, in the very police station where it all started, while the police and the national guard prowl helplessly around outside. Finally, talked out by the colonel who trained him, he walks free, the crowd parting to let him through.

The book differs from the movie in complexity. There is a whole exploration of the sheriff's character: his own Korean past is paralleled with Rambo's Vietnam experience; he develops paternal feelings for Rambo; and his own relationship with his uncle/surrogate father is explored. And, in contrast to the movie, Rambo is killed at the end.

At this point I am going to include a personal response. I shall do this at a number of points throughout the book in order to remind the reader of the self behind the researcher. Of course, my accounts of texts will be flavoured by my personal interests and predilections in any case, but I think it will be helpful to include these more clearly personal comments, for these, too, may throw light on my account of my research. So, as far as *First Blood* is concerned, in the book I was particularly taken with the fatherhood theme that runs through it. The sheriff is still exploring his own relationship with his father, and Rambo becomes the son he never had, whom he must kill. It struck me that this theme paralleled that of the fatherland disowning its own sons as the Vietnam veterans came back from the war. In the movie this parallel between the personal and the political is much less obvious, and the moral is turned, as the father figure of the colonel who trained him does finally come to his rescue. In the movie I felt much more powerfully the force of the violation of the individual as Rambo was restrained and ordered around at the start.

The boys had read the book, skimming parts of it in the manner indicated in the previous chapter, and they showed every evidence of being aware of the differences between book and movie, expressing irritation, for instance, with the psychologizing of the sheriff's character.

I divide the discussion of violence that follows into three sections – the school, the individual, and the politics. In the first of these the group talk about violence in the playground and among themselves and their mates. In the second I concentrate on one boy, John, who seems to bring together many of the themes of this chapter in one individual response. In the third I bring wider political and ideological perspectives to bear.

Violence: the school

This group of bottom-stream boys 'digress' with great ease. Discussion of one element in the book/video soon sparks off ideas and stories about the world and their own experience. The material of the present section emerges out of just such a digression. We are talking about the American setting of the story. In America:

> *John:* You know there's sort of right all these gangs, fights and that lot, poor streets and all that.
> *Tony:* It's like this place, this school.

I pick this up and they start telling me stories about violence in school. Some seem to be stories shared by all but witnessed by none of this group in particular, others bear the stamp of personal experience.

> *Matthew:* Like the fifth years, they started, these couple of kids in the fifth year, they all ran around and they broke this girl's arm.
> *John:* Yeh.
> *Matthew:* It was by accident. And then the fourth-years ran around, 'cause the fourth-years got angry and they put this kid's head through a window.

They are talking about the previous year's year 11 who have now left the school. On one occasion I was in the staffroom and rumour spread that these last year's leavers were waiting outside the gates. The head came in and advised all staff not leaving by car to leave in pairs. Thus the view of this group of boys is not isolated, and indeed they speak of what they take to be common knowledge.

Matthew: The fifth-years were nutcases.
Tony: This school's, this school's, this school's a nuthole.
Matthew: They just go round and beat them up.

They then describe to me a game that is built around male aggression (it is clear that when they say 'everyone' they mean all the boys).

John: I mean I must admit I played it as well, murderball, right.
Tony: Everybody in the fourth year played murderball.
John: All the fourth-years right. Now you just get one ball and you kick it ...
Tony: Kick it – – –
Matthew: Whoever gets the ball you got to get them.
John: Whoever gets the ball, you just go up to them and punch them in the face.

Later:

John: Like me, say I got the ball now, right ...
Tony: Everybody'd jump.
John: Next minute all my mates and sort of banging hell out of me, in my face, but I'd still be friends with them.

The game is stopped by the authorities when someone gets hurt:

Tony: They stopped us, someone got, someone, someone broke their leg or something.
Matthew: No. Mickey Heath had his nose broken in three places.

The account of murderball is an account of actual involvement in an event. The account of the previous year's year 11 year is a common knowledge that may or may not be confirmed by direct observation. There is, in addition, direct observation itself. Here is John:

John: I'll tell you two incidents, one incident was when um the black people, and the white people, now I found this bloody confusing ...

and he goes on to tell me about a fight he has observed between a group of black and a group of white youths which promptly stops the moment a teacher walks past.

The distinctions between events participated in, events observed, and events in the common knowledge, blur and overlap as they tell me, and each other, stories of their actual experiences, stories of their personal observations, and stories that are current in the fourth-year culture of that particular school. Thus the general culture of the 'common knowledge' is informed and revitalized by the personal experiences of the participants in that common culture, and vice versa – the personal stories are given currency by their clear relationship to the general. Other vital elements in this mixture are cultural artefacts: in particular, visual and, to a lesser extent, written fictions. John is specific about making the link:

> *John:* It's kind of like, I mean if you honestly had've filmed that lot and you tried
> to work it out, really this school's kind of gang warfare.

As we have seen, John, at another point, has admitted to finding something he has seen confusing. What he seems to be suggesting here is that a film of events in the school, provided it was an honest record, would offer an opportunity to understand those events in terms of the cultural construct 'gang warfare'. Such a process, i.e. the filming, and such an artefact, i.e. the completed film, he seems to be suggesting, would have a vital *cognitive* function.

But where does *First Blood* fit into all this? At this stage it is only informed by the same general assumptions about violence and aggression that are made by these year 10 boys. Otherwise it presents individual rather than collective action. Such an individual perspective strikes an answering chord in a clearer way with this group, and with John in particular.

Violence: the individual

In the constant and, at this age, crucial negotiation of personal identity, as traced by John Schostak in work I have already discussed, and by Paul Willis, in *Learning to Labour*, among others, individuals interact with the culture that surrounds them, defining their path through it, deciding which groups to identify with and what behaviours are appropriate to those groups.

John, who tends to dominate discussions with this group, talks almost obsessively about wanting to fight. It is a recent change that both he and the others recognize. Here is Matthew describing John's change:

> *Matthew:* Like Jonathan, when he was younger he was alright, but now he hangs
> around with harder people he's a hardnut, he really, he reckons he's it.

John does not demur at this characterization:

> *John:*   I've never liked fighting. I've always used to be scared, but I mean now,
> if I go in a fight, say a kid comes in here now and pushes me around,
> even though he's bigger than me I'd have a go at him. * * * It's the way
> I just hang around with a lot of hard people now. I know the only way
> to be one of them is to fight.

While this aggressive way of life is, on the evidence of the others, no figment of John's imagination, he does also devote a lot of his talk to conjuring science fiction scenarios about being contained within a limited area with a limited amount of food, being given the necessary weapons and being forced to fight it out. At one stage he talks about being contained in large domes, an image from a science fiction film he has seen, and at another about putting a wall around the estate and being contained within that. These compulsive images, he suggests at one point, act as a metaphor for the condition of youth itself:

> *John:* I mean I'd love to go out, to just dump off going to school. I'd love to fight for my living. I'd love to sort of like if there's food there, my personal way, I'd love to sort of like fight for it. * * * I'd rather just fight for it and live in a dump, not a dump place but ... I'd rather fight where there's violence all the time and there's no schools, windows smashed, there's no true houses. If you sleep there one night you have to sleep somewhere else just 'cause someone comes to there. Sort of like that. Now that's really what youth's like.

'Youth', then, for John, seems to be a violent wasteland, isolated from the mainstream of society, where survival depends upon fighting and winning. At one point he even suggests that the violence of youth is best dealt with by isolating them and letting them fight it out, though at another he suggests that such containment would lead to eventual break-out.

So intense is John's vision at times that it is easy to lose sight of its fictional status. However, in one revealing moment he makes a link with childhood games with their fictional scenarios, played so as to make them as 'realistic' as possible:

> *John:* and they built the wall so much that you couldn't break out, right, and they'd let you have that certain area and you'd split into your own armies, like the blues and the greys, or the Yanks and the Germans – whatever – that army goes there and that army goes there and you kill (??) yourself. I'd rather do that because then I'm risking my own life and it would be more better. I'd find it more realistic.

He also makes the link to Vietnam:

> *John:* That's what I want to do, fight in Vietnam. If I was allowed to go – – – there I would start the war back up.

When we examine *First Blood* it is striking to what extent an external fiction matches with the internal fiction of a particular reader/viewer. In *First Blood* the hero has to survive by fighting. He is effectively isolated from the mainstream of society and his isolation serves to isolate the sheriff and the national guard in their turn, who have to fight it out on ground of his choosing. At the end of the movie, though not of the book, he effectively walks free and inviolate. This is a point of vital importance for John – it is a symbol of Rambo's strength and integrity. John's desire to restart the the Vietnam war is startling in the light of the fact that the movie *Rambo* had not been released at the time, yet that is precisely what the character does: goes on and refights the war. The character of Rambo is also defined in his refusal to be pushed around any more. It is the violation of his personal liberties that causes him to break out. Here he is, for example, talking to himself about being constantly moved on: 'In fifteen goddam towns this has happened to me. This is the last. I won't be fucking shoved any more' (*First Blood*, p. 19).

As Schostak has pointed out, above, many adolescents in school share that sense of personal violation. John places it in a wider context than just school:

John: But I mean us, it ain't fair because, just 'cause I'm a skinhead, just because, 'cause I want to be who I want to be, just 'cause the citizens – – – the people, the rich people don't want to, they don't want me to be like that, they reckon they can rule my life, change me, make me become one of them.

And later:

John: It's my life. I want to do what I want to do, you only live once so I do it.

He explicitly links the teachers with that process:

John: And then there's the teachers, the army, the police and that lot that are making it hard for us.

[Thus, as on one occasion I follow John through the playground, I watch as he removes his ear stud when he sees a teacher approaching, and puts it back in the moment the teacher has passed: 'To censor dress is to violate community; this is as true of punk dress as of Sikh dress; but the latter is legitimized through religion' (*Maladjusted Schooling* p. 142).]

Later in the tape I read an extract from the book for another purpose, but John makes a crucially pertinent interjection:

CS: 'Because I have a right to decide for myself whether I'll stay in it or not. I won't have someone decide that for me.' (*First Blood*, p. 19)
John: That's my point.

It will be clear to the percipient reader that I am, almost wilfully, ignoring the political dimensions of what John and, to a lesser extent, the others have to say. I shall be examining them next but I was anxious to emphasize the individual here. The meeting point between the reader/viewer and the printed page/screen is an individual one. John's evidence is particularly useful in that it focuses these wider aspects within the individual vision, the individual response. He allows us to make the links between wider cultural, social and political processes and an individual actor within those processes. It is the individual nature of response, so much emphasized in the literature, that requires such focusing.

Violence: politics

The politics of *First Blood*, in particular of the video, are contradictory, a point most clearly exemplified by the sequel, *Rambo*, directed by Cosmatos in 1985. The character is to go on to refight the Vietnam war in the later movie. His gung-ho patriotism is exemplified in his question 'Do we get to win this time?'. Such patriotism informs the first movie, and the book. However, as I have suggested, the betrayal that underlies the plot is the betrayal of its ex-soldiers by their fatherland. It is implicit that Rambo has returned from the war and discovered that he has no place to go. It is that fact the sets off the train of events that leads to the violence and the slaughter. It is the agencies of the state in the form of the police and the national guard that are set against the individual, and that individual ends up opposing the very state to which he owes his first allegiance.

We have already seen that John specifically relates the police, the army, and teachers as together being in opposition to him. This is a view shared by all four boys in the group. Furthermore, we have also seen that John sees the rich as the group that want to prevent him from being a skinhead:

> *John:* Just 'cause I'm a skinhead, just because, 'cause I want to be who I want to be, just 'cause the citizens – – – the people, the rich people don't want to, they don't want me to be like that, they reckon they can rule my life, change me, make me become one of them.

In discussions the group are somewhat divided as to how they see themselves. Tony thinks they are middle class but both John and Matthew call themselves the poor people. Such a characterization, it should be said, is specifically placed within a discussion in which the distinctions between rich and poor are the issue. However, there is no doubt that they are not the rich. The rich have big gardens, swimming pools, bigger houses and so on. They are a different class:

> *John:* They're upper class, right.
> *Matthew:* They're snobs.

Later:

> *John:* They don't want to be us, they want nothing to do with us. They want to be them. They want to teach their children their things.

When I ask them if they think that teachers, the police, and so on, represent the views of the rich, Tony says:

> *Tony:* Course they do.

For instance, they all agree that people are much less likely to get stopped by the police and asked to account for their actions if they are rich. By contrast, they have frequent experience of police harassment. John, for instance, gets stopped just because he is a skinhead:

> *John:* just 'cause I'm walking along the street, policeman come up to me and say, 'What you doing out this time of night?'

Matthew, too, has had recent experience of being stopped and asked why he was carrying a tape-recorder. John offers a somewhat cryptic enactment of how the police would deal with the rich:

> *John:* ... if it was a rich person walking round the streets: 'Oh hello, good morning, see you, bye,' walk off.

But he has more subtle perceptions of the operation of hegemony:

> *John:* They [the rich] rule us and then there's the police, the teachers, the lot * * *
> they do what the higher people say. Now us, we're the very bottom.

So far, so straightforward, but he develops his argument with a somewhat unexpected analogy. It is, he suggests:

> *John:* as if we're the pets, as if we don't have the right to exist, as if we don't have
> the right to do what we want to do.

A little analysis of the status of the pet might help to explain John's analogy. The pet is contained, its freedom is severely constrained, while at the same time it is fed, even well fed, and often generally pampered. Indeed it is that very process of feeding and pampering that constitutes the method of constraint. It is not my purpose here to pursue the subtlety of John's perception and the ramifications of all his arguments in detail, though it would make a fascinating study. Suffice it to say that it is a crucial element in his perception of the world that he is not simply forced to do what he is told but that he sees himself as cajoled and bribed. Indeed, he even suggests at one point that the authorities have instilled the habit of obedience into him to such an extent that he agrees despite himself to do as he is told. His puzzlement and anger at this state of affairs recur again and again.

It needs to be said at this point that John's 'official' politics are right-wing. Essentially he characterizes himself as a skinhead, and this means that he is British Youth Movement and that his 'natural' enemies are Blacks and Asians. All the gang fights that he describes are racist in nature. The others in the group, all of whom are white, share his racism to lesser extents. Here is Tony:

> *Tony:* When you're going down the street * * * and there's a Paki or and Indian
> or a Paki in front of you * * * you tell him to walk on the other side of the
> road. You tell him, 'Oi, Paki, move out of the way', and he doesn't move
> out of the way you start beating him up for no reason.

But Tony has an Asian uncle:

> *Tony:* My aunty, right, * * * she's married to a ... an Indi ... a Paki, right * * *
> and he's a kind man * * * he's a nice bloke.

Tony's complex experience, evidenced in his uncertainty about using the insult 'Paki', is not unique in this group. Matthew has mates who are black and he has to take care not to let them meet his skinhead mates. And John, the most extreme of the group, has contradictory perceptions about those very divisions in which he partakes so violently. He instances the riots in Brixton:

> *John:* You know the Brixton riots, that started off with one skinhead against one
> coloured. It got bigger and bigger then eventually the skinhead and coloured
> went together and fought the police.

In a further discussion we are talking about banning the bomb. All the groups want to ban the bomb, they claim, including the British Youth Movement. This is evidenced in the music to which different groups listen. If all the groups banded together they could do something:

John: So it's stupid, 'cause if us lot all ganged together, be able to do it, be able to ban the bomb completely * * * so why can't we all join up against ... fight the – – – fight all the governments.

Matthew: There'll be a war then Jonny. You said they don't want a war.

John: Revolution. We don't want the bomb to go off, that's what we don't want.

Matthew: If we start a revolution they'll set the bomb off.

John has a sense of being trapped in something he can't control, and much of one of the tapes is taken up with his pursuit of such questions. Though it is never clearly expressed, the division of youth into destructive warring factions seems to be part of that trap.

Their view of the role of school and teachers in all this is uncompromising. They are an agency of control. School is for:

John: Keeping us off the streets, that's what it is, * * *

Tony: It's just to keep us off the streets * * *

John: That's it.

The energy of youth they seem to be suggesting, above, could amount to a potentially revolutionary force. Here is Schostak again:

It is through the energy of youth that revolutions have been able to ignite and transform societies intellectually and physically (cf. Heer, 1974). The energy of youth is dangerous hence the institutions of 'growing up' are essentially instruments for the control of individuals in order to maintain traditional social behaviours.

(*Maladjusted Schooling*, p. 136)

Here is John expressing similar views:

John: They know fair well [*sic*] that the youths can take over the world, if they really wanted to * * * and they know ... they can sort of make us think it's nice to go to school, and stuff like that, but really in their mind they're keeping us off the streets, they ain't bothered about us.

There has been little within the school to counter such views. John and Matthew were in the remedial class for the first three years of their school life and it was a bitter experience for them:

John: We hate the school now, do you know why, because when we was first years they tried this experiment * * * and it failed.

Matthew: And they left us there.

John: * * * and they just left us there for three whole years.

John's bitterness is tangible:

> *John:*   For three horrible years. Now we're out and they still look at us as if
> we're remedial. For three years, that really got me, ate into me badly,
> three years, I hated that, every day and every lesson.

When I ask if it was the lessons or their relationship to the rest of the school that
was so bad, John says succinctly: 'Both.'

   In this section I have tried to sketch the political perceptions and insights of
these four (mostly three) boys. A number of contradictions seem to emerge.
They are potential National Front members, racist to a degree, violent and
anarchistically destructive in their talk – Matthew at one point even describing
having fun as going and busting something up. On the other hand, they have a
clear notion of themselves as at or near the bottom of the pile in a society
divided by economic status and class; and they have a clearly expressed view that
the agencies of the state, the police, the army and the school serve the interests
of the wealthy. Furthermore, I would argue that they recognize that to change
things, both collective solidarity and a revolution are required. In the absence of
either, we could argue that they turn for their sense of identity within the collective experience to various groups that could be described as more or less
pernicious. We could also argue that, in the absence of a constructive political
outlet for their energies, they are driven to individualistic acts of rebellion and
destruction, or to gang warfare on the streets and in the football stadiums, or to
racist attacks upon people of their own age. In the very process of being involved
in racist gang warfare they seem to recognize the destructiveness of the activity.
The alternative is perhaps a retreat to a feeling of grievance and bitter resentment, or an increasingly cynical resignation.

   A fiction like *First Blood* seems to me to encapsulate and express such resentment with remarkable clarity. When we first meet the hero he is everyman. Here
is the very first sentence of the book: 'His name was Rambo, and he was just
some nothing kid for all anybody knew, standing by the pump of a gas station at
the outskirts of Madison, Kentucky' (p. 9). Pushed around by the forces of law
and order until he can take no more, there is effectively a magical transformation
into an individual of phenomenal power. He becomes a one-man revolution. In
the forest where he hides out he sets traps which catch various members of the
police force and the national guard. Thus his power is even extended beyond his
physical presence. When a high-powered tool of modern warfare is sent after
him, a helicopter gunship, he zaps it out of the sky. He becomes an unstoppable,
indestructible force, and his achievement is to redefine the world in his own
terms. But while, on the one hand, Rambo's characterization and actions are
those of a superhero, on the other the violence and the corresponding emotions
are portrayed, as we have seen, in graphic detail, generating an emotional intensity that is traditionally not found in superman-type adventures.

   I have tried to portray the depth of bitterness with which these boys, and
John in particular, regard their school experience. I have tried to give some taste

of the intensity and obsessional nature of John's science fiction scenarios of urban gang warfare. There is an argument to be made that the intensity of their feelings is an individual psychological phenomenon, but it is not an argument that I wish to pursue here. I wish rather to argue that their feelings also emerge out of a specific economic and political situation of which they are well aware but to which they can see no practical political solution. They are left only with the individual response. It is perhaps not surprising, then, that they appreciate fiction where that individual response is given its head and allowed to run with such intensity.

The video/violence controversy

It is not possible to conclude this chapter on violence without touching on the video/violence controversy. The Hungerford massacre, in which a lone gunman, Michael Ryan, ran amok, killing a number of people, and injuring others, and the fact that *First Blood* was a video that was allegedly found among his effects, means that it would be wilful to ignore it. In a tendentious article by Davies and Peart in the *Sunday Telegraph* of 23 August 1987, the story of the movie is run beside an account of Ryan's exploits. The question that is popularly asked is whether watching violence on television or video causes violent acts in real life. By all accounts the evidence is inconclusive. Here, for instance, is the DES looking at the matter in 1983, making the rather cautious statement:

> Watching scenes of violence may in the short term make some young people more aggressive, and it may act as an outlet for others: considerable research has already been done. Long term effects are less amenable to research ... (p. 10)

and writing in the highly controversial report *Video Violence and Children* edited by Barlow and Hill in 1985,[1] Simms and Melville Thomas state: 'So far as violent viewing is concerned it is not possible in this survey to submit any conclusions regarding the *long-term effects* on minors in a representative way' (p. 86, original emphasis).

Given the inconclusiveness of the evidence it is perhaps legitimate to ask why the authorities want to ban such videos. The answer to such a question may, of course, be quite simply that so long as the evidence *is* inconclusive there is a 'better safe than sorry' case to be made. Discussion with the boys certainly did not shed any further light on the supposed psychological damage of such viewing. John offers both scenarios, that it could cause him to be violent and that it could relieve emotional tension. Here, first of all is his most frightening scenario:

> *John:* Say I watched more violent films than I did anything else, I would want to do something violent.

and later he suggests:

> *John:* The films trigger the people off. They pull the trigger and you can't just leave a gun without firing.

At this point John clearly feels that if he watched too much violence he could, in his words, 'go crazy', that he wouldn't know 'what's right and what's wrong'. However, at another point, in a later tape he suggests quite the reverse, that watching such material is good for him in that it calms him down and helps him to sleep. John echoes precisely the contradictory findings quoted by the DES above, that video violence may act as a short-term trigger, or it may act as a release for violent emotions.

However, when I ask the boys about why the authorities want to ban material they do not touch on any of the above controversy directly. Instead they offer a somewhat different analysis. They see it as a class issue. The issue arises first of all with reference to the banning of both the song and the video of Frankie Goes To Hollywood's performance of *Relax*:

> *John:* as soon as the sort of like upper class people realized it was dirty and that, that's it.
> *Tony:* They banned it.
> *John:* Banned it. You can't hear it on the radio.

I broaden the discussion to include violence and ask why it is that the rich and wealthy want to ban that:

> *John:* the reason why they don't want it to be on telly is because they think it's us.

Brake, in *The Sociology of Youth Culture and Youth Subcultures*, suggests that, since the war, the young working-class male has been portrayed as a 'folk devil'. John seems to echo this in his comments. When I ask him to expand he says:

> *John:* They don't want to be us, they want nothing to do with us. They want to be them, they want to teach their children their things. They don't want to, they don't want their children to become us, poor people ... It's hard to explain.

Matthew agrees with this analysis, so does Tony to a lesser extent. So I ask if the rich see violent videos as threatening:

> *Matthew:* everything they do they reckon is right and everything we do is wrong, and we threaten them, right.
> *John:* It's threatening, that's it. And they don't want to be threatened by us, it's right. Even though they've got more power over us ...

The argument they are making is that the wealthy associate violent material with working-class youth. And even though John is clear about where the power lies, none the less the violent material becomes threatening by association. John adds a further dimension to the analysis by suggesting that the rich regard the local estate, Fen Common, which the school serves, in much the same way as they (the boys) would regard violent films:

> *John:* You see Fen Common.
> *CS:* Yes.
> *John:* And that, to them is like us to the scenery of violent films.

The argument I am making is that *First Blood* and material like it actually represents the experiences and feelings of what it is like to be at the bottom of the pile, both in school and in society at large. In a way in which the phrase is not generally used, it is 'their culture'. This is not to say that *First Blood* and material like it does not find a wider audience than just those at the bottom of the pile. Indeed, that is possibly part of the problem for the powers that be, for if such representations are going to find a wide and sympathetic audience by virtue of the fictional form in which they are cast, then perhaps the powers that be have cause for concern. This is perhaps another way of saying that the expressed fear of the authorities that violent material will produce copycat behaviour in unstable individuals contains within it a political dimension. If such material represents the experiences and feelings of the oppressed in society then perhaps there is a danger that *groups* might copy that behaviour and, in the worst of all possible scenarios direct violence against the state itself. Let me make it clear that I am not suggesting that *First Blood* is a revolutionary tract, far from it. What I am suggesting is that in the intensity of its presentation, in the insistence of its felt experience (to use a Leavisite term for once, albeit in a very alien context) such material brings the feelings of the oppressed to the notice of the general public in a way that the authorities would very much rather it didn't.

Conclusions

In this chapter I have considered violence from several perspectives. In the first place, I have sought to show that these young people live in a real world where violence is a normal part of existence, experienced both within school and outside it. Second, I have tried to show how an individual perspective, sitting within that violent context, finds meaning in, and appreciates the felt experience offered by a fiction such as *First Blood*. Third, I have placed that experience within a wider political context. Fourth, in touching upon the video/violence controversy, I have suggested that there could well be political undertones to the ostensibly purely humanitarian desire to protect society by controlling the violence in such material. Finally, as the chapter heading indicates, I have ignored the female experience of violence. The parameters of the argument have been defined by boys, and the details of the discussion have never challenged the view of an all-male world. In subsequent chapters I hope to redress the balance.

Note

1 For an account of the controversy surrounding the Barlow and Hill report, see Brown, B. (1984a, 1984b) and Barker, M. (ed.) (1984).

4 Girls, gender, violence and the paranormal

Introductory

This chapter is dominated by issues of gender, issues which fall into two categories. There is, first of all, material where the difference between the responses of boys and the responses of girls to the same material emerges and can be related to cultural differences between the sexes. Second, there is material that is raised by the girls, but which is defined by them in some way or another as relating to a male-dominated society. The issue of girls' fear of attack on the streets is a prime example of the latter, for it is quite clear that they do not fear attack by other women, it is men who are the problem.

Sheila Rowbotham, in *Woman's Consciousness, Man's World*, argues that the role of woman in society has to be seen in terms of the economic structure. Women are, she suggests, marginalized from the mode of production. Men have a value in the cash nexus, offering their labour for economic reward. The woman's role is to reproduce the workforce and service its needs in an unpaid capacity. That Rowbotham's analysis might be somewhat different in a time of higher male unemployment and increasing, low-paid, part-time female employment does not, in my view, affect her main thesis. She suggests that when the ruling class become sanctimonious about the preservation of the family they are really talking about the need to maintain the division of labour between the sexes and the need to ensure that one half of the labour force remains unpaid. 'Women's work' in the workplace is that which most resembles women's work in the home – cooking, cleaning, child care, making clothes. That work, she argues, is not seem as 'work' in the home, where it is unpaid, and it is therefore very poorly paid in the workplace.

Macdonald in 1980 echoes such arguments, and suggests that such social definitions of femininity and the subject choice that they lead to in school, become internalized in a sort of *gender code*. This includes specifically an association of girls with the home, and of boys with the outside world, of girls with inner concerns of personal life, and of boys with action.

Walkerdine in 1981 suggests that such gender identity is somewhat more complex and shifting. Recognizing that individual identity is part of a wider, complex, and changing social world, she suggests that women and girls can be in positions of power at one moment and of powerlessness at another. And Steedman, in 1982, traces some of that complexity in the meanings that three 9-year-old girls negotiate in their writing.

In the present chapter I discuss the readings of girls. It seems to me that many of the meanings that they bring to and take from texts stem from their position in the world as young women, in particular their concern with home, and with inner life and their perceived helplessness and vulnerability in the outside world. However, we shall also see that simple fixed distinctions between boys and girls are not adequate to explain the complexity of response from the girls, that while in some cases they may confirm expectations, in other cases they confound them.

The chapter features the discussions of one group of year 10 middle-stream girls in particular – Tracey, Mary, Deborah and Rosie. Of these Tracey is black, the other three are white.

Girls v. boys

My initial survey and, in particular, early questions about what sorts of book are liked by boys and what sorts of book are liked by girls confirmed the conventional wisdom which suggests that girls like animal stories and boys like adventure stories, that girls like love stories and that boys like violence, that boys like heroes and girls like heroines. When, for example, I ask the bottom-stream boys if they will read Lena Kennedy's *Maggie*, the book chosen by the year 10 bottom-stream girls, they are adamant in their rejection of it because it is a girls' book. John evidences both the cover design, featuring a woman in 1930s dress, and the title itself, suggesting as it does a female protagonist. (*Maggie* is shelved under 'Romance' in the bookshops, and it would be difficult to find fault with such a marketing strategy for there is no doubt that it thus finds a wide audience.)

Here are three year 10 middle-stream girls discussing the issue:

> *CS:* Go on, tell me about love stories then.
> *Tina:* They're just good * * *
> *Carol:* Yeh, well if you wanted to have a love story you can't have it too – – –
> *Sara:* You can't have it to a class * * *
> *Sara:* Yeh, 'cause the boys, you know what they're like.
> *Carol:* The boys, the boys wouldn't be interested, that's why we've got books like *Mice and Men* and they're class readers. They should have something like *The Rats*, everyone would like *The Rats* and *The Lair*.

The Rats and *The Lair* are popular horror stories by James Herbert, and here Carol has immediately identified a genre that crosses the gender boundaries and denies the simpler notions of gender-differentiated preference. In the same bottom-stream boys' group I mentioned above, Tony expresses great enthusiasm for Stephen King's *Carrie*, which has a female protagonist but which is also a horror story. *Carrie* will feature quite a lot later in this chapter, but first I wish to look at distinctions between male and female *readings* which will perhaps tell us more than the simple statistical surveys offer.

In the previous chapter I looked in some detail at *First Blood*. It was a book that spoke to a culture of violent male-to-male relationships, and it seemed to me unlikely that any girls' group would be interested in reading it at all. I was thus somewhat surprised when two of the middle-stream girls decided to read it. Both of them were familiar with the video and had opted for the book on the strength of that. In contrast to the boys, they prefer the ending of the book, where Rambo and Teazle are killed, to the end of the film where Rambo walks free and inviolate. We have seen how important it was to John that Rambo did walk free at the end of the film – it was a sign of his integrity and power. Furthermore, the boys were irritated by the psychologizing of the book, feeling that it interrupted the action. Rosie, by contrast, has picked up on the more complex psychological exploration of the characters in the book, and is aware of the paternal feeling that Teazle develops for Rambo. Thus, in contrast to John, she feels that the end of the film is merely preparation for a sequel and wishes instead that the film had ended with the two deaths:

> *Rosie:* It would have had a more sort of psychological meaning to it.

I take up the issue of whether the book is a boys' book or not. I point out that, by and large, it features men without women, that the movie is an all-action movie and the book is pretty well an all-action book, and that it has lots of violence and blood. Tracey likes the violence and blood, a common reaction from lots of girls and many boys. It is Rosie, however, who suggests there is more to the book than I have indicated:

> *Rosie:* Yeh but the thing is they've all got, they've all, it's got er, they've all got feelings. * * * It tells you about their past and how they feel, that sort of thing ... and it says about Teazle's wife leaving him so it does bring it down on to a more sort of human level.

Furthermore, in the film, despite a popular view that Stalone represents the ultimate in macho, for these girls it is not the case:

> *Rosie:* Sylvester Stalone hasn't sort of got that really macho image.

and the girls go on to instance his eyes in particular, which suggest that he's really nice and kind underneath.

The distinctions in response between boys and girls, so far as *First Blood* is concerned, do initially suggest that girls prefer feelings and boys prefer action. The boys' reading of *First Blood* concentrates on male power and integrity, which are exemplified in the action. The girls are much more responsive to details that render the characters human, in Rosie's term, recognizing that they have feelings and past histories that affect their behaviour in the present. It is not, however, that girls do not read for the action, as we shall see in Chapter 9, it is rather that they also read for the relationships and the characterization.

The arguments, noted above, that boys and girls develop different notions of self in accordance with their different economic positions in society, would support a notion that the enculturation of boys leads to a male self-image that is concerned with work and earning power. It follows, I would argue, that the emphasis in that enculturation will be on the competitive individual achievement of boys and men, an emphasis that is reinforced by unemployment with the struggle to get a job in the first place. For girls, by contrast, as Rowbotham and Steedman suggest, the emphasis is still on homemaking – an emphasis, I would argue, that highlights, along with domestic skills, personal relationships. The casual, and not so casual, conversation of many of the girls' groups, both on and off the tapes, is about boyfriends, other girls, and the everyday moralities of social intercourse. The boys rarely raise such issues or such topics. Such cultural differentiation, I suggest, is reflected in the choice of and response to the books they read and the films they watch. In the case of *First Blood* it is not that the girls reject the text altogether because it looks like a boys' book. It is rather that they find things in the book that enable them to read it differently from the boys. They exploit, in other words, the *plurality* of the text.

There are texts, and readings, where the girls do not so much read different parts of the text from the boys, as read the same parts with quite contrary effects. Umberto Eco suggested in 1981 that ideologically closed texts are open to 'aberrant' readings. (I shall explore this idea more fully later.) What happens in the next section, I would suggest, is that the girls succeed in reading *against* the ideological closure of such texts.

The macho and phallic deflation

This 'counter-reading' emerged in discussions of *First Blood* when the book offered particularly specific symbols of male power. Here, for example, is the description of Rambo observing Teazle's gun:

> Rambo shifted his eyes down to Teazle's left side and the hand gun he wore. It was a surprise, not the standard police revolver but a semi-automatic pistol, and from the big handle Rambo decided it was a Browning 9 millimetre.

(pp. 13–14)

After establishing further detail about the power of the gun there is this curiously intimate couple of sentences:

> Rambo had to admit that Teazle carried it awfully well, too. Teazle was five foot six, maybe seven, and for a smallish man that big pistol ought to have hung awkward, but it didn't.

(p. 14)

When I asked the boys about this description of the gun, John saw it in terms of the respective characters' pasts and the future development of the story as Rambo and Teazle fight each other using just such weapons. The girls do not pick up on that, nor do they see the gun as a symbol of power, on the contrary:

> *Rosie:* Makes him look like a big wet I think.

And they continue:

> *Tracey:* You can imagine him sitting in this car, this great big pistol down there
> * * *
> *Rosie:* As though his hardness is measured by the size of his gun. I thought it was really pathetic.

It is very tempting to read such comments in Freudian terms. Once attention is drawn to the possible sexual symbolism it is difficult to resist the temptation to giggle. However, none of us did. What does seem clear is that the girls regard the gun neither as proof of virility nor of power; it is rather a sign of weakness. The 'phallic deflation' interpretation is, however, reinforced by the comments that follow in a later tape when the same group of middle-stream girls discuss James Herbert's *The Fog*. The evidence comes from a fairly extraordinary tape and it is necessary to offer a careful analysis in order to make the link that I am suggesting. On the tape the girls concentrate almost exclusively on two scenes in the book: one is a scene in which two lesbians make love, and the other, dwelt upon at some length, is a notorious passage set in the gymnasium of a boys' boarding school in which the boys engage in an explicitly described sado-masochistic sexual orgy, attacking the PE teacher and beating him to a pulp. On to this scene arrives the sexually repressed deputy head, closely followed by the caretaker brandishing a pair of shears. … Both Mary and Rosie find this scene funny and it is with the analysis of that laughter that I am concerned here.

The agenda for the discussion is set largely by the girls themselves: Tracey, who has elected not to read the book, asks how the film of the same name, which she has seen, differs from it, and Mary immediately relates the scene in the boys' school to her. (In fact the John Carpenter film of the same name bears no relation to the book at all.) Mary had read both this scene and a scene with two lesbians more than once when she read the book originally. She had enjoyed the book, in contrast to Rosie, who was familiar with the book because both her mum and her aunt had copies, but who had refused to read it when she had the opportunity. However, in the course of the tape it is Rosie who finds the passages in the text and Mary who reads them out loud. Mary first of all reads out the lesbian scene (pp. 113–14) and Rosie says:

> *Rosie:* I don't know how you can sit there and read that, girl.

Rosie finds the scene disgusting. It is, she suggests,

> *Rosie:* Just the sort of thing that you get in dirty porno films, that's all …

Despite her comments, Rosie later finds the boys' school scene (Herbert 1975, pp. 64–7) and asks Mary to read it out loud. Mary proceeds to read virtually the whole scene. At the end of the reading Rosie says:

> *Rosie:* I thought that was so funny, I did. That bit I thought was hilarious.

Rosie is referring to the whole scene, not just the end, and I would suggest from the evidence of further discussion that her laughter can be interpreted in a number of ways. In the first place she finds the scene to be full of incongruity, for when I ask what is funny about a scene that I find horrific she says:

> *Rosie:* I don't know, it's, it's queer funny. It's not funny ha ha, it's sort of, 'Eh? Funny.' Do you know what I mean?
> *CS:* Oh I see what you mean.
> *Tracey:* 'Oh, so that's what they do.'

The behaviour presented in the scene is so bizarre that it makes her laugh:

> *Rosie:* I laughed at it ...
> *Mary:* It makes you laugh ...
> *Rosie:* and I had to read it again to sort of believe it.

However, as well as this she finds the scene arbitrary within the structure of the book. Indeed it is her case against the book that it gratuitously strings together scenes of sex and violence with no underlying story to otherwise relate them. Thus the very inclusion of the scene she describes as 'laughable'.

I would suggest that there are a number of things going on here, and that part of the laughter arises from the very activity of reading such sexually explicit passages out loud. Such laughter arises from making explicit the culturally taboo, a theme that gets a fuller treatment in a subsequent chapter. (The dual nature of Rosie's response as she both complains about the gratuitous and pornographic nature of the scenes, and yet encourages Mary to read them, will, I hope become more comprehensible in that chapter, too.)

It is quite possible, too, that the laughter covers revulsion to, or at least embarrassment at, the homosexuality. In discussion both Mary and Rosie admit ambivalent feelings of revulsion and tolerance, which does, I suspect, contribute to their response.

It is clear also that the three girls bring individual psychologies to bear upon the process, but this is not a path that is pursued here. That does not leave us, however, with nothing more to say, for it is still pertinent to ask what the girls laugh *at*, and to discuss the issues that then arise.

In the middle of the tape Mary reads this passage from p. 65: 'Several tore off their own shorts and vests and began rubbing at their own already enlarged penises ...'. There are giggles as Mary continues reading and then Rosie virtually repeats the comment she made about Rambo's gun (above):

> *Rosie:* It's pathetic. It's so funny.

When I ask Mary later what is funny about the scene she is both specific and explicit:

> *Mary:* Boys masturbating, that makes me laugh, that makes me laugh.

Though I have already quoted Rosie's comment at the end of the passage and suggested that it refers to the whole scene, it comes, along with an interesting comment from Tracey, after the climax of the scene (p. 68) in which the deputy head has his 'huge swollen penis' cut off by the caretaker with the pair of shears:

> *Tracey:* He's no longer a man, he's a woman.
> *Rosie:*   I thought that was so funny, I did. That bit I thought was hilarious.

The laughter, then, is specifically placed at points of maximum male sexual assertion. I would suggest that to find the scene horrific is to take that assertion seriously and these girls undermine the horror by refusing to do so. In addition, it is a scene of exclusively male sexual activity culminating in the emasculation of one of the main characters. Tracey's comment suggests that to lose the penis is to lose masculine identity, and her tone of voice on the tape carries with it a certain satisfaction at such an outcome. It would be possible to argue that that satisfaction, together with Mary's hilarity at and Rosie's contempt for the masturbating boys, sees the seriousness with which both the boys and the text take the activity as absurd.

A number of boys' groups read *The Fog* but I never succeeded in getting them to talk at any length about the boys' school scene. None of them, however, thought it was funny. It takes girl readers to puncture the priapic presumption of the scene, and to reveal an essential absurdity that lies beneath.

So far I have looked at examples of gender-differentiated response to material that was read, and enjoyed, by both boys and girls. We have seen how the same material is susceptible to different *readings*, in some cases mutually exclusive readings, and I have suggested that those differences are rooted in gender-differentiated cultural points of view. Next I want to look at concerns that are specific to girls, but which also relate to differences between the sexes.

Violence, girls' fear, and the supernatural

Stephen King's *Carrie* was chosen by a year 10 middle-stream girls' group. It was made into a film by Brian de Palma with Sissy Spacek in the lead, and many of the pupils I talked with saw it in the course of my investigation as it was shown on television that Christmas. It was a book that was popular with the groups, both boys and girls, and I was nagged constantly by groups who wanted to be next with it.

Before discussing the book in further detail, however, I want to sketch in the background culture of violence and fear that emerges in discussion with this group of middle-stream girls. The issues emerge out of their descriptions of un-explained noises at home, wardrobe doors that seem to open and close on their own, typical teenage experimentation with Ouija boards and so on. First of all they talk about spirits coming to get them:

> *Rosie:* Experts say that if you worry about that sort of thing it's more likely to ...
> *Tracey:* happen ...
> *Rosie:* happen to you, because you're giving off heat and that * * * 'cause you're worrying and erm ...
> *CS:* You attract them.
> *Rosie:* They say spirits can sense that and they come to you. I mean I worry about it all the while (*laughter*) 'cause I mean they tell you not to worry about it but I do.

Such worries are real enough even if what these girls are ostensibly worried *about* is, I would suggest, the product of adolescent fantasy. If they attempt real solutions to such imagined threats, however, they are promptly presented with real threats:

> *Mary:* What I do is I try and get out more at nights * * *, and go round friends, but it's worse now because if you go out at night on your own and you're on your way to your friend's house you can get attacked, and that worries you.
> *Rosie:* Mmm. Especially in the dark.
> *Tracey:* Yeah, 'cause I get off the bus right and there's quite a lot of people down, going down Blackburn Park but as soon as you turn up Coventry Road there's hardly no-one up there, and you've got all alleyways leading out the housing and you think some of them will come and attack you. It's really bad.

Such fears are still at the level of what they imagine might happen to them. However they have real experiences of being accosted to support such fears. Mary, for instance, used to have to walk home through a street frequented by prostitutes:

> *Mary:* I was walking down that road you know, to go to my Mum's, and a car stopped, you know a bloke stopped and he kind of looked at me, and I just walked on, and he realized, you know I just wasn't anything to do with that street.

If they haven't been attacked they know someone who has:

> *Rosie:* I'd never walk through City Meadow – – – in the dark * * * there's been about ten rapes down there in the past three years, and my aunty walked through there once and she got attacked but luckily she got away.

Fear of the unreal comes to mirror the fear of the real. As Rowbotham and Macdonald suggest, above, girls are enculturated to regard their domain as the home. Thus, I would argue, they come to regard the outside world as threatening, in contrast to the boys of the previous chapter who find it challenging. That the threat is specifically sexual is implied by their conversation so far. Mary makes the point explicitly and draws the parallel most clearly:

> *Mary:* It's, it's quite frightening, I mean if you, if you stay in you can worry about what can happen to you with spirits and if you go out you worry about if you're going to be raped.
>
> *Rosie:* Mmm.
>
> *Tracey:* Yeh.

Finally, and in a way that unites these two concerns most graphically, there are the videos they watch. More often than not these involve the supernatural, and almost always, as they relate the plots, they involve a female lead who is the victim of physical assault and sexual violation.

We see thus that meaning is made of the world by the combination of shared stories of fear of the dark on the streets and of teenage fears of the supernatural. These fears of what they imagine might happen to them are supported by real experience of being accosted themselves, or of their relatives being accosted. Thus what at first might appear to be imaginary fears turn out to have a real basis in the real world. At the same time as I was doing my research, for instance, the exploits of a local rapist were filling the headlines of the national press. Is it, then, surprising that their conversation is full of the videos that so dramatically represent their salient concerns?

So far we have seen how these girls' emerging sexuality puts them in positions of vulnerability in the outside male world, and we have suggested that many of the videos they watch dramatically represent just that vulnerability. *Carrie*, by contrast, offers a precise, if horrendous, reversal of that situation, for it is the story of a girl whose emerging sexuality gives her tremendous power.

Carrie has been born with powers of telekinesis – the ability to move objects just by thinking about it – which develop enormously after the onset of menstruation. The only child of a single parent, she has been brought up by a religious fundamentalist mother who regards sex as sin and who even regards the onset of menstruation and the development of breasts as sinful. Thus, when, at the age of sixteen, she has her first period in the showers at high school, Carrie does not know what is happening to her, though the other girls do, and a scene ensues in which they taunt her mercilessly. Here is a sample:

> Then the laughter, disgusted, contemptuous, horrified, seemed to rise and bloom into something jagged and ugly, and the girls were bombarding her with tampons and sanitary napkins, some from purses, some from the broken dispenser on the wall. They flew like snow and the chant became: 'Plug it *up*. plug it *up*. plug it –'
>
> (p. 13)

From this first incident the rest of the plot flows (and I choose the word advisedly) with increasing horror and inevitability. The lawyer's daughter who led the assault upon Carrie is banned from prom night, the leaving dance that is *the* social high spot for all the characters, and she and her disreputable boyfriend plan a revenge in which a bucket of pig's blood is poured over Carrie at the climactic moment. Carrie meanwhile develops her powers of telekinesis by exercising them on larger and larger objects, and uses them to fight her mother for her independence. Through a complicated plot development she ends up going to the prom night with the handsomest boy in the year, wearing a blood red evening gown, and the couple are elected king and queen of the ball. At this point the pigs blood is tipped over her, and Carrie proceeds to take the most dreadful revenge, in the first place on all at the prom night, who are trapped, and then burned to death, then on the town, which she sets ablaze, and finally on her mother, whose heart she stops. Only at this point does the flow of both the blood and the plot cease. The book is full of images of or references to blood of various sorts, hence my emphasis here. One cannot open it without finding a phrase or an image – 'the blood of the lamb' and Pilate washing his hands, to take two at random from pages 112–13.

You will have already detected a personal element to my account of the book. Let me, at this point, focus my response in more clearly personal terms. *Carrie* has a number of narrators, as we shall see below, and I must confess, I became quite fascinated by the skill with which King deploys them to persuade readers of the 'truth' of what he is describing. There are little Hitchcockian jokes (one of the learned accounts is by someone called McGuffin) neatly placed to draw the reader's attention to the game he is playing, and I was reminded by nothing so much as Hitchcock's own description of *Psycho* as a joke, a game played on the audience. Furthermore, I was struck by the deployment of the imagery that I have mentioned above. It is certainly true that I felt manipulated as reader, and that I resented it. But I have to confess that I did somewhat rejoice at the awesome revenge that Carrie takes on the world. The film dispenses with such narrative complexity, but otherwise follows the story pretty closely. I find de Palma's camera work beguiling. He sets up scenes in long fluid takes and the whole thing is a very elegant piece of film-making. And there is a wicked shock effect at the end, as Carrie's hand emerges from the grave, that had me shitting bricks, to resort to the vernacular!

Foucault in 1978 suggests that the discourse of sexuality is also a discourse of the operation and distribution of power in Western society. It is tempting to read *Carrie* in this light, for Carrie's mother attempts to construct her daughter in a discourse that completely denies her biology. When that discourse is punctured by the inevitable emergence of that biology, the power that was contained by that discourse is released upon the world: to juxtapose Yeats and a more modern colloquialism, the centre cannot hold, and all hell is let loose.

Such an interpretation may be considered an over-interpretation, but it is true to say that the sudden and unprepared emergence of female sexuality does release the most awesome power. It is possible to read the story both as an exemplification of male fear of the power of female sexuality, and as a very celebration of that power over a helpless, male-dominated world. As we shall see, the girls make a number of links that make the nature of such readings quite explicit.

Carrie's mother's religious extremism takes the form, as we have noted, of total sexual repression, both in herself and in her daughter. She is portrayed as really believing that if Carrie had led a sinless life then she would never have developed secondary sexual characteristics at all:

> *Rosie:*   I think her mum's a bit of a nut actually.
> *Mary:*   She was.
> *Tracey:*   Yeh so do I. She went really over the top about that.
> *Deborah:*   Yeh, same with me.
> *Mary:*   She was, she was a fanatic.
> *Deborah:*   She was really weird.
> *Rosie:*   'Cause it says here that erm when Carrie was about um three she was, her neighbour was sunbathing topless.

Rosie finds the passage in the text and reads the incident complete with the assertion that the development of breasts is a sign of sin, hence Mrs White's name for them: 'dirtypillows' (pp. 32, 33). Mary picks up on this and relates it to a much older tradition of male fear of and suppression of female sexuality:

> *Mary:*   Hundreds of years ago it was erm, people thought you were bewitched if you came on, if you passed blood in that way.

And she continues:

> *Mary:*   They thought that was, you were bewitched, you had the devil in you and they wouldn't have nothing to do with you.
> *Deborah:*   But that's every woman then, innit?

Deborah's pertinent comment leads Mary to elaborate:

> *Mary:*   The men were the ones that erm were mostly religious 'cause a lot of women were coming on and they thought they were bewitched, they were evil, and when they came off they thought they were alright ...

Mary here suggests one implication of the argument, that religious repression of female sexuality is male repression of female sexuality. The analysis is complicated by the fact that the spokesperson for the repression of sexuality in the book is, of course, Carrie's mother (and is further complicated by the fact that the book is written by a man, which leads us down paths of authorial intention, narrational independence, and so on, which in the end will not help to clarify this particular discussion). But Mrs White's fundamentalism can certainly be seen in the light of a specifically paternalist biblical tradition that makes it perfectly clear that it was the woman who tempted the man to eat the forbidden fruit and thus brought sin into the Garden of Eden.

Tracey's view of Mrs White is rather different from the view of the others. Her comments raise a question that stems, I would suggest, from the very complication I have outlined above, that it is a female character who is the spokesperson for the repression of female sexuality:

Tracey: In her way I think her mum's protecting her as well.

When I ask her to expand on this she does:

Tracey: Even though she was sort of mad and religious and everything I think she, down to earth, to the base of it she's trying to protect her daughter from all that sort of stuff because she got pregnant and she's gone through a lot, she's gone through a real lot with her husband being drunk and everything, and now she's trying to protect her daughter from going through the pain and suffering that she'd been through.

Tracey's suggestion, then, is that while Mrs White's religious behaviour is without doubt over the top, beneath it is a real insistence that women should have control over their own bodies and not just be the victims of men. Indeed, her comment can in one sense be seen as a critique of the book, which only allows of one form of female independence — to wit, religious mania. (Tracey's single-parent family background may give her a unique insight into this contradiction, though this was not an idea I followed up.)

We thus have an analysis that, on the one hand, suggests that the repression of female sexuality is the product of a paternalist culture, no matter that that repression is mediated by a female character. On the other hand, within that paternalist framework, such repression is an, albeit negative, sign of women's assertion of the need for control over their own bodies, and independence from male demands and male control.

In a way that should no longer surprise us, it is beginning to emerge that *Carrie* is deeply riven with contradiction. In one sense it is a violent plea for female independence, while in another it clings to those very values that it challenges. The story is about the conflict between 'normal' male-dominated sexuality and the repressed and distorted sexuality of the heroine which challenges it. That female independence can only be achieved through religious mania in the mother and paranormal powers in the daughter does not for a moment undermine the vigorousness of that challenge; on the contrary, it allows King to play it to the hilt. But the fact that it is couched in those terms allows of only two resolutions — either that Carrie 'rejoins' the normal sexuality of her peers or that that female independence self-destructs. In fact, with some cunning, King has it both ways. Carrie has both her moment of triumph at the ball and she and her mother do destroy each other, taking the town with them for good measure.

The moment of triumph at the ball is deeply conventional. Carrie's independence from her mother (another major theme in the book that we have barely touched upon), her recognition and acceptance of herself as a sexual being, and her 'arrival' in the normal world are all achieved in terms of male approval and ratification by the conventional paternalistic culture. Here, for example, is the moment when Carrie's date, Tommy Ross, calls to pick her up to take her to the ball:

She opened the door and he was there, nearly blinding in white dinner jacket and dark dress pants.

They looked at each other, and neither said a word.

She felt that her heart would break if he uttered so much as the wrong sound, and if he laughed she would die. She felt – actually, physically – her whole life narrow to a point that might be an end or the beginning of a widening beam.

Finally, helpless, she said: 'Do you like me?'

He said: 'You're beautiful.'

She was.

(p. 118)

And with that final 'She was' the objective narrator (and, as I have suggested, it is a book with a number of narrators) endorses the judgement. It is Mary who recognizes this, and with implicit approval:

> *Mary:*   There's one person that I thought, that I really liked for doing something
> and that was Tommy Ross.
> *Tracey:* Yeh.

In the film, though not in the book, Tommy kisses Carrie:

> *Mary:*   Yeh, he kissed her in the middle of the dance floor.
> *Deborah:* Oh yeh.
> *Mary:*   Really long as well.
> *Tracey:*   And I thought, yeh, that was nice.

It is the boy, then, who gives Carrie the seal of approval, who establishes, by his approval, her achievement of personal independence and sexual maturity, and who marks the achievement of her most dearly held desire, 'to be like the others'. Here is Mary both emphasizing the point and suggesting, none the less, that boys have to behave in ways that are acceptable to girls:

> *Mary:* I felt as if he did like her and he realized that she wasn't different, that
> people just treated her different * * * And he did like her and it showed. I
> mean some boys can be right pains but you know he wasn't.

Of course a bit of judicious casting can make all the difference:

> *Rosie:* Who played Tommy Ross?
> *Mary:* I don't know but he was ever so nice! (*Laughter*)

The response of readers/viewers to characters can thus include as 'simple' a matter as sexual attraction, whether they fancy him, or her, or not, and a character can win approval for his or her action simply by being played by a certain actor. Once the film of the book has been seen it becomes impossible to entirely disentangle such cross-fertilization. It is noticeable, however, that it is the three girls who have seen the film that are so vocal in their approval of Tommy Ross; Rosie is silent on the subject.

What I am suggesting, after Catherine Belsey, a critic whose work has an important influence on all my analysis here, and whom I shall be discussing in more detail later, is that *Carrie* interpellates – calls forth – a reader who is herself divided by the contradictions of the ideological construction of 'girl' or 'woman' in present-day society. The central contradiction of the book, I would suggest, is between Carrie's need to find her own identity and autonomy and the fact that that identity is ratified by male approval in a paternalistic world. The responses of the girls seem to echo some of that complexity, some of that conflict.

Mothers and daughters

In this brief section I want to draw attention to an interesting phenomenon that emerged in specific discussion of the film. As already indicated, the book contains a major scene in the showers when Carrie has her first period. This scene is faithfully reproduced in the movie and thus contains plenty of nudity. In other respects also the film pulls no punches, the lawyer's daughter and her disreputable boyfriend, for instance, engage in felatio just before the final show-down. It is discretely filmed but there is no doubt about what is going on. At the end of the film Carrie uses her powers to throw kitchen knives, scissors, and so on, at her mother, pinning her against the wall in the form of a crucifix as she bleeds to death. And at the very end of the film a hand emerges from a grave in a shock effect that I have already mentioned, and that left these girls gasping, too. There are, in other words, a number of elements about the film that might lead it to be considered 'unsuitable' viewing for girls of this age. I asked them directly about this, and discovered that far from being considered unsuitable it was actually treated as family viewing for the three girls who did see it. (Rosie's mother saw the film but told Rosie that it wasn't suitable for her because it would frighten her too much, a verdict that Rosie does not resent, though she adds that her boyfriend has recorded it so she will probably see it anyway.) Here is Deborah's family:

> *Deborah:* Yeh. Well my dad had gone to bed, because he'd got to go, to get up for work. Anyway um … yeh my mum, my mum and my sister were with me. They always watch things like that. Most, my mum was the one that wanted to watch it mainly. * * * So I came in a bit through it, you know, I came in a little bit when it was already on and she said 'Right shush, sit down, I want to watch this film!' (*Laughter*) So … I just sat down and watched the film.

Mary blackmailed her family into it:

> *Mary:* See I said to my mum and dad 'Right, I'm going to watch *Carrie*' and I said 'It's for my work at school and if I don't watch it I'll miss it and I'll have to watch it on video. We haven't got a video now so we're

watching it and I don't care what you say, we're watching it!' So we sat
and watched it.
(*Laughter*)
Deborah: So they had no choice.
Mary: And they, they quite ... they had no choice.

Mary indeed has an argument with her dad, not about the suitability of the film,
but about who was in the plot to pour the blood over Carrie. Her dad hadn't
particularly liked it, but her mum:

Mary: My mum quite enjoyed it, she said it was different.

In all three of these families mums and daughters get together and enjoy the
film and the men are in one way or another excluded. This becomes explicit as
both Mary and Tracey describe how their families watched the nudity in the
shower scene:

Tracey: My mum was well into the film at the beginning – – – it was funny.
Mary: My dad was going ... especially you know all the girls were naked, he was,
his eyes ...
Tracey: (*Laughs*) My mum was going to her boyfriend 'Shut your eyes, shut your
eyes'.
Mary: My mum was sitting there going ... looking at Dad.
CS: So she wasn't embarrassed about having you there?
Mary: No, 'cause she knows, she thinks that I know more than what she does.

In both cases the nudity unites the mothers and daughters across the age divide
against the prurience of the men. There is, then, a sense in which, and in a way
that the term was never traditionally used, *Carrie* is a 'women's picture'.

Conclusions

I have tried to place the responses of girls in the context of the social construction of gender, outlined briefly at the beginning of the chapter. In the first place
books are chosen because they appear to have an appeal to one sex or the other.
Once the book is chosen, if the text has the requisite plurality then it is open to
alternative readings by boys and girls. If, on the other hand, texts, or parts of
texts seem to be ideologically *closed*, then it seems to be possible to read *against*
the closure, as I argue the girls did with parts of *First Blood* and *The Fog*.
   In the next chapter I return to *The Fog*, revisiting some of the evidence I have
touched on in this chapter.

5 Cultural order

Introductory

This chapter and the next are concerned with the ways in which fiction is a source of cultural information and the ways in which young people read for cultural information. It will, once again, concern itself with popular forms and examine the ways in which those forms offer sites of cultural typification and definition. One of the elements in such defining processes is, of necessity, arriving at negative as well as positive definitions. In the social construction of reality that culture is, it is necessary to learn the boundaries of cultural order, and to learn what those boundaries are it is just as necessary to learn what is beyond them as to learn what is within them. In the learning process, then, the concept of the cultural 'other' is crucial, and we shall see in the course of this chapter that much attention is given to the various 'others' we construct for ourselves to project beyond the boundaries of cultural order in order to both identify and question those boundaries.

In the introduction to her book *Fantasy: The Literature of Subversion*, Rosemary Jackson suggests:

> The fantastic traces the unsaid and the unseen of culture; that which has been silenced, made invisible, covered over and made 'absent'.

and:

> From about 1800 onwards those fantasies produced within a capitalist economy express some of the debilitating psychological effects of inhabiting a materialistic culture. They are peculiarly violent and horrific.

and:

> [The] introduction of the 'unreal' is set against the category of the 'real' – a category which the fantastic interrogates by its difference.
>
> (all quotes p. 4.)

This chapter is about the ways in which young readers use fiction as a virtual world in which to both define and, in Jackson's word, 'interrogate' cultural order. The text which features in this chapter, James Herbert's *The Fog* (1975), is certainly a fantastic text, but we will see that the net spreads wider than any conventional definition of fantasy. In the sense that any fiction is unreal, fantasy, then, becomes only a special case of fiction, defined in terms of a particular genre, and some of the functions of fantasy that Jackson outlines can be found operating elsewhere. Jackson's highlighting of the violent and horrific nature of the material is very pertinent to the present study, for, as we have already seen, the books that many adolescents revel in are both violent and horrific.

The subject matter of *The Fog* is sex, violence and death; of *First Blood*, violence and death; of *Carrie*, sex, violence and death. It is in these fields that the battle for cultural order is fought; the first two, sex and violence, are of salient importance to the young, and, as we shall see, they are not uninterested in death either.

Stevi Jackson points out in *Childhood and Sexuality*, that bringing children and sexuality together 'breaks a particularly powerful social taboo: that children and sex should be kept apart'. Furthermore, adolescents 'inhabit a strange in between world, no longer children but still not adults, told to "grow up" but denied the opportunity of participating in adult life' (pp. 27–8). She traces the complex web of censorship and control that categorizes the explicitness of sexual content in films and on television, and shows how the transmission of sexual knowledge from the older to the younger generation is hedged about with caveats and caution. In school, too, the transmission of sexual information is very carefully monitored. Indeed, Stevi Jackson argues that the protection of the child, most often used as a reason for this careful control, is not the real reason. The real reason, she suggests, is the need to protect the moral values of society at large, particularly those that pertain to the family. The furore in the late 1980s over the 'promotion' of homosexuality by local authorities, for instance, can, I would argue, be seen in these terms, too. Sheila Rowbotham places the family within a political context, as we have already seen, and indeed, as Foucault has suggested, the whole discourse of sexuality is one that is imbued with power relations disposed in one form or another.

We have also noted, in Chapter 3, the work of John Schostak, who suggests that violence has also changed from the overt to the covert in both family and school, as methods of control have become more subtle, and as, in Gramscian terms, forceful suppression has been replaced by hegemonic coercion. Foucault, too, traces the rise of the idea of non-violence as it became paradoxically necessary to value life more highly in order that it should be protected by the state with more and more potentially devastating weapons. And yet, as I have already noted, we live in a century when millions of human beings have been killed by other human beings.

If we accept the arguments outlined so far then we will see that both sexuality and violence are hidden away from children and adolescents by the institutions of the family and the school, and the chief weapon of that hiding, I would argue, is adult hypocrisy.

It is instructive to look briefly at how we deal with such subject matter in the wider social sphere, particularly when confronted with behaviour that is widely condemned. At around the same time as I was doing my research the multiple rapist known as 'the Fox' was captured. Here is the *Daily Mail*'s headline of 27 February 1985:

THE FOX – EVIL BEYOND WORDS

Inside there is a double page spread with the sub-heading:

UNMASKED: CRUEL MR. NOBODY WITH A MONSTROUS SECRET

When faced with unacceptable behaviour we resort to definitions in terms of non-existence, and, in order to emphasize the non-human, to animal imagery. The evil is unsayable, 'beyond words', and the ambiguity of the sub-heading allows both that the secrecy is monstrous and that the content of the secret is monstrous.

The arguments of this chapter should be seen within the framework that I have outlined. There is initially an investigation of cultural norms and stereo-types which are established by society and which are then used in the nego-tiation of individual identity. There is secondly the investigation of material which is kept hidden by conventional cultural discourse, despite the fact that what is not talked of is perfectly acceptable behaviour. There is finally the inves-tigation of the culturally unacceptable, in order to both better identify the acceptable and also at the same time to question it.

Sites of cultural typification

Let me open the discussion of *The Fog* with a personal response. The book featured in my opening chapter and, as I suggest there, on first reading I certainly thought it exploitative. The construction, in particular the use of cliff-hanger and interrupted narratives, was blatantly obvious. I felt highly manipulated as a reader by Herbert, and I felt that the book was deliberately put together so as to revel in the sex and violence: indeed, I entirely agreed with Rosie's comments reported in Chapter 4: 'it's just the sort of thing you get in dirty porno films, that's all'. None the less, I was totally gripped and read it at a sitting! When I first read it, in the mid-1970s, it was the first time I had read such sexual detail in such graphic form – it was certainly arousing stuff! Add to which the most notorious scene combined two 'hidden discourses' – homo-sexuality and sadism. Perhaps that was my starting point in rethinking the book. The question of why two such socially forbidden discourses should appeal so widely became an interesting one for me, and subsequent readings have found more and more of interest in the book, as will be evident from the discussion in this chapter and elsewhere. I am left admiring Herbert's skill at racing the reader along: the book is like a well-constructed roller-coaster. That said, I always did prefer the dodgems.

Character

I talked to a group of top-stream year 10 boys about the book. In order to follow the discussion it is necessary to summarize the plot. In a sleepy Wiltshire village there is an 'earthquake', subsequently revealed to be the result of underground weapons testing. Through the fissure that opens up in the ground a fog emerges. Instead of dissipating in the normal course of events, it coagulates and grows. It is subsequently revealed to be the result of chemical warfare experimentation, a deadly 'microplasma'. When people pass through it, it attacks their brains and makes them 'mad'. The madness is manifested in the form of monstrously violent or sexual behaviour – in one notorious passage a combination of the two – or in a death wish. Thus, after the fog has settled on Bournemouth the entire population of the town commits suicide by walking into the sea. The hero, Holman, is an undercover agent working for the Ministry of the Environment. His job is to uncover pollution and other misuses of the environment by big business, by the Ministry of Defence and by other government and non-government agencies. He survives the fog, becomes thus immune to its effects, and is then crucial to the plot because he is the only person in the land who can approach the fog in order to get a sample from which an antidote could be prepared.

In popular forms character is often defined in action and can be categorized in terms of function within the plot, a theme I shall return to later. Suffice it to say here, in relation to *The Fog*, that Holman is the hero and thus has to do heroic things. He has a number of 'helpers' who aid him in his task, and a number of 'hinderers' who obstruct him. Some are ambivalent, most noticeably the policeman who has to look after him, and who provides the sting in the tale by nearly finishing him off even after the fog has been destroyed. The villain is the fog itself, but there is a whole succession of characters whose role effectively is to be 'manifestations of the villain', these being the characters who get caught in the fog and then go mad.

Such an analysis of character is purely in terms of plot role, but it is possible to examine the characters and their relationships from a slightly different perspective. Here are the boys talking about the hold the caretaker in a boys' boarding school has over one of the teachers. They have met previously in the forces. I ask them why we have this digression into these two particular characters' pasts:

> *Peter:* It explains the hold the caretaker had over him, 'cause he, it said he had a hold over him.
> *Kenneth:* Yeh, Yeh.
> *Peter:* But you didn't know what.
> *Kenneth:* It helps you to understand the characters as well, it goes into more depth in them.

Kenneth's recognition that to tell the reader what a person has *done* will deepen one's appreciation of his or her character reinforces the point that in popular fiction character is presented and developed through action. Peter brings out another feature, however: the way in which Herbert uses these characters to sketch in a whole variety of social vignettes. This is how Roland, another of the group, expresses it:

> *Roland:* He does that though, in his books, he sort of picks out little scenes – – –
> separate stories of people's lives and then puts that in with the overall
> story. It's like, it's just like all different little books in one book.

These social vignettes bear some further examination. They are presented, generally, in terms of oppositional pairs: the vicar and his congregation, the poacher and the landowner, the drinking husband and the nagging wife, the lesbian and her unfaithful lover, the homosexual schoolmaster and the boys, the corporal and the two privates who run him ragged, the airline pilot and his unfaithful wife, and so on. These conflictual relationships are drawn from what I. A. Richards called 'stock'. They are representative rather than unique, typical rather than unusual. Thus the vicar wants to broaden the minds of his congregation from their narrow concerns, the poacher hates the landowner, the strict disciplinarian has a secret desire for his charges, the lesbian's lover has finally found 'the right thing' (p. 116) in heterosexual love, and so on. The fog then intervenes in each of these relationships and certain actions follow.

In *The Structural Study of Myth*, Lévi-Strauss suggests not only that characters in myths are always associated with certain actions, but also that these character–action associations can be grouped and an underlying organizational principle discovered. So it is here. Each of the actions that follows the intervention of the fog violently resolves the conflict that is inherent in the vignettes. In addition, these resolutions have ideological import in that each of them, with one exception, involves an underdog gaining revenge on an oppressor. These ideological implications are revisited in Chapter 6, as is the exception. Here we can further note that actions occur in answering pairs. Sexual betrayal is followed by revenge; animals are tamed, then go wild; the colonel beats the poacher and in return the poacher kills the colonel.

In this chapter, for the moment, I wish to explore a little further the representative nature of the social relationships. As I indicated earlier, I would argue that such generalizations are of vital importance to adolescents learning about adult relationships. Popular fiction constructs generalities, values, and views of relationships which the young can use in order to begin to understand the world and their place in it.

Herbert's social vignettes sit at these sites of cultural generalization about human relationships, and the fog releases particularly dramatic representations of those relationships. If, for instance, the *essential* relationship between a vicar and his flock is that of a religious and moral authority set over the ignorant or the uninitiated, how apt that the fog should release the underlying obverse of that – contempt – by making the vicar pee on them from the pulpit. Or if the *essential* relationship between a jilted husband and his wife's new lover is one of sexual jealousy, how apt that the lover should work in the Post Office tower, of all places, and how apt that the husband, by good fortune an airline pilot, should be in such a unique position as to be able to destroy it by flying his airliner at it. (I trust I don't need to labour the phallic symbolism any further!)

Such *essential* relationships are, of course, also sites of cultural generalization and typification and as such constitute particular ideological formulations. Young people, in the negotiation of their own individual courses through the culture, need some signposts against which to chart their own directions. 'Marriage', 'love', 'normal sexuality', 'normal relationships', 'right', 'wrong', 'order', 'chaos', are all cultural constructs. If we want to know how such categories are currently constructed by the culture, then the first place to go will be the primary means of cultural communication – the popular arts: television, video and popular literature.

Cliché

In *The Role of the Reader*, Umberto Eco argues that cliché acts as linguistic generalization that, contrary to the received opinion of many English teachers, is replete with meaning. This group of boys are well aware both of the received opinion and of the communicative power of cliché. They had for instance, not met one English teacher who had not warned them off Herbert, and as often as not the reason was to do with his use of language. Here is Peter:

> *Peter:*   You're supposed to read something that's more um ... advan, advan-
> tageous to your reading sort of like, to your vocabulary.

And here is Roland backing him up:

> *Roland:* [Our English teacher] said it didn't use a very good vocabulary. His
> writing wasn't a brilliant sort of, using all the right phrases.

We examine an extract, chosen by them because it is a 'good bit' because it is about death. I question them about the style. It is the passage where Mavis, a lesbian, is trampled to death by the suicidal population of Bournemouth (*The Fog*, pp. 119–20):

> She was knocked again, and this time went under, losing her grip on the boy, her
> lungs filling with salty water. She emerged fighting for breath, blinded by the salt
> water, screaming and kicking out in panic.

When I ask them to criticize that passage from the point of view of their English teachers they pick on the repetitions of 'salty' and 'salt'.

> *Roland:* 'Cause there he uses er ... in two sentences he uses 'salty' and 'salt'. If we
> did that in an essay the teacher'd say, 'Oh you could have thought of
> another word.'

He continues:

> *Roland:* He sort of gives you the direct, what people would think first.

The boys argue that precisely because Herbert does not hunt around the houses for another word, the communication is more direct. Similarly, they pick on 'fighting for breath'.

> *Roland:* 'Fighting for breath', he uses cliché ...

They expand on this:

> *Roland:* He just gives you it straight out, the sort of clichés and that, a sort of slangy sort of style.
> *Kenneth:* Yeh.
> *Roland:* It's easy to read.

Because Herbert uses cliché, they as readers are familiar with its meaning, and, once again, the communication is more direct.

'Fighting for breath' is a phrase that occurs in everyday speech in a whole variety of situations, and can be found in plenty of texts other than *The Fog*. Such intertextuality, to use Eco's term, enriches the meaning: what is lost in precision is gained in universality. The phrase carries with it more than its ostensible meaning. This directness of communication allows these readers much greater freedom to respond to cultural messages contained within the text without having to believe them lock, stock and barrel. They recognize, instead, that meanings and interpretations of the world are being offered in a communication between equals rather than being handed down from teacher-accredited literary authority. So, when Herbert describes death it is assumed by the boys to be just one view among many. The passage we have been discussing continues as follows:

> There was no pain. There was no recollection of her life, no memories to taunt her in her dying. Just a misty blankness. No thoughts of God. No questions why. Just a descending white veil. Not a veil of peace, nor one of horror. Not even one of emptiness. Nothingness. Free of emotion and free of coldness. She was dead.
>
> (pp. 119–20)

The Leavisite view on this passage, as luck would have it, is available to us:

> To speak of matters of life and death in these tones is not only to deprive our existence of all dignity but also to cast a very disturbing light on our post-industrial way of seeing ourselves.
>
> (Grixti 1982, p. 47)

Such a view, I would argue, distorts the importance of the text by recasting it in the guise of scripture, and also drastically underrates the intelligence of 14- and 15-year-old readers. Here are Roland and Kenneth:

> *Roland:* I like that 'cause that's giving one person's view of what death would be like.

> CS: Yes.
> Roland: 'Cause I think about it a lot myself what it's going to be like to die.

It is a subject that interests them:

> Kenneth: Me and him had a discussion once in Maths about it – – –
> Roland: About religion and things. We're always talking about that.

The subject matter is salient for them, the language is straightforward and the communication direct. It thus allows them not to have to believe every word, but to add it to the evidence available in an ongoing discussion about a matter of interest and concern to them.

In continued discussion of the book the boys point out a further use that Herbert makes of cliché, and this time it is not individual phrases but a whole narrational structure. I read them the very beginning of the book, a description of a sleepy Wiltshire village. They explain to me that it is the classic 'calm before the storm' opening:

> CS: So you know, you know that what is being set is like the calm before the
>   storm?
> Roland: Yeh.
> Kenneth: Yeh.
> CS: Because it's James Herbert? Because it's got that sort of cover?
> All: Yeh.

Roland adds:

> Roland: It's sort of erm how films like that start, of disasters and that, it's like a
>   peaceful sort of little village, and you know, all the horror starts. People
>   start killing and that. It's a, it's sort of a cliché again, that sort of image,
>   the quiet before the storm.

In continuing discussion they reiterate the directness of the communication – Herbert just goes straight in and it makes it easy to read. Popular fiction finds a wide audience because it draws on common knowledges of the world and of other texts. These boys draw on genre expectations, on the semantics of presentational symbolism, and on concepts of authorship and authorial consistency to help them to generate meaning. And Roland's specific intertextual reference to current horror films draws on information which is salient in the culture of many 14- and 15-year-olds. Clichés, whether of language or of narration, are, as I have suggested, replete with cultural information, and encouraging young people to unravel them will, I would argue, give teachers and the pupils themselves a unique window both on to their culture, and on to how the text in question draws upon and interacts with it, thus allowing readers to construct meaning.

The culturally hidden

The particular culture, the particular set of meanings that characterize the relationships between the young and the adult are, as we have noted, noticeably quiet about certain aspects of human behaviour, most particularly sexual behaviour. This hiding, this quietness, often takes the form of naming but not describing the activity in question. Any explicit descriptions in plain language, particularly if they attempt to convey emotional content, run the risk of being branded as pornographic, exploitative of both the content and audience. In that hidden area no aspect is more named and less described than homosexuality. In the examples that I discuss below it is specifically homosexuality which is the subject matter, for the boys, lesbianism, and for the girls, male homosexuality.

The book is still *The Fog*, and the two groups are the top-stream year 10 boys and the middle-stream year 10 girls. In the case of the latter I am revisiting some of the evidence I have already discussed in Chapter 5. In each case the groups spontaneously discuss the scene themselves, and it is noticeable that both groups talk about the scenes involving homosexuality in the opposite sex. The boys refuse point blank to discuss the scene in the boys' school, no matter how hard I try to raise the issue. The girls are more equivocal and more prepared to discuss both:

CS: Is the thought of another girl touching in that sort of way, in real life, is that a horrible thought?

Mary: Well I think ...

Rosie: It's entirely ... It's more to ... I think it's more to accept that men do it, because we're girls, but I couldn't ... oohh (*shiver of revulsion*)

Tracey: Makes you cringe.

It is not clear from the transcript but from the context of the discussion Rosie, I think, is suggesting that it is more difficult, perhaps more horrible, to imagine boys' homosexuality. However, when Rosie finds the lesbian scene in the book and Mary reads it out (*The Fog*, pp. 113–14), Rosie, as we have seen, finds it disgusting. Let me quote her again:

Rosie: It's ... To me it's just the sort of thing that you get in dirty porno films, that's all ...

Rosie's response here places the extract squarely in the realm of sexploitation, and she rejects the scene as a result. Indeed it is her case against the book that it strings scenes of gratuitous sex and violence together with no relevant linking story. However, both groups produce comparable responses when talking about the scenes of opposite-sex homosexuality.

Two of the boys had read the book when they were younger. At the age of 12 the episode in which the lesbians make love had surprised, or even shocked them. It was new information for them:

Kenneth: I think it's all a new thing when you first read it. At 12 years old I mean it's all new.

However, as Peter pertinently suggests:

> *Peter:* You've got to start to learn about it some time.
> *CS:* Yeh. So that there is a sense in which you actually read it to learn about it, yes?
> *Kenneth:* In a way I think it is.
> *Roland:* Yeh.
> *CS:* To find out what lesbians *do*?
> *Kenneth:* Yeh.
> *Peter:* Yeh.
> *CS:* And to find out what homosexuals do?
> *Roland:* Yeh. 'Cause you hear people always talking about 'He's a queer' and ...
> *Kenneth:* 'He's gay' and ...

It is a common insult between younger boys without their really knowing what it means:

> *Kenneth:* And then you see something about it, you want to read it to know what it really is.
> *CS:* Yes.
> *Roland:* Yes.

My *Concise Oxford Dictionary* grudgingly allows that a lesbian is a female homosexual, but keeps noticeably quiet about desire, pleasure, flesh, arousal. Other dictionaries are not inclined to be more forthcoming. Herbert, however, does give the reader all those details, clearly spelt out and with no obfuscation or coyness. Indeed, he owns up to the fact that lesbianism is not just a category, it is also an activity. It is, thus, the greedy eagerness of 12-year-olds for sexual information that leads them to pass the book around with the pages marked:

> *Kenneth:* She had the page, well a couple of pages, that was really bad all marked off, and you sit there and pass it round the class like, 'Page 81, read that' ...

We saw in the last chapter that the middle-stream girls laugh at the scene in the boys' school from the same book. Though I discussed that laughter there, it is relevant to revisit that evidence here. I would suggest here, then, that part of their laughter arises from a similar disclosure of an activity hitherto named but never described. Rosie laughs, among other things, at the unexpected incongruity of the activity:

> *Rosie:* I don't know, it's, it's queer funny. It's not funny ha ha, it's sort of, 'Eh? Funny!' Do you know what I mean?
> *CS:* Oh I see what you mean.
> *Tracey:* 'Oh, so that's what they do.'

Tracey's quotation marks are quite audible as she characterizes a reader discovering precisely what the nature of the activity is. As Rosie says:

Rosie: I had to read it again to sort of believe it.

We can go right back to Aristotle's *Poetics* for a comment on this. He suggests that people like to see aspects of life shown and imitated because they actually enjoy learning from the portrayal:

> The reason for this is that learning is a very great pleasure, not for philosophers only, but for other people as well, however limited their capacity for it may be. They enjoy seeing likenesses because in doing so they acquire information ...
>
> ('The Art of Poetry', p. 35)

The evidence from the pupils in this section very much appears to bear this out. School, with its role as the official face that adult culture turns towards the young, has to walk a tightrope when passing sensitive information across the generation gap. Sexuality is dealt with in a scientific, medical health context, or within a very closely monitored moral framework. Only fiction can offer the felt experience of sexual acts, and here, too, teachers have to be very cautious. The teacher of the top stream, for instance, felt that neither *The Fog* nor *Carrie* would be acceptable as texts to be included in a review folder for the examination board, and he told me stories of complaints he had had about using much less explicit texts. His experience is not uncommon, and was reflected in my discussions with teachers and librarians during the pilot study, all of whom were concerned about where to draw the line with such material. Teachers, librarians, members of exam boards are thus all witting or unwitting contributors to this hiding of sexual experience from the young in a manner that can be construed as cultural hypocrisy. Such hypocrisy, I would argue, is part of the relation of power and dependence that exists between the adult and the young person. *The Fog*, and texts like it, offer young readers an exposition of some of those elements of culture that are hidden by this ideological edifice that is adult hypocrisy. The text comes thus to have a double function. For young readers it is quite simply informative, telling them about feelings and sensations in straightforward and direct language and narrative, giving them information that is simply not available elsewhere. For adults, particularly those adults acting as official representatives of adult culture, the dissemination of such material among the young, to say nothing of the young's appreciation of it, can come to be seen as subversive of established cultural norms and values.

So far we have seen how the text offers sites of cultural typification and how linguistic and narratorial analysis can offer us windows on to current cultural signposts. We have also seen how young readers read texts of this nature in order to peel back the carpet of cultural discretion to reveal what has been brushed beneath it. It remains for us to investigate the cultural 'other' and the ambiguity with which it is received, an ambiguity which reveals the way in which the 'other' interrogates the known and ordered.

Ambiguity, the insidious appeal of evil, and the interrogation of cultural order

The geography of the 'other'

Rosemary Jackson's suggestion, above, that the fantastic is the domain of the cultural 'other', the 'unreal' that interrogates the 'real', is interestingly broadened in a number of discussions that I had with readers about America. It is the setting for many horror films, and films of contemporary violence. Specifically, both *First Blood* and *Carrie* are set in the States. Such a setting gives readers access to a ready-made landscape of the imagination where anything could happen.

For instance, the bottom-stream boys, in their discussion of the American setting for *First Blood*, suggest that it is the place where whatever could happen in Britain in a small way could happen there in a large way. 'America' thus becomes an agent of dramatization:

> *John:* You know it's something important because England's small and America is big.

and he continues:

> *John:* The policemen carry guns around. Everybody knows there's violence and there, the lot, and you know it's kind of, you know, there's sort of right, all these gangs, fights and that lot, poor streets and all that.

As we saw in an earlier chapter, this violent landscape of the imagination was of crucial, almost obsessive importance to John, but he is not alone in attributing to 'America' aspects of extreme or unusual behaviour. Here are three middle-stream boys talking about the American setting of *Carrie*:

> *Gavin:* It makes it more lifelike, you expect things from America to be sort of you know, weird, you know, erm ... You wouldn't expect, say, go down [Bigton] and see [the] town fall to pieces you know.

The context suggests that Gavin is here using the word 'lifelike' to mean 'vivid' or 'believable'. 'America' is the source of the unusual, the 'weird'. Damon picks up this theme, and relates it to the common culture of horror movies and so on:

> *Damon:* Those sort of films that are way out, they always come from the States.

America is a place of pressure, of natural disaster, they suggest, and they return again to the business of size:

> *Gavin:* It's just that it's a greatly massive place and you get more things going to happen, you know.

Ted takes up the theme:

> *Ted:* The fact that it's a bigger country and there's loads more people, there's more chance of there being people that, that kind of power [Carrie's tele-

kinesis] and so it's much more likely to happen over there than it is over here.

The American setting, then, is not simply a geographical landscape or townscape. For these readers it is a fictional construct that becomes the domain for the extreme or the alien. The unreal that Rosemary Jackson talks about does not, in other words, need to be the fantastic as such. Other things can operate in ways to be set against the real. 'America' is an unreal to be set against the real of Britain today.

Crossing the boundary

The Fog is not set in America, it is set in Britain. It comes closer to the sorts of fantastic text that Rosemary Jackson discusses. In it Herbert not only reveals the 'normal' but unsaid and unseen of culture, he also examines the 'abnormal'. In tracing the abnormal, the normal itself is given boundaries and more clearly defined. Again I would argue that such boundaries and definitions are of vital importance to adolescents coming to terms with their burgeoning sexuality and with the casual, and organized, violence of playground and street. And such definitions of normal and abnormal as are offered by the text are cultural signposts, markers of cultural value which have to be identified before they can be discussed, thought about, changed, or negotiated around.

If, as I am suggesting, at its core the book is about the culturally hidden, what Freud in 1919 calls 'das Unheimliche', literally 'the unhomely', then one rapidly discovers that the text offers a whole variety of references that reinforce such an interpretation. The fog of the title is the agency that causes monstrously violent and or sexual behaviour. It appears out of a 'frightening black void' (p. 13), 'a bottomless pit' (p. 14). In other words, in its initial appearance it is given a totally metaphysical origin in nothingness, a nothingness that echoes the unnamable character of the rapist in the *Daily Mail* headline above. Once the fog has emerged it is rapidly associated with another of Western culture's current demons, for as it ascends into the sky it forms a mushroom cloud 'like the aftermath of a hydrogen bomb' (p. 20). We finally discover that it is the result of biological warfare experiments gone wrong, yet another popular version of Armageddon. The hero's job is to fight pollution, a much nearer and more intimately experienced threat for many readers, and there can be no doubt that whatever else the fog is, it is certainly some form of pollution. Finally, there are suggestions that the fog itself has some sort of animal-like instinct, and Holman relies on 'instinct' in his encounters with it. In their final drive through London, Holman and the man he is with observe that the people affected by the fog resemble 'a flock of birds' (p. 225), that they are 'losing their individuality, flocking together the way animals do' (p. 225). Again there are echoes of the rapist, christened 'the Fox' by the media.

When I talk to the top-stream boys about the function of the fog in the book they have picked up on much of this imagery. Roland, for instance, suggests that the fog makes people behave 'like animals' and Kenneth adds 'just like wild animals with no restrictions to anything', or again Roland suggests that the characters behave as if 'they're not civilized any more'. In discussion of the fictional nature of the book, Roland suggests:

> *Roland:* It's an unbelievable situation they're in, everyone's going mad ... Nothing would ever happen like that you know ... nuclear war maybe.

In the contemplation of this 'unbelievable situation' both Kenneth and Roland are clear on which side they stand:

> *Roland:* It makes you think what you'd do if you were in that position if there was a mad person after you, trying to kill you.

And Kenneth adds:

> *Kenneth:* If I was in like Holman's position where you've got to defend yourself, I think I could do that if a load of madmen came running at you or you was in a car and they was all just charging along the road you wouldn't think, I don't think I'd think about stopping, you'd just go straight through them. But I don't think I'd be able to chop someone's head off, it's just that if you had to defend yourself and you knew they was mad then I don't think I'd care about them ...

By contrast, John, whom you will recall from an earlier chapter, is clearly on the other side, wanting to start the Vietnam war back up so that he can go and fight. Roland and Kenneth were pillars of the establishment. When they got into year 11, the fifth year of this 11–16 comprehensive school, Roland was made head boy and Kenneth was made a prefect. They are a far cry from John at the other end of the scale, with his bitter resentment of school and hatred of all things associated with it. It is perhaps not surprising, then, that Roland and Kenneth imagine themselves on the side of cultural order. Nor is it perhaps surprising that John identifies so closely with a hero who rejected all forms of cultural order when he came across them. For bottom-stream John, Rambo is the classic underdog who becomes the lawless all-powerful outsider who attacks the order that has excluded him. For top-stream Roland and Kenneth, Holman is the hero of the hour, repelling the disorder that threatens to destroy society from all sides.

For all that these top-stream boys take a position within the imaginary experience of the fiction that reflects, among other things, their political position within the school, they none the less reveal that the evil has an insidious appeal. It is this appeal, I would suggest, that most tellingly constitutes the interrogation that the unreal performs upon the real. Where Roland and Kenneth take up clear positions, Peter is more equivocal:

> *Peter:* You've all got your feelings like you'd, like you'd want to do it, but you know you'd never ...

and here is Kenneth making an interesting suggestion:

> *Kenneth:* Like the bus driver, he just goes round smashing into things, it must be something he's really wanted to do like. I think he uses it [the fog] to show that everyone's evil really, they've got evil inside them. They're just doing what they'd love to do.

This feeling that the fog releases emotions and actions that people would 'love to do' is experienced by many readers. I would suggest that it accounts for the fact that Rosie, while condemning the book, keeps finding passages for Mary to read out, a point I noted in Chapter 4. When I talked to the teacher of the top stream about the book he confessed to both disliking the book and being totally gripped by it. This ambivalence, which I share, is felt particularly by those who have a statutory responsibility for forming the minds of the young.

Such ambiguity can be found within the text, most noticeably when Herbert shifts narrative perspective, and the narrator moves from being objective to being focused through the perspective of one of the characters. Here, for example, just before the climax of the boys' boarding school orgy scene, is the impotent deputy head entering the gymnasium: 'He saw the boys watching him, his boys, so pure in their innocence, so evil in their deviation. Standing before him, magnificent in their nakedness!' (*The Fog*, p. 67). Here we are plainly seeing things through the perspective of the deputy head; two paragraphs previously the deputy head isn't even there and the narrative is objective, not focused through any of the characters in the scene. If such shifts generate ambiguity in themselves, then the content of this particular quote is even more ambivalent. The boys are both innocent and evil and both pure and deviant. On the one hand, they represent some Utopian pastoral idyll that threatens our normal existence, and on the other they represent some evil deviation that threatens our normal existence. We thus see that in many ways Herbert manages to have his cake and to eat it. On the one hand the fog and its effects are portrayed as evil, to be condemned and vilified by the reader, but on the other, many readers feel that the text in some way glories in the very material that they are invited to condemn. I would suggest that this double thrust is in the text, to be read by any reader who chooses to do so, and I would also suggest that it is that double thrust that generates what readers often characterize as the insidious appeal of the text.

Conclusion

Earlier in this chapter, in the discussion of what I have called sites of cultural typification and in the discussion of cliché, I have, in one sense, been demonstrating how readers find themselves in texts. The suggestion is that Herbert uses language that these readers recognize as being their language, and presents situation, character and relationship in ways that are current in the culture. In the next chapter I shall be developing this particular picture with further examples of how readers find themselves in texts, and I shall follow that in Chapter 7 with an example of how and why readers reject texts, a common experience in school where readers have no control over the texts that they have to read.

In this chapter also I have largely concentrated on one text, James Herbert's *The Fog*. It is a particularly popular text by a particularly popular author, as Pauline Heather's (1981) survey shows. It is a text that is often mentioned to me by teachers, even when they have not read it, as being 'the one with the scene in the boys' school'. In my analysis I have tried to draw attention to the negotiation of cultural order and disruption that constitutes a major theme of the book, and to relate that to a similar negotiation that adolescents need to make as they grow up in a world where particular knowledge is hidden from them, or where their access to that knowledge is severely monitored and constrained. There is a further aspect to the appeal of the book, and that is the ideological thrust of the sub-plots, an ideological thrust that counters the more reactionary framing ideology of the book. This I discuss in Chapter 8.

6 On finding yourself in the text

Introductory

The meeting between text and reader is a unique interaction. Yet so far I have sketched broad themes, and outlined general arguments. In the second half of this chapter I concentrate on the more unrelated and quirky responses of readers to text. These may arise out of individual histories, or divergent politics, or from more individual aspects of personality. The chapter, as a result, does not take such a clear line as do earlier chapters, and the reader may experience some discontinuities. However, I feel that it is important that these should be explored. If there is a grand theory of response that applies to the readings that people bring to texts it is that there is no theory that will adequately explain all the varied responses that texts generate. I hope that this chapter, at least in part, will demonstrate that.

In other ways, however, I am continuing a general theme from the previous chapter, for I am still exploring how readers match their culture to the text, and thus, contrariwise, how texts offer readers aspects of their culture that allow them ways into texts. Among other things, I shall be examining the response of younger readers to a popular text, and showing how one of the books chosen by older girls almost directly mirrors their everyday concerns and experience. In other words, I shall demonstrate how readers 'find themselves' in texts, and, indeed, how texts 'find themselves' in readers.

From life into text

I have already suggested that we have alternative ways of regarding character. The Russian formalists, such as Propp, and their structuralist descendants, like Todorov, have suggested that characters are presented in popular literature in generalized terms, as types, or caricatures, offering readers empty categories into which they are at liberty to inject their own characteristics, their own motives, their own psychologies. This was nowhere more clearly demonstrated than with a group of year 7 boys who read and thoroughly enjoyed *Super Gran* by Forest

Wilson. I discuss their response to the book more fully in Chapter 9, but I wish to examine one aspect of their response here.

The story concerns one Granny Smith who is hit by a ray that gives her 'super' powers. The ray, it seems, has hit her by accident. The machine that makes it has been stolen by the villain of the piece, the Inventor [with a capital *I* – 'His big ambition in life was to rule the world, no less!' (p. 16)], and his incompetent sidekick, Tub. Super Gran, her grandson Willard, and Edison Faraday Black, the daughter of the man who actually invented the machine, set out to thwart him and get the machine back. In the meantime Super Gran has a number of unrelated adventures and escapades: she plays football, climbs trees, rescues a drowning girl from the municipal boating pond, foils a bank robbery, and so on.

The Super Gran books are in a category that, in terms of a personal response, I find very difficult to appreciate at any level. The characters fall straight into stereotype. The humour is knockabout farce of the banana-skin type, and the book has a sly nudge at knowing adult readers, a trick I always find particularly irritating when it carries with it an implicit patronization of the ignorant younger reader – the name of the little girl, Edison Faraday Black, being a case in point. She is, I have to admit, one of the saving graces of the book, a character full of energy and intelligence. So, I suppose is Super Gran herself, though the transformation causes such an obviously delineated power reversal as to really fail to engage my interest. To read the book was thus a duty rather than a pleasure; but this was, thankfully, offset by the kids' responses to the book, and I was able to get some pleasure by proxy, as it were.

Given the apparent lack of realism of the characterization, I ask the boys how they relate the book to life:

> *Wayne:* I place the gran as somebody I know, then I place myself as somebody in it, then I place all my mates in it right, as people.

As Wayne continues to describe the process I would suggest that it is the *relationships* between the characters in the book that are particularly meaningful to him:

> *Wayne:* Like Edison, or not Edison, the professor who stole it, you know, they're sort of like some of my mates who I've known, people to steal from me and that, and not pay me back or anything, and then Tub, who's really scared and the professor bosses him about and I've been like that, bossed about and that you know, and it just seems to all come together.

The bullying relationship between the mad inventor and his sidekick particularly reminds Wayne of being bullied himself:

> *Wayne:* Like in here where the professor's bossing Tub about it reminded me of me being like Tub ...

and he produces a specific example:

Wayne: This big kid, he, there was this big kid who, you know, he kept making me go to the shops for him, and all that kind of thing ...

The Inventor bullies Tub mercilessly, makes him run errands, uses him as a guinea pig in his experiments, ignores everything he says. Tub is described as 'an untidy, not-too-bright, fat teenager' (p. 16). Despite the fact that Wayne is none of these things the relationship that Tub has to the Inventor, that of 'being bullied', allows Wayne to bring his own experiences of being bullied to the text, and Tub emerges as about the most unlikely role model that you could imagine.

The other two boys in the group had similar experiences reading the book. I am arguing that what appear to adults to be stereotyped characterizations and clichéd relationships, are far from that for these 11–12-year-olds. We find, instead, something very reminiscent of the characterization and relationships presented in *The Fog*: that for these younger readers the characterizations and relationships are once again sites of cultural typification, but that in this case the culture is not the wider adult culture, but the specific culture of childhood itself.

Finding the text in yourself

Stranger with My Face by Louise Duncan is a story about an American teenage girl, Laurie, who discovers she has a long-lost twin sister. The discovery occurs when her twin transports her spirit half-way across America and appears to Laurie, and half her friends, by a process known as 'astral projection'. In the course of the book Laurie discovers the same powers in herself. This device fuels a thriller plot in which the twin uses her powers to isolate Laurie from her friends, her family, her boyfriend, and finally from her own body. The twin lures people into near-fatal accidents and so on, but all is resolved in the end. The context for this plot is an everyday story of teenage love affairs, of social acceptance and rejection, and so on. The book was chosen by a year 10 top-stream group of girls because one of them had read an extract in *Jackie*. It was very popular with the three groups of girls that read it.

So far as my own personal response is concerned I liked this book a lot. The paranormal paraphernalia are well constructed to keep you reading. More interestingly, however, they allow an exploration of the teenage quest for identity. The spectral twin who is the opposite of everything represented by the protagonist allows Duncan to dramatize the essentially internal conflicts of identity, and Laurie is enabled to play out her drama by acting in and on the world as well as by thinking about herself. In a sense it is a sort of *Carrie* without the religious hysteria, and without the gore; mind you it lacks one of *Carrie*'s central themes – the revolt against the parent.

When I discussed the book with the group of year 10 middle-stream girls that have already featured in Chapter 4 I had difficulty in 'keeping them to the point'. As a result, in the middle of the tape they start to discuss a friend. The story concerns Louisa and her boyfriend Tim. In the course of their discussion they debate the nature of the relationship, the morality of the behaviour of the two people, their probable motivations, and so on:

> *Rosie:*   Right. Tim thought that Luke was trying to chat up Louisa and that, just because they get on really well, and Tim wouldn't come in, and he just sat there all night being miserable.

Tim's behaviour makes Louisa and her friends feel miserable. These girls start to debate Tim's behaviour:

> *Mary:*   Yeh. I feel, I know that Tim's very moody and he has, he's ...
> *Deborah:* I think he's just caring. He's just trying to protect the relationship.

and Louisa's behaviour:

> *Rosie:*   Yeh, but Louisa wouldn't go, go off with anyone else I don't think.
> *Deborah:*   I know, but it's the way she acts, isn't it.
> *Mary:*   Yeh, well she's very friendly towards other people.
> *Deborah:*   She's really gay, you know what I mean, the way she acts and that. He thinks she's, he's going to lose her and he likes her so much.

but Mary disagrees and cites another story of a visit to Great Yarmouth:

> *Mary:*   Louisa was talking to her friends and he turned round and he goes, he said, 'Aren't you talking to me or something', and she goes, 'No, it's alright, I'm just talking to my friends', and he was in a right mood just 'cause she wasn't talking to him, and he felt left out, and she, and in the end she had to leave her friends to go off with him on her own, which I don't feel is right. I know he's protective about her and he must really like her, and I understand that. The fact is that I don't think that any boyfriend should take you away from your friends and not let you go out with them.

I quote this transcript at some length in order to convey the detail of these girls' discrimination in their judgements of Tim and Louisa's behaviour and also because the substance of the story shows how a boy and girl trust and mistrust each other, and understand and misunderstand each other, and the ways in which that relates to their friends.

At the beginning of *Stranger with My Face* the heroine, Laurie, writing in the first person, describes how she has started dating Gordon this summer, and as a result has become part of the 'in' crowd on the island where they live and of which Gordon is a handsome leading light. When the time comes for the final party before they go back to school for the September term Laurie is sick and can't go. Laurie's twin appears on the beach and is seen by Gordon and Natalie, his previous girlfriend, as they kiss on the beach. They mistake her for Laurie and the next day, when they see her, accuse her of lying about being sick. The argument develops over succeeding days as Laurie discovers that Gordon has kissed Natalie. Finally, Gordon 'forgives' Laurie for, as he thinks, lying about being on the beach and they get back together again. Laurie makes a new friend in school, Helen, who is definitely not of the 'in' crowd and that produces more tension. Then, as she learns about the existence of her twin and about astral projection, she finds she can only really confide in Helen, and finally in another boy, Jeff, who has one half of his face badly scarred from a burn and who is also definitely not in the 'in' crowd. In the course of all this Laurie reflects upon her own behaviour and that of the others.

It will not need a particularly discerning reader to relate the fictional story I have just outlined to the story that Rosie and the others were telling above. When I ask how they have enjoyed the book they have no trouble in making the link either.

Deborah:	I liked that because it was sort of, you know, social gathering, things like that.
Mary:	I like ...
Deborah:	and sort of girlfriend boyfriend type situations. I liked that.
Tracey:	Mmm.
Rosie:	Mmm.
Mary:	I like the way they, the phrases [*sic*] they go, the phases they go through with girlfriend boyfriend, you know.
Tracey:	Yeh. Trouble and all that.
Mary:	Show what arguments you have, how you feel and so on.
Deborah:	It's like you know, it's like the stage we're in really, us going out with people and you know, breaking up and having arguments about things and that. It happens now.

The top-stream girls who originally chose the book say much the same sort of thing at greater length. For instance, when I ask them to tell me about the book they retell the story starting with the fact that Laurie is going out with Gordon at the beginning, moving on to the twin, astral projection, and so on, and finishing:

Pippa:	and she went out with this Jeff boy at the end.

The social setting and contexts of the story:

Pippa:	made it more realistic.
Caroline:	Mmm.
Tricia:	Yeh, you could relate to it more.
Pippa:	'Cause if they'd just said about this astral projection you wouldn't have believed it otherwise.
Tricia:	Yeh, it made it more, seem more down to earth sort of thing, that you can picture it actually happening ...

It was set:

Tricia:	in real life.

The appearance of the twin, Lia, in the book serves to dramatize Laurie's social relationships which are made and broken as Lia intervenes in her life. There are issues of whether the characters trust or believe each other, and these are exposed to the sharpest tests at every turn by Lia's interventions. In discussing the book the top-stream girls concentrate on the social effects of the plot development. They bring out the complexity of behaviour of the characters in the book in ways that are reminiscent of the complexities of the observations of the middle-stream girls on a real-life situation above. For instance, after Lia's initial appearance the top-stream girls had been distressed at the other characters' refusal to accept Laurie's word:

Pippa: I thought, 'Well surely they can see it, they'll realize that there's two different people' * * * 'cause she was getting sort of kicked out by friends and that.

Tricia: Yeh. I thought it ... Yeh.

CS: Oh so that that made you ...

Tricia: feel as if you thought you'd just stand there and just shake them and make them think, realize.

Pippa: (*Laughing in sympathetic agreement*) Yeh.

Their distress at the behaviour of the characters fuels their interest in how the plot develops. They want to read on to see what happened, to see when and how the situation was going to be resolved.

These girls relate to the book by recognizing that the characters are behaving like they would behave. Despite the fact that the social milieu of the characters is very different from the social milieu of these Bigton girls, none the less the characters make the same decisions and judgements and discriminations about their behaviour, and that of their friends, as these girls make in real life. They also recognize Laurie's actual judgemental processes in themselves. The point emerges in a more general discussion of what they feel they have in common with Laurie:

CS: Could you identify what it is in her that you have that she has in common with you?

Caroline: Boyfriends.
(*Laughter*)

CS: So boyfriends is one ...

Tricia: Her age as well, I mean. Although she is seventeen you can picture her more our age than she is.
* * *

Pippa: and she could look on and, and see, you know, all the peop ... things people were doing to impress others and that kind of thing.

Tricia: You know, she could see through it.

Pippa: You know, and that's the kind of thing I'm always doing ...

Tricia: Yeh.

Pippa:	always thinking, you know.
Tricia:	'cause a lot of groups go around, you think well, you can see straight through them.
Pippa:	You can think why they're doing that sort of thing, you know.
Tricia:	Yeh.

There is a double effect here, for, within the fiction, Laurie takes on the spectator role, observing her fellow characters, trying to understand and predict their behaviour, and judging their actions. In the same way, these girls in real life observe their peers, seeking to understand and predict their behaviour and judge their actions. But at the same time, of course, they are taking the spectator role with respect to the fiction and are thus enabled to reflect on their own thinking processes in relation to their own society. And it needs to be reiterated here that these are girls doing this sort of reflection. Nowhere on the tapes do boys produce these sorts of discussion about behaviour, either between the sexes or within single-sex peer groups. It is, of course, what tends to get dismissed by paternalistic culture as 'gossip'.

In the first two sections of this chapter I have outlined ways in which the culture of book and reader match and fit together. If there is a distinction to be made it is a subtle and perhaps minor one: in the case of the boys and *Super Gran*, they seem to project themselves into the generalized categories and relationships offered by the texts as empty spaces, almost, to be occupied by readers; and in the case of *Stranger with My Face*, the detail of the text reaches into the lives of the readers in such a way that they find the text reflected in their own lives. Hence the distinction between the boys finding themselves in the text, and the girls finding the text in themselves. (Pippa, indeed, talks about characters that relate so strongly to her that she imagines what that character would do in her place in life; and John, incidentally, in the bottom-stream group also talked of a similar experience, in particular of imagining that he was Rambo.) It seems to me in any case more than probable that both processes are two sides of the same coin, but that the boys' evidence emphasizes one direction of the process while the girls' evidence emphasizes the other.

Individual perspectives

In this section I move to the consideration of the more individual and disparate responses of readers. Books will always have specific appeal for readers for more or less personal reasons, but though these reasons will always have individual psychological explanations they also have social and cultural dimensions. It is the ways in which these dimensions are delineated in the individual response that is unpredictable and even quirky. I shall look at just a few examples of particular readers and their response.

Books in the head

I start with the continuing discussion of the top-stream girls about *Stranger with My Face*. Laurie's parents in the book are a successful writer of science fiction and a successful painter of land- and seascapes. I ask about this creative artist background. One of the girls says 'Well somebody's got to do it I suppose' but for Pippa it has a much more direct relevance and appeal.

> *Pippa:* I thought that was nice, you know, I thought that would be nice, have an artist as a mum and a ...
> *Caroline:* She should know about the ...
> *CS:* Yes.
> *Tricia:* Yeh.
> *Pippa:* I thought, I wonder what it'd be like having parents like that you know, if they'd always be rushing around with books in their head, that kind of thing.

Pippa herself has phrases that run through her head.

> *Pippa:* I used to write them down when I was little. * * * Especially in English less ... I'm always picking up little sentences that he says and writing them back down again (*laughs*) writing the essay.

Though Pippa's response may look somewhat individual, the social context of teacher and taught and her position as a girl in a top-stream places that response firmly within a socio-cultural framework: that of a learner within the academic tradition.

The discovery that Laurie makes in the book that she is adopted fuels speculation about what it would be like if they had had different parents – Pippa had even asked her parents after she had read the book if she was adopted. The answer had apparently been no! However, she again throws an individual light upon such speculation – to, it may be added, the hilarious response of all:

> *Pippa:* It wouldn't bother me that much because I was an accident anyway!
> (*Laughter*)

Gavin prefers non-fiction

The above group of girls clearly shared experiences, judgements, and values, while obviously retaining their individuality within the group. By contrast, Gavin, in a group of year 10 middle-stream boys, stood out from his peers. At 15 he read the 'serious' papers, watched documentaries rather than fiction films on television and was generally interested in facts rather than fiction:

> *Gavin:* I just want to know the truth about something you know.
> *CS:* Yes.
> *Gavin:* I don't want to be told a load of lies so I don't ...
> *CS:* Yes.

> *Gavin:* You know, anything that is true, you know, I want to pick up on, make
> sure, say, if something happens to me in later life I know what's going to
> happen.

As a white boy, Gavin preferred people of Asian origin to people of Afro-Caribbean origin, a reversal of the racism generally endemic within the white pupils of the school, and was a member of the Young Conservatives. He had ambitions to be a politician when he grew up. Given his avowed dislike of fiction it is surprising that he agreed to read *Carrie* at all and even more surprising that he enjoyed it. The reason for his enjoyment lies in the way that the book was written.

The book contains transcript from the inquest, extracts from the autobiography of one of the survivors, extracts from a journalistic/academic account of the affair, extracts from textbooks on telekinesis, newspaper reports, and so on. The top-stream boys enjoyed these devices in a dissociated way: it was, they thought, an interesting way to write a book; and all the other readers were to a greater or lesser extent irritated by them, feeling they got in the way of 'the real story'. Gavin is the only reader I talked to for whom these devices were a crucial element in the book. It seems fairly clear that as he originally read it he actually took it as a true story. However, the minute he starts talking about it he amends this response. He read it rather *as if* it were real:

> *Gavin:* sort of looking back, 'cause it's got, it's having all them reports in it and it's
> got the bit at the back with all the death certificate.
> *CS:* Yes.
> *Gavin:* I read it as if it was a real thing.

He expands on this:

> *Gavin:* I found all them little bits popping up more interesting 'cause I thought it
> was something real and I wanted to get in what actually did happen, more
> of the facts than or what the story said.

He likes the alternative perspectives:

> *Gavin:* It gives me sort of different options about what's going on,
> *CS:* Yes. Ah.
> *Gavin:* 'cause they had a newspaper, or whatever it is, reports it and what the
> actual author is saying.

For Gavin, then, narrational devices have been important in that they enable him to read the book as if it were non-fiction, but they also allow him to set one view against another, and free him, as a reader, to come to his own decisions. That cognitive process itself, then, becomes a vital part of his response.

When it comes to telekinesis, the power that Carrie develops to move objects by thinking about it, Gavin is not nearly so isolated from his peers. In this case they share his interest about whether or not it is something real, and share too his requirements that evidence for it should be presented in non-fictional form. It may, indeed, be argued that King recognizes this and is skilful in the way he handles the issue, for the text contains quotes from '*Telekinesis*: *Analysis and Aftermath* (Science Yearbook 1982), by Dean K. L. McGuffin' (p. 50), the little Hitchcockian joke I've already mentioned. Gavin, and the other boys in this group, have seen documentaries on television about the subject and firmly believe it exists. In this they do not differ from many of their peers. I don't think I spoke to one reader who categorically denied that it existed.

Once Gavin has found ways of reading *Carrie* as if it were real, he makes links between the book and the world in the same way that many other readers do. For instance, the character of the religiously fanatical Mrs White reminds him of a woman who lives down the road:

> *CS:*   Do you find that she was a believeable character?
> *Gavin:* Um. Maybe, I don't know, there's this woman down our road she's got her kids, they're not allowed to go out with a girl until they're about seventeen, you know.

Once he has made the link, he describes how the children of this woman are right little tearaways though the woman herself will not have a word said against them:

> *Gavin:* they're going around or beating up people, you know, spitting all over the place, sometimes smoking, you know, she wouldn't believe that they'd do things like that sort of. She keeps them in her mind as they're good (??)
> *CS:*   So her kids are actually a bit of a terror on the, on the estate are they?
> *Gavin:* Yeh, some of them, well the smallest one ...
> *CS:*   The smallest one.
> *Gavin:* You know, he goes round burning things like that, an arsonist.
> *CS:*   And yet she won't have it that there's anything wrong with them?
> *Gavin:* No she won't say anything against them.

I try to draw a direct parallel between Carrie and these kids, suggesting that both might be rebelling against their mothers, but neither Gavin, or Ted, another boy in the same group, will have that, suggesting, rather, that Carrie is in rebellion against being isolated from the rest of the world. There are striking echoes, though, since Carrie herself becomes a fire-raiser at the end of the book.

Gavin's individual approach, and initial response to the text, leads him back to some of the themes that are salient for many readers of the book, leads him back, as it were, to the mainstream of adolescent culture with its need for the assertion of independence and its quest for identity apart from its parents, but his search for his own identity is not within the common culture of most of his peers. It could even be suggested that it is defined in opposition to the dominant peer-group culture, and this is suggested in his response to *Carrie*. He likes those aspects of the book that they do not like, and dislikes those aspects of the book that they do like.

A footnote on the blood

A totally different response to *Carrie* relates to the blood that, as we have already noted, flows through the book. The middle-stream girls mention a particular application of that imagery not over-emphasized in the text, i.e. the use of the word in the expression 'in the blood', meaning that something is inherited. Having observed, above, that these girls, in common with many readers, found the multi-narrational devices and the pseudo-scientific asides irritating, it was, none the less, one of these asides that suggested that telekinesis was inherited:

Mary: Some things run in people's families don't they.

Mary, who in her own words is 'chubby', points out that such chubbiness runs in her family. But it is Rosie who specifically reintroduces the notion of blood, thus picking up on this major theme in the novel and giving it yet another slant:

Rosie: Like a disease that's in my blood. We got, our family are, my dad's side of the family, they've got this illness that causes blindness ...

The issue that engenders these specific observations is, once again, that all-important one for adolescents, the relationship between parents and children, and the ways in which struggles for independence are inevitably limited since the family is written into the child's very genetic make-up itself. It is, indeed, 'inscribed in the blood'. But the individual perspectives that these readers bring to the texts, though part of that wider adolescent culture, contain elements of personal and family history that are inevitably unpredictable. Thus Mary's 'chubbiness' and Rosie's family's history of inherited blindness find particular and quite unexpected echoes in *Carrie*, a book that is saliently about neither.

Reading yourself into the text

Finally, in this rag-bag of examples, one of the year 7 girls describes how she uses a specific reading technique to read herself into a text. Quite simply, she reads to herself more expressively:

Victoria: You could really get into a good book if you was reading it in your mind, and um if there's a boring bit in it you can make it more exciting by reading it more um what it would be like in real life, how you'd say it in real life if you was there, type of.

Victoria then makes up a couple of examples of sentences and says the second with more expression than the first:

Victoria: Put a bit more exaggeration in.
CS: Yeh. Put a bit more expression into it.
Victoria: Yeh.

and a bit later she says:

> *Victoria:* Yeh, 'cause I, 'cause it's seems as if you can actually hear what you're
> saying ...
> *CS:* Yes. Yes.
> *Victoria:* if you really get into the book enough.

The point that Victoria is making, I would suggest, is that such expressive reading brings the text to life, makes it more exciting, makes it more realistic – in her words, it makes the book 'what it would be like in real life'. To read with expression is not to distort real life but to import real life into the text:

> *Victoria:* And it just seems as if it's alive in my head.

Conclusion

In this chapter I have further pursued ideas about how young people relate to text by finding themselves in it. In the case of *Super Gran* the empty categories created by the stereotypic characterization allow year 7 boys to find their own experience dramatized in fictional terms.

Super Gran relates to much of the popular fiction we have considered, in that character is identified in action. With *Stranger with My Face* the situation is somewhat different. The book fits more clearly into the category of expressive realism outlined by Catherine Belsey in *Critical Practice* and this is despite the supernatural content. It fits into that category because it places the individual psychology back in the centre ground, and sees action as dependent upon it. The resolution of the story is a resolution of the central character's dilemma about whether to live life in the fast lane or whether to go for relationships of more 'value', i.e. permanent and monogamous. All the girls who read the book appeared to read *with* this closure. In this way their readings differed from the readings I have been discussing elsewhere, in which these same young people, and their peers, read *across* or in spite of the ideological closure of more obviously popular forms.

Finally, in this chapter, I have looked at more individual and quirky response, and tried to show how that relates to more general cultural factors, but in unpredictable ways.

7 On not finding yourself in the text

Introductory

This chapter is a reverse, a sort of photographic negative of the previous two. It concerns the processes that go on when readers reject a text.

The text that I look at in some detail is John Steinbeck's *The Pearl* (1948), a book that was a set book for the middle-stream class that I worked with. It was a very frequently used text at examination level as Mike Hayhoe (1980) has shown, and I guess it still is. Gail Rodes, the teacher of this group, had not chosen the book out of any particular enthusiasm, but because it was the only one left in the stock cupboard that she felt she could use. The middle-stream pupils who had to read *The Pearl* because it was a set book, and the top-stream girls who read it at my request, were united in their dislike and rejection of it. In all cases it was clear that they were familiar with the text and that they understood it, but that it was a barren and tedious experience for them. They fail to do what I described them as so successfully doing in the last chapter, that is, they fail to find themselves in the text.

Denial of reader experience

Let me first of all briefly recount the story. The setting is Central America, a fishing community. Kino, the fisherman, and Juana, his wife, have a baby, Coyotito, who is stung by a scorpion. After Juana has sucked the poison out to the best of her ability they go to the doctor who refuses to see them because they are poor Indians. They go out pearl fishing and find a very large pearl. The doctor gets to hear about it and comes to visit the baby. That night there is an intruder who tries to steal the pearl. Next day they take the pearl to the dealers, who are in a cartel, and who offer so little that Kino refuses to sell, and decides to go to the city where he hopes to get a better price. Juana by now fears for the consequences that the pearl will bring and the following night takes it to throw it into the sea. Kino gets it from her in the nick of time, and then is set upon by an assailant whom he kills. Their hut is burned to the ground and their canoe holed. They leave for the city but are followed. Kino attacks and kills his pursuers but in the fight Coyotito, the baby, is shot and killed. They return and throw the pearl back into the sea.

The book is written in a style which eschews both exciting action and internal psychology. Instead Steinbeck resorts to other means to portray the inner life of his characters. Here is Kino, the fisherman, waking up in the morning at the start of the book:

> Kino heard the little splash of morning waves on the beach. It was very good – Kino closed his eyes again to listen to his music. Perhaps he alone did this, and perhaps all of his people did it. His people had once been great makers of songs, so that everything they saw or thought or did or heard became a song. That was very long ago. The songs remained; Kino knew them, but no new songs were added. That does not mean that there were no personal songs. In Kino's head there was a song now, clear and soft, and if he had been able to speak of it, he would have called it the Song of the Family.

> (pp. 7–8)

The story that the book tells is, in this and other ways, distanced, placed within a context of the oppressed culture in which the Indians find themselves, and the characters become representatives with representative histories rather than individuals with individual histories.

In the case of *The Pearl* I find it particularly difficult to disentangle personal response from the wider purposes of the research. Thus, as I was reading the book I had a dominant feeling of irritation that it is so widely thought to be suitable for year 10 pupils. I felt the only real reason it was there was that it was short. Politically I find the story deeply nihilistic, as I do *Of Mice and Men*, another favourite in school at this age. The poor are shown as trapped within an economy in which they have no power, but the closure of the book, as Kino throws the pearl back into the sea, seems to suggest that there is no way out. Individual attempts to climb the ladder are doomed, and there is nowhere any suggestion of the collective action that would be required to overthrow the system. Nevertheless, I appreciate that Steinbeck's sympathies lie with the underdog, and under other circumstances I would be more disposed to appreciate the detailed evocation of the life of the poor, and the mythic structure of inevitability with which Steinbeck structures his story.

Here are Mary and Tracey, two of the middle-stream girls we have already met, expressing general dissatisfaction:

> *Mary:*   I couldn't get into that book, there was no way I could get into it.
> *Tracey:* I couldn't get into it, no way.

and here is one of the top-stream girls:

> *Nina:*   It's sort of, if I like a book I can sort of picture it, everything, but with his [Steinbeck's] books I can't picture anything.

Being unable to 'get into' a book is a universal cry. Here is a year 7 girl talking about *The Last Battle* by C. S. Lewis. She had found it boring:

CS: Can you explain any more what that means when you say something's boring
Angel: I couldn't understand it. I couldn't get into the book, it was just boring.
CS: What do you mean when you say you couldn't get into the book?
Angel: I couldn't understand what they, what it meant, all the words meant and that. What was on, what was happening.

The suggestion that something is boring because it is difficult to understand opens up possible avenues for exploration, but we have to return to the year 10 pupils' discussion of *The Pearl* for further elucidation:

Rosie: It was so different we couldn't imagine how it was like.

In the first place, a major stumbling block for many pupils was that characters behaved in a way that was totally foreign to their experience of how people behave and what they are like. The doctor, for instance, is portrayed as grasping, mercenary, and entirely unprincipled. When he perceives that the baby is recovering from the scorpion sting under its own steam he deliberately gives it something to make it sick so that he can then come and 'cure' it.

Rosie: I thought the doctor was unlifelike because if he was a doctor he wouldn't go around steal ... literally stealing things from the beggars. If he was a proper doctor he would treat everyone, and he wouldn't charge them much.

It is not as if these middle-stream girls do not understand that the doctor is being portrayed as a monster:

Mary: 'Cause his family and that doctor and his family had always fought, and um always been against each other and the thing, the thought of this child being treated by the ... an enemy didn't agree with him ...
Rosie: The doctor was prejudiced as well weren't he?
Tracey: Yeh.
Rosie: He would only treat white people whereas Kino ...

They understand what Steinbeck is saying, but they refuse to take it on. When I press this particular group of girls on the character of the doctor, and on the behaviour of the beggars in front of the church, and on the behaviour of the friends and neighbours in the book, they are quite aware of the differences between what the book has to offer and their own experience, but each instance is yet another nail in the coffin of the book's acceptability to them. When I raise the question of the doctor's characterization with the top-stream girls, they reject the book on different grounds. If the doctor was like that, they argue, the poor people would have known, and thus would never have dreamed of going to him. Furthermore, they would have had doctors of their own.

The fact that they can't relate to the book as fiction means that it feels like a history lesson:

Mary: We've done it, we've done all that in History.
Rosie: Mmmmmm.
Mary: It's a bit too much. It bores you as well don't it, the book?
Rosie: You expect to learn about English things like Shakespeare and that, not people from other countries. I'm not prejudiced or nothing but ...

We may comment that such compartmentalization of knowledge, which they have learned, *inter alia*, from the structure of the school curriculum, may do them no service, nor does it help the book. But that is the situation that they find themselves in, in the subject that is known as English.

Reader response theory has shown us that the reader needs to share a knowledge of the world, a cultural repertoire with the text in order to take that text on board, and we see here how that simply isn't the case. At every turn these readers reject the text because the differences in the two repertoires are too great. They are faced with two alternatives, either to abandon the attempt, or to take pains to acquire sufficient repertoire to take on the text.

Ideological

So far I have discussed the pupils' knowledge of the world and in particular how people behave in the world, and how that knowledge is so distant from the alternative views offered them in the book that they cannot relate to it. However, the examples we have looked at also have ideological overtones. The young people I talked to were directly aware of the ideology of the book, though not quite in the way that Steinbeck intended, one suspects. Here are two of the top-stream girls talking about it:

Nina: I think what it's trying to say is that erm man's desire to obtain what it can't is destroying other people around it and sort of that you should sort of be grateful for what you've got and not sort of go after things you haven't got ...
Carole: I think it's a boring moral for a story 'cause, well it's just so normal ain't it, it's boring. (*Laughter*)
CS: So it's it's, it's normal is it, the sort of ... normal from whom?
Carole: It's things you sort of like get told about in assemblies and that, it's boring, do you know what I mean?
Nina: It sort of, get sort of ...
Carole: Do this, don't do that and ... be good and all that, it's boring. You don't want to know.
Nina: You're told in assembly, right and then if you do sort of humanities subjects or something like that, you're told there, and then you're sort of in reg ... in form time, you're told there as well and then you're told by

your parents, and then you're told by – – – people, and so on and so on
and so on, and when you sort of read a book about it ...

CS: As well?

Nina: You sort of think, 'Oh my God, not again!', you know. It would have been
different if there was more excitement in the story or more adventures or
things like that, but it was so erm ... dull.

These girls are alerting us, once again, to alternative readings of a given text.
On the one hand, it is quite possible to argue that Steinbeck is exploring the
delineation of white Western greed, and the oppression and hopelessness that
results from it. Such a reading would invite the reader to take a stance of shared
guilt for such exploitation and to look to ways of redressing the evil. We might
even argue that Steinbeck expected his ideal reader both to share such liberal
humanist views and, simply by virtue of being a member of Western society, to
share responsibility for its exploitation of the Third World.

However, this is plainly not the way in which these girls have read the book.
Young people in school are in a situation where they are to a greater or lesser
extent powerless, so that paradoxically they are nearer to the situation of the
impoverished Indians in the story. A brief examination of the plot makes it
perfectly plain that no matter what efforts Kino and his family make to alleviate
their condition they are doomed to failure. Not even great good fortune in the
form of unexpected wealth can do anything for them. Thus, though white liberal
guilt can be relied on for one reading of the book, where readers are not prepared
to assume that stance an alternative reading emerges, which is that, no matter
how hard you try, the oppressors always win, and that the only resort in the face
of such odds is to be grateful for what you've got.

That these particular girls forcefully reject the moral they perceive, is evident
from the tone of their comments, but they are more specific. So also are the
middle-stream girls:

Rosie: You know, the moral was sort of um ...

Mary: Be good.

Tracey: It was split up.

Rosie: Don't wish to have more than what you've got because it will only bring
bad luck ...

CS: And what do you think about that as a moral?

Rosie: I think it's stupid, because everyone's got ambition that they want more
than what they've got.

Tracey: Everyone's got to have ambition.

Rosie: And it doesn't always bring bad, does it?

And here is Nina, one of the top-stream girls, taking a slightly different tack:

Nina: But I mean if you work hard and have the ability to er do something ... I
don't think that, you know, they should sort of say, 'Oh you can't change
this just because you think you've got the ability to, you've got to go

through this, this, this, and the other', but 'cause if you feel that something needs changing I don't see why you shouldn't.

The book is open to two readings and the reading that occurs will depend as much upon the ideology of the reader as upon that of the writer (in so far as it can be known). What is clear is that the reading these pupils have made is perfectly justified by the structure of the plot, and, I would argue, they make equally clear their rejection upon ideological grounds.

It might be thought that such ideological rejection is solely the domain of the older pupils. This proved not to be the case. I have already mentioned C. S. Lewis's *The Last Battle* and suggested that it was not much liked by some of the year 7 pupils. It, too, was a class reader.

In terms of personal response, it is difficult to come to any of the *Narnia* series cold. As a youngster I was entranced by *The Lion, the Witch and the Wardrobe*, not least because I first came across it serialized on the radio. Subsequent reading did not disappoint. I didn't read the whole series until I was an adult, and I have always found *The Last Battle* by far the weakest. Lewis is so concerned to get the allegorical detail right that the story all but disappears, and as a result the deeply uninteresting final vision of an infinitely expanding, infinitely receding Platonic heaven dominates the book. Add to which, in a more recent rereading I realized that the whole set-up leading to the battle that occurs in the first half of the book is appallingly racist: it is perfectly clear that the white imperialists, plus the friendly natives, have the one true god, and that the dark-skinned invaders from across the border worship the devil, and are to be well sorted out at the last trump, if not before.

At the beginning of the book Shift, an ape, uses Puzzle, a foolish donkey, to deceive the population about the coming of Aslan, the presiding deity of the series. One reading is that this is part and parcel of the Christian allegory, with true gods and false gods battling it out as the end draws nigh. Such a message is, however, passed by by all the younger readers that I discussed the book with, but Belinda and Angel recognize a different aspect of the relationship. Here is part of the description of the relationship, from the opening chapter.

> At least they both said they were friends, but from the way things went on you might have thought Puzzle was more like Shift's servant than his friend. He did all the work. When they went together to the river, Shift filled the big skin bottles with water but it was Puzzle who carried them back. When they wanted anything from the towns further down the river it was Puzzle who went down with empty panniers on his back and came back with the panniers full and heavy. And all the nicest things that Puzzle brought back were eaten by Shift; for as Shift said, 'You see, Puzzle, I can't eat grass and thistles like you, so it's only fair I should make it up in other ways.' And Puzzle always said, 'Of course, Shift, of course. I see that.'
>
> (p. 7)

Again in terms of the Christian allegory, it is perhaps necessary for Puzzle to be meek in order that he should inherit the earth (which is what he does at the end of the story). As far as these girls are concerned, however, his meekness is stupidity, and they resent *not* Shift's domineering and bullying ways, but Puzzle's stupidity in allowing himself to be exploited:

CS: Does it irritate you the way Shift get, keeps, is, gets, gets better, gets the better of er of ...
Belinda: Yeh.
Angel: Yeh, that's stupid.
CS: of Puzzle. Now what's stupid about, is it stupid because Puzzle doesn't do anything about it?
Angel: Yeh – – –
CS: Or is it stupid, stupid because Shift is wrong ...? I mean I know Shift's wrong in one sense but I mean like people like Shift don't exist.
Angel: Well they do exist.
CS: Yes.
Angel: But Puzzle should do something about it.
           (my emphasis) ... and Belinda agrees.

It is tempting to read Shift as entrepreneurial capitalism and Puzzle as the exploited working class. Angel is a black girl so it may be that the relationship raises other echoes in her mind. Whichever particular exploited group Puzzle might be read as, there is no doubt that his acceptance of the exploitation is an important factor in that exploitation. It is this that is so categorically rejected by these two year 7 girls, just as the similar over-arching moral of *The Pearl* – that to try to better yourself is doomed to failure – is rejected by year 10 children.

Prediction

We know, these days, the importance that prediction has within the reading process, and the subject is dealt with at length in Chapter 8. Here, it is the thwarting of the prediction process that irritates readers of *The Pearl*. In the first place, they dislike the reflective style of the book, in particular the use Steinbeck makes of references to music and song to characterize the nature of relationships and emotions. We had just read such an extract and Tracey had groaned:

CS: So, so Tracey when you said 'and the music started up in his head again' you went 'Urggh!' as if it was, as if it was a right turn-off for you.
Tracey: Yeh. But it was all, the writer's, John Steinbeck or what ever his name is right.
CS: Yes?
Tracey: He's always bringing this music in his ears, it really does turn you off.
CS: Yes.
Tracey: That makes it even worse.
Mary: You think you're just going to get good to, a good part.
Tracey: Yeh.
Mary: In the book, and all of a sudden this music.

It may be that these three girls are rejecting these episodes because of their unusualness and unfamiliarity. But the fact that these episodes also function to prevent the reader from becoming involved with the action, that they distance the reader from the drama and excitement of the story, means that these three girls' demands for excitement, demands that the book should engage them emotionally, are continually being thwarted.

Something else is also going on here too, I would suggest. The girls are predicting what is going to happen in the text. They construct what they hope will be the underlying story, the *fabula*, to use the structuralist term. Their previous experience of other texts tells them that their constructions are possible, indeed they would not be able to make them without previous experience of other stories. Here they are, demonstrating the point. We have just read a bit of the text where Juana, the baby's mother, has sucked the poison out after the scorpion has struck:

> *Mary:* No, one thing I'd like is if she sucked the poison out and swallowed it herself. (*Laughter*)
> *Rosie:* Yeh, that would have been better …
> *Mary:* The fact was I thought she was going to swallow it, I thought she was going to swallow it, that's why I read on, but she never. I thought, 'Oh you boring girl' …

When young readers reject a text, one of the things they have done is to make predictions that have been radically disappointed: they have attempted to construct an underlying story that is at odds with what they are offered. The question of prediction into the text is however a complex one, for it cuts both ways: we were talking about the finding of the pearl:

> *Mary:* Well you knew he was going to get it the way that um, you know, he saw something bright in the water so he picked it up. You think 'Oh well he's got it' but it didn't take long. I mean if we went diving for pearls we wouldn't find it in about five seconds flat would we?

So here are the same three girls saying, on the one hand, that the development of the story is too far away from their own predictions; and, on the other, that they predict precisely what is going to happen, and it promptly does. Once again there is a mismatch between what one might surmise to be Steinbeck's purpose, as exemplified in the text, and the requirements of the readers. At this stage in the story Steinbeck does not seem to be interested in raising suspense about the action. Thus by his style he distances the reader from concerns about the immediate action, or else allows so little time for suspense to be generated before it is resolved, that readers are not given the opportunity to feel any suspense for themselves. Later on in the story he does allow suspense about the action to be generated:

> *Nina:* Well I wanted to know what would happen to the family 'cause, 'cause they sort of escaped didn't they, and sort of, I wanted to know if they would die

or if they would live but that was about just, the point, that's the only point that I got really interested in.

Some of these reactions are echoed in the differing responses of the first years to the *Narnia* stories of C. S. Lewis which I shall be considering in the next chapter. For the moment I wish to conclude this consideration of the rejection of texts by looking at issues of relevance and choice.

Interest – in what and on behalf of whom

In this final section on rejection I want to look at the same issues from a somewhat different perspective. In a frequently formulated point of view, pupils were simply 'not interested' in the book. They found it boring. First of all the book gets rejected along with much of the rest of the school curriculum, as irrelevant. Here are three year 10 middle-stream boys:

> *Ken:*   At school they don't teach you enough about when you go on the dole, they should write a book about that.
>
> *Nemesh:* Special brew!
>
> *Ken:*   They don't, they don't know what forms to fill in and that and they have to go to this place ...
>
> *Jagdish:* Like Nemesh says, special brew dole queue!

I later discovered that a special brew was a fart, though at this stage all I recognized was that it was a generally disruptive noise. My initial tape with this group is peppered with such jokes. Beneath such jokiness and subversion of the interview situation there is an underlying seriousness in the demand for what they perceive as some relevance in the curriculum. They are capable of being more specific. They complain that the book is too old-fashioned:

> *CS:*   So you, are you saying you're not interested in books that are about olden times, you'd rather read books that are about now?
>
> *Ken:*   Some, some, but it'd have to be um, it would have to be something interesting like, I wouldn't mind say reading something like about Hitler in the war or something.
>
> *CS:*   Yeh, yeh.
>
> *Jagdish:* (*In Black English Vernacular*) What you on about man, Hitler in the war? Hitler in the war.

Ken's interest in Hitler is no accident in an area where groups like the British Movement and the National Front are recruiting at local football matches, and Jagdish's dialect move from the local accent to Black English is a recognition of the implications of such a suggestion. I have little doubt that if one were to offer these three boys a choice of reading a book about Hitler, a book about life on the dole or a video from the local video shop they would opt for the video every time. Their disillusion is as much to do with school and the whole curriculum as it is to do with *The Pearl*. *The Pearl* is merely a small part of the whole picture. However, it is worth saying that young people just coming up to leaving school are understandably interested in the present and the future. They see *The Pearl* as offering them a view of the past that has no relevance to either.

A second issue is the question of choice, and whom the pupils perceive as being interested in the book:

> *Ken:*   Sir, like we're given these to read but everyone says they don't like them, but no one takes any notice, we just have to read it …
>
> *Nemesh:* Yeh, we don't get, we don't get no say in these books 'cause the teachers choose them and we have to make do with them.
>
> *Ken:*   Yeh, and we see all the other classes, they get really decent books and that, and then we come up with the ones that are left over.

Here is Mary again:

> *Mary:*   I suppose Miss must have liked it more than we would because I mean for a start she's older, and she's got different points of view to what us young people have …

Here are the top-stream girls suggesting initially that Steinbeck writes what he is interested in, and then that it might interest the teachers:

> *CS:*   So you can answer me this question, why do you think Steinbeck writes like that? What's he playing at if he writes it like that?
>
> *Nina:*   He could be a pouf! (*Laughter*)
>
> *Carole:* I suppose he thinks it's interesting.
>
> *Nina:*   Maybe what he thinks is interesting is not interesting to others. He just writes what he thinks is interesting for himself …

and later she says:

> *Nina:*   It's probably the teachers find it interesting.

The year 7 girls provide graphic evidence of the consequences of this lack of choice on their behalf. Belinda is describing reading lessons where they are required to read the class text silently to themselves:

> *Belinda:* I just sit there reading it even if I, even if I don't enjoy it. Got no choice.
>
> *CS:*   So what, what do you sit and do, I mean do you sit with the book open in front of you and doodle on the pad underneath the desk or something?
>
> *Belinda:* No I just get the book and start going through the pages til I get to the end, then I go back to the front, just keep doing it.

I ask what would happen if they read another book at this time, or if they read stories that they had written themselves in their own English book, an activity that Belinda does enjoy. They would, in Belinda's words, 'get done'.

The teacher who takes them for their one reading lesson a week is a History teacher. When I talked with him he explained that he was not qualified in

English, and simply did what was suggested to him. It needs to be added, too, that other pupils had enjoyed *The Last Battle*, and that Belinda and Angel were both enjoying *The Weathermonger*, their current class reader.

Returning to *The Pearl*, a third issue that arises is why it appears so frequently on the syllabus. Beyond suggesting that the teachers might be interested in it, the pupils I talked to were by and large unilluminating about the reasons. Here is Catherine, however, with one suggestion:

> *CS:*   Er, but why is it that schools go for it then?
> *Catherine:* Because of the description and imagery in the book.

Catherine, a top-stream girl, reintroduces what we have learned to recognize as Leavisite perspectives here, and such perspectives take us back to the liberal humanist message that, I have suggested, lies at the heart of one reading of the book. If I am correct about that reading, i.e. that the whole point of Steinbeck's portrayal is to alert his readers to the results of prejudice and greed, then it is possibly for this reason that it appears so often on syllabuses. The response of the pupils I talked to suggests that if such is the aim then it is misfiring completely.

Conclusion

Use of language and moral imperatives, are but two of a whole host of reasons that individual teachers may have for using *The Pearl*. I have already noted Gail Rodes's reasons. But it is clear that many young people feel excluded from the choosing process completely. They feel instead that texts are foisted on them whether they like them or no, and that they have no say in the matter.

In this chapter I have endeavoured to show that when pupils reject texts it may well not be because they do not understand them. On the contrary, in this case, all the pupils I talked to showed every sign of understanding *The Pearl* very well. Having understood, they then reject the text on experiential grounds, on ideological grounds, on grounds of lack of emotional satisfaction: because, in my shorthand, they do not find themselves in it.

In the next chapter I look at some of the requirements that texts should offer young people a relevant, and preferably positive gloss on their future.

8 Inventing the future

Teacher: Again [what happens in *Charlie and the Chocolate Factory* is] all quite
unreal isn't it or does it seem possible?

Wayne: It could be possible but I doubt it, I doubt it would be, maybe in a long
time.

Teacher: Does it have to be possible enough for you to like it?

Wayne: It has to be *virtually* possible, but not completely.

Teacher: Yes, yes I think I understand.

Introductory

This chapter examines two related topics which emerge from the data: cognition
and prediction. To that end in this introductory section I need to relate play and
virtual experience.

James Moffett, in *Teaching the Universe of Discourse*, suggests that narrative is
of vital importance in the cognitive development of children, and Piaget makes
similar claims for play in *Play, Dreams and Imitation in Childhood*. They are
clearly related activities. In his discussion of symbolic play, Piaget talks of the
child removing events and emotions from his or her immediate context in the
real world and placing them in a play situation where the child can control the
parameters. The decontextualization of experience (cf. Margaret Donaldson's
Children's Minds) in play allows children to take experience and rerun it in a
controlled context. The child is thus enabled to examine both the way that the
world is and how she or he feels about it. Susanne Langer has suggested to us
that the experience of reading fiction is the experience of a virtual world, and
this virtual world, like the world of play, is one in which events and emotions are
removed from the real world.

The young make specific links between the play world and the virtual world of
fiction, as I have shown elsewhere in an article on Blyton in 1985. There I was
concerned to trace the links between play and the reading of fiction as demonstrated to me by a group of 12-year-olds talking about Blyton. In this chapter

I wish to develop the ideas raised then, and, in particular, emphasize the cognitive aspect of the game element in reading fiction. Relevant here is what Roland Barthes in *S/Z* calls the hermeneutic code of fiction, whereby fiction raises questions or constructs puzzles, and then provides explanations or solutions for them.

The other strand of the chapter is concerned with the ways in which, as Margaret Meek has suggested for instance in 1987, young people read fiction (or watch videos) in order to construct potential futures. To use Langer's term, for the young, fiction is a virtual future, or to use Wayne's term from his comments about *Charlie and the Chocolate Factory*, above, fiction is about the virtually possible.

We shall see that such construction of futures consists, on the one hand, of local predictions within the fiction itself. Prediction exercises have been recommended classroom practice for some time (see, for example, Lunzer and Gardener's work on *The Effective Use of Reading*) and are familiar to many English and language teachers. In them the sorts of prediction game described below by the boys in relation to *Super Gran* are formalized and structured so that they can be played by groups or even whole classes. There has thus for some time been a recognition of the cognitive relevance of prediction. While not wishing at this point to enter into debate about the somewhat dubious desirability of dragooning and regulating response in this way, I would wish to build on the underlying assumption that prediction is a vital part of the hermeneutic process itself. When readers start playing these prediction games, the reading is one in which the evidence is weighed, potential outcomes are predicted, and then measured against 'what really happened'.

On the other hand, the construction of futures is not restricted to prediction within the text, for the young make wider cultural judgements about fiction, measuring it against their cultural needs as growing and developing people. I quote again the demands of the three middle-stream year 10 boys from the last chapter:

> *Ken:* At school they don't teach you enough about when you go on the dole, they
> should write a book about that.

This second wider cultural perspective is much more clearly related to the general thrust of my wider thesis as a whole, and will be dealt with in the second half of the chapter. First, I wish to examine the hermeneutic process in action within the fiction itself.

Playing the narrative game

The group of year 7 boys that had read *Super Gran*, as I have said, had thoroughly enjoyed the book: it was 'excellent', 'brilliant', and so on. I want here to concentrate on some of the structural features of the narrative.

The book opens with a scene in a park where Granny Smith is hit by the magic ray. The narrative then alternates between providing explanations of how the machine had been invented and stolen, and scenes where Super Gran discovers her new powers. The boys are quite aware of, and particularly enjoy this structural skipping about:

> *Paul:* At the beginning it says, it starts ...
> *Wayne:* It explained about what the gran was like.
> *Paul:* Yeh, then it, then it kind of went back a little bit, and say how she got her powers in the park.
> *Wayne:* * * * it was if, as if somebody ripped the pages out and stuck them in back in ord ... in different order.
> *Paul:* So it explains it better like that * * *
> *CS:* Yes, yes. So, but that didn't worry you, that jumping about. That was ...
> *Wayne:* No that that made it more exciting.
> *Paul:* No, that, that made, that ...
> *Dave:* Mmm.
> *Paul:* 'Cause you had to read on to see *how it happened.*
>
> (my emphasis)

What I want to suggest is that at every point they relate the structural intrigue of the text to processes of explanation. The book enables them to remove the very business of explanation itself from the real world and examine it to see how it works. For example, when Wayne says:

> *Wayne:* Yeh. It says something like 'The gran was playing football', you kind of think 'How's the gran playing football?'

he is simultaneously asking the question about the gran playing football and, I would argue, reflecting on the experience of asking the question.

The genre of the book, a comic, almost comic-strip superheroine fantasy, allows of any number of unexpected outcomes to situations. Social realism, the boys argue, would not give them nearly such a free reign. The genre allows them to play the game of explanation:

> *Paul:* You read the end of the paragraph, right, then you think what's going to happen ahead. You think just let's say for about ten minutes or something, then then then you just open the book again and start reading and see if you're right, and – – – little game with that.

The others do this too.

> *Wayne:* I do sometimes, like I think, I read a chapter tonight and I just read one chapter and all that night I'm thinking, well, 'If that happened then, then this is going to happen next.'

It is a game where they can play at thinking:

Paul: Really it's, this is like a game, sort of, if you really think about it it's like a
game, 'cause erm as I said you think on, and then you actually find out …

The year 7 pupils talked of this structural game playing on a number of tapes, more so than the fourth years. Both girls and boys talked about it, though few groups were quite so explicit as this one. If there was a distinction then it was in academic rating. In year 10, for instance, the group that liked the structural complexity of *Carrie* was the group of top-stream boys, though we have seen that a single middle-stream boy also responded to it. Among year 7 the groups that were most interested in discussing structure were those that the teacher rated as potential top or second set. Year 7, if you remember, was mixed-ability, but in year 8 they were to be divided into four sets for English.

I have argued that, in reading *Super Gran* this group of boys was enabled to play explanation games. It was not a book that was universally popular by any means. The group of girls I shall be discussing in the next section could not stand the book. They disliked the very genre conventions that the boys so enjoyed. The fact that they could predict that Super Gran was going to win through every time, meant that they had no interest in investigating the method by which she did so. However, when presented with a text to which they did relate, they too took the opportunity to play the investigation game.

Investigating the fictional world

Prince Caspian is another book in C. S. Lewis's *Narnia* series. The series differs from much formula fiction in that it does not take one set of characters and run them through a different adventure in each book. Consisting of only seven books, it instead takes a number of different characters and explores a wholly invented world from creation to day of judgement. By far the most popular, indeed one of the most popular of all children's books ever written, as the surveys have shown, is *The Lion, the Witch, and the Wardrobe*. The others tend to get mentioned quite a lot, too, but as I have already suggested, in discussion with the young people who had filled in my questionnaires, it emerged that as often as not these titles were included by them on the assumption that since they had liked *The Lion, the Witch, and the Wardrobe* then they would like the others in the series. Furthermore, it also transpired that part of the reason for the frequent appearance of the title on recent lists was accounted for by a popular full-length cartoon film of the story shown regularly on television at Christmas and on other high days and holidays. It is also frequently read as a class reader in junior school.

Much of *The Lion, the Witch, and the Wardrobe*, is devoted to the discovery of a whole secondary world, Narnia, reached through the back of an old wardrobe in an old house. Much of the drama of that book is created by the conflict between those children who do believe such a world exists, those who do not, and those who do but lie about it. In an unpublished paper, Peter Rowe in 1987 has argued that the book is about the very process of reading fiction itself, likening the invitation that is offered to the characters within the book to explore a secondary world to the invitation that is offered by all fiction to explore a virtual world. In all the other books in the series the entry to the secondary world is peremptory and sudden. There is little or no drama or story surrounding the entry. Indeed in *The Horse and His Boy*, another in the series, there is no entry at all, the entire story is set within Narnia. To add to the complication, the first book to be written was *The Lion, the Witch, and the Wardrobe*. This is generally the first book to be read in the series, but it is not the one in which the story of the creation of Narnia is told. To add yet further to the complication, in the case of this particular study, as I have already mentioned, the year 7 pupils I talked to had had *The Last Battle* read to them during the course of my research.

Victoria, a year 7 girl, had read the whole series at least once, and knew *all* of this. She was in the process of rereading the series in fiction time order, and had fitted her reading of *Prince Caspian* into that process.

The main objection raised to *Prince Caspian* by many readers was that it took too much getting into. This is, they explain, because the book starts one story, breaks off to sketch in the background of a second story, breaks off yet again to tell a third story. Both boys and girls who failed to get into the book make this complaint. An examination of the text soon reveals the grounds for such an analysis.

The book opens with the four children from *The Lion, the Witch, and the Wardrobe* (the title of the earlier book is specifically referred to in the first sentence) on a railway station. They are magically transported to an island which they spend the first chapter exploring. In the second chapter they start to piece together the evidence and discover that they are in Narnia, some hundreds or even thousands of years after their visit in the previous book. In the third a dwarf turns up, and in the fourth and fifth he fills in the historical gap between their last visit and the present day. It is not until some half-way through the book that the children themselves get to partake in the adventure.

In terms of a personal response, my own problems with the book are very similar to those mentioned above. In the first place the four children spend ages discovering what I already know by the third page, that is, that they are in Narnia. That, of course, is something to do with the fact that I know how the game of fiction is played. My second objection is more thoroughgoing. The four children are introduced, I assume, because they are the protagonists. It is by their agency that things will be done, yet for the first half of the book they are entirely passive recipients of information, information that they are indeed in Narnia as they piece together evidence that has no relevance whatsoever to the remaining story, and then information about the intervening history. To enjoy the book I would have had to be engaged by both those processes, and I wasn't. In common with many of the children who read it, or attempted it, I kept going 'Yes, yes, yes, but for goodness' sake get on with the story.' And I have already hinted at my objections to the muscular Christianity and assumptions of white imperialism and feudal social order that underlie that series as a whole. In this book, for instance, it emerges that only the human characters can aspire to rule the country – so much, to fall, for a moment, into the intentionalist fallacy, for Lewis's views of democracy!

Victoria, however, saw and felt things differently. Her response to the book is dependent upon her knowledge and enthusiasm for the whole series. Like the children in the story, she too pieces together the evidence in order to relate what she is being told to what she knows, but of course the whole thing is done at a fictional level. She is relating new fictional information to pre-existing fictional information.

> *Victoria:* You've got to read the other books in the series before you can read, say, this book ...

This book carries on from the previous book:

> *Victoria:* 'Cause, erm, it tells you things that you haven't learned before, and then it comes on to the next book type of.
> *CS:* So that you sort of fit it into the ...
> *Victoria:* Yeh.
> *CS:* Into the whole, into the whole pattern.
> *Victoria:* Yeh.

The reading of this book is dependent upon the reading of the series:

> *Victoria:* 'cause you can't just really read this book on its own...
> *Lakshmi:* without ...
> *Victoria:* without reading the, all the other six books ...

She continues:

> *Victoria:* And it's really good when you carry it on 'cause you say, 'Oh that's how that happened, and that's how that happened,' and you find out: 'Oh that's good!' Things like that.
> *CS:* Yes, yes.
> *Victoria:* And you discover what's happened.

The series enables Victoria to play at learning, to play at fitting things together to make a pattern, to play at relating pieces of apparently disparate information, to play at generating explanation. The fact that Lewis constructs a whole cosmology aids and abets her in this. Each book, she argues, is like a chapter in a larger book which is the whole series. The whole drift of Victoria's argument, i.e. that the interest in the books is in how they fit together as a series – indeed, in how a whole world is created, has a history, and is concluded – means that other sorts of question, alternative hermeneutics are excluded.

As I have mentioned, yet another in the series, *The Last Battle*, was read to this year 7 class as a class reader. As we have seen, in that book a monkey clothes a donkey in a Lion's skin to pass him off as the presiding god figure in the whole series. This information is clear from the opening chapter. Thus when rumours spread subsequently that Aslan is coming, the reader is in a position to recognize that such a rumour is false and one strand of suspense is closed to the reader, though not to the characters. Here are the boys arguing that the reader should have been left in doubt too:

> *Wayne:* I think they should lead us to believe it's Aslan as well, so …
> *Paul:* They shouldn't have told us, they really shouldn't have told us that it's a lion's skin.
> *Wayne:* I think they should have led us to believe it was Aslan as well.
> *Paul:* So we kept, so … C. S. Lewis should have made us keep, keep reading on like.
> *Wayne:* Made us guess.
> *CS:*   Why would that have made it, why would that have made it better?
> *Wayne:* Because you'd be, you'd be say reading through it and would be turning the pages and going, 'Well I wonder if it really is Aslan', and you'd be saying that to yourself and thinking, 'Well if it is Aslan, why is he making them do mean things like that when he's good', and if he was dying he'd be kind, he wouldn't make them die with him.

That such a strand of questioning is denied to the reader is perhaps not surprising given the allegorical nature of the whole series. A reader alerted to the Christian parallels may recognize that questioning the good of God/Aslan is not an 'appropriate' response. The young readers here, that both like and dislike the books, are not primarily interested in the allegorical nature of the books, nor in the religious arguments that are being propounded in the development of the action of the series (though Lakshmi at one point does pick up on the fact that there is a religious debate going on, but only in so far as that debate helps her to follow the action rather than vice versa). The boys who reject the book, do so because it denies their particular enjoyment of 'explanation on the run', if I may so characterize it. Victoria's appreciation of the book(s) arises from her enjoyment of entering into the construction of a whole fictional world. She is interested in both how it fits together as fiction and in how it fits together as a world. Indeed, the two processes are inseparable. *The Magician's Nephew*, for example,

> *Victoria:* tells you how the wardrobe got there, the witch got there. How Aslan, how Aslan created, created…
> *Lakshmi:* Narnia.
> *Victoria:* Narnia, and how the Queen and King got there.

Rowe's (1987) suggestion that *The Lion, the Witch, and the Wardrobe* offers the experience of getting into fiction has obvious application to Victoria here. On each occasion that she picks a new book in the series she re-explores that experience. Where I would wish to develop Rowe's thesis is in suggesting that the 'getting into fiction' experience is itself a game of cognition, a game of understanding, a game in which the actual process of understanding can be decontextualized and held up for examination. We have seen the boys doing it with *Super Gran* and we have seen Victoria, with Lakshmi's support, doing it in a more thoroughgoing way with the whole Narnia series.

There is another theme from the series that we discuss, and that is the play that is made with time.

Virtual futures

We have seen how, in the process of explanation making, the boys reading *Super Gran* predicted into the virtual future of the text and then checked their predictions against 'what really happened'. Let us, for the moment, take up Rowe's suggestion that the shift from the primary to the secondary world in the *Narnia* series offers readers a fictional rerun of the reading experience itself. We could then suggest that the series offers readers a fictional rerun of the experience of the *virtual future* that reading is for young people. The girls shed some light on just that question. I ask them why the time shift between the everyday world of the characters and the secondary world of Narnia is so fascinating. Victoria talks at length about the ability that the fiction allows for a lifetime to run in Narnia while no time runs in the primary world of the characters. I pursue the question of why this play with time so fascinates them:

> *Lakshmi:* It would be nice to do that really, you know if you could grow, you grow up and wear lipstick and everything and suddenly you can go back when you, when you don't feel like being old anymore, you know.

The point to emphasize is that time in the secondary world of Narnia bears no relation to time in the primary world. Characters grow up, become adults in Narnia, and then at the end of the book return to being the same age, and even waiting for the same train in the same station, waiting to go to the same prep school. Rowe's analogy is persuasive, for while we spend three or four hours reading a book, or one and a half or two hours watching a video, the characters can encompass weeks, months, even lifetimes of experience. Lakshmi takes up the theme and puts it even more forcibly:

> *Lakshmi:* Yeh, it would be nice if say you were living in this wonderful world of paradise for, for, until you were about 999 years old, you know, if that, you could live that old in Narnia and suddenly you feel, 'Oh God, I'm going to die' and you could just suddenly go back in the wardrobe ...
> *Victoria:* Yeh!
> *Lisa:* Mmm.
> *Lakshmi:* ... and you're a little young again, and that would be good, and you can carry on your life and go back, you know. It would be really good to be able to do that.

The womb/wardrobe that the characters can re-enter at their will, ready to venture forth again when the going is not so tough, is an idea that would seem to have had a potent effect upon Lakshmi here as she sums up so poignantly the feelings of a young person on the brink of adulthood. The future beckons with paradisaical offerings: in the case of Narnia, that right will triumph, with a little help from us, and we shall all live happily ever after, or at least until the next book; but the future also offers the inescapable threat of death. The biological and social imperatives of growing up, encapsulated here by Lakshmi in the realization of that final imperative of death, require that we continuously have to attempt to control the future. This is nowhere more keenly felt than by the young. Part of the very cultural definition of youth is that it is a process of change, a process of becoming adult. What I am arguing is that the *Narnia* series offers those young readers that enjoy it a unique opportunity to decontextualize that process and both play at it and examine it at the same time.

If we accept Rowe's thesis, i.e. that the move from the primary to the secondary world in the *Narnia* series is an image of the move from the real world of everyday life into the virtual world of fiction itself, then the time-shift that offers the *characters* within the series possible alternative futures becomes also the move from the everyday to the fictional that offers *readers* virtual futures. There is nothing in the evidence that these girls offer that denies such a suggestion, and a good deal that supports it. But also, the argument would run, the series offers readers the opportunity to decontextualize the experience of reading fiction. It offers them, in other words, the opportunity to both decontextualize and examine the experience of experiencing virtual futures. Well, maybe. I have no evidence that would support that degree of reflexivity on the part of 12-year-old readers. But it could be an intriguing path to explore.

The chase

There is one constantly recurring feature of many of the videos and some of the books that the older pupils that I talked with watch and read, and that is the chase. In many ways, for instance, *First Blood* consists of one long chase. The chase performs for readers/viewers much the same sort of function as the narrative predictions that we saw the year 7 boys exercising with *Super Gran*, but faster. While it may often be assumed that such action appeals more to boys than to girls, and indeed such suggestions were made to me by both boys and girls, in fact both boys and girls spoke in similar terms about the appeal of the chase. Thus, in discussing *First Blood*, it is the year 10 middle-stream girls who are most articulate at spelling out its appeal, developing and exploring the complexity of the response. I ask the direct question:

CS: What is it about chases that are so appealing?
Rosie: Oh they really build you up don't they Tracey.
Tracey: Some can leave you in suspense.

Rosie's reply suggests both physical and emotional involvement, and Tracey's comment should by now alert us to hermeneutic processes. They talk about the most immediate of all presentations of the chase, that when the camera is put in the driver's position in a fast-moving vehicle. Rosie describes swaying to avoid things:

Rosie: It's like you're actually there in it.
Tracey: Doing it.

So I ask:

CS: So, so do you feel, you feel the physical sensations of what it would be like?
Tracey: Yeh, and the mental.

I ask Tracey to develop that last point:

Tracey: You sit there, right, and you're sort of thinking like they're thinking.
Rosie: Mmm. Sort of planning like – – – detective – – –
Tracey: Yeh, you're planning ahead.
CS: You're?
Tracey: You're planning ahead of what's going to happen. You're sort of thinking, 'Now right, there's a top corner coming up, turn that corner.'

We see that the same planning and predicting processes that we have discussed above are going on here, too. In this case though the physical and emotional involvement are more overt:

CS: And what about the emotional?
Tracey: You're getting all excited.
Rosie: Mmm.
CS: So all three things are running at once?
Tracey: Yeh.
Rosie: It doesn't always show though * * *
Tracey: * * * you're watching telly but everything's running through your brain.

These girls suggest, then, that the chase generates physical (kinesthetic), emotional, and cognitive response, all running simultaneously; and, of course, that while all this is happening in their head they are to all intents and purposes sitting quietly in front of the television.

I would argue that the enthusiasm of the boys for *Super Gran* and of Victoria for *Prince Caspian* is also an indication of emotional involvement. The excitement of the chase is an excitement of planning and prediction, an excitement of cognitive process. It is also, and at the same time, an excitement of reading, an aesthetic effect generated by the text.

Taking a positive path through the text

In this final section I want to return to analyses more central to my thesis and to revisit a text that we have discussed at some length elsewhere, James Herbert's

The Fog. Jack Zipes, in *Breaking the Magic Spell*, suggests that, although popular culture clearly promotes bourgeois ideology, none the less there sit within it elements of, admittedly individualistic, utopian fantasy that offer opportunities for autonomy and self-determination, and insist that people can still be the subjects of their own social change. Such notions can clearly be applied to *The Fog*.

The overall framing of the story is both reactionary and paternalistic. Even though at one stage it looks as if the fog will be defeated by carefully planned collective action – collect a sample, develop an antidote, spray the fog, and cure the people – in the end all that is virtually set at nought by the fact that the fog is actually destroyed by an opportunist maverick action by one of the scientists in the team. And such collective action as there is relies very heavily upon, and is focused very strongly through, the hero, a loner by inclination, who by the end of the book has gained a girlfriend but otherwise made no links with the rest of the world. The book ends with the isolated nuclear couple, archetypal unit of present-day capitalist Britain. The retreat to his flat, looking for support only to each other, and, to quote the last sentence of the book: 'He closed the door behind them' (p. 284). Just as bad is the sexism of the central female characterization. Called 'Casey' throughout, we discover that this is the hero's name for her, and that he has named her after his dog. She is portrayed throughout as helpless victim, first of her stepfather's barely contained desire for her, then of the fog itself. She needs 'rescuing', so along comes the hero, someone she can finally 'depend on'. During the final action she is left in the flat on her own – the little woman at home – a decision that makes absolutely no sense in plot terms, given the breakdown in order going on around her; she merely becomes more vulnerable and thus more in need of a man's care and protection. (We have seen elsewhere how one group of girls at any rate was able to read the book in such a way as to deflate its phallocentricity.)

Against such reactionary framing, and the sexist nature of part of the context, must be set a number of factors. First, it is clear that Holman's job is to counter the corporate interests of big business, and to expose both the denial of individual rights by the state apparatus and the concomitant secrecy that follows such denial. Utopian individualism certainly, but holding out the offer of autonomy, self-determination, and hope for individual rights within the capitalist corporate state. Not only is Holman shown to win in this case, it is also made clear that if he loses on any particular occasion then he bounces back to fight again.

Second, in the sub-plot episodes, where the fog causes the personal conflicts of the characters to be acted out in a particularly violent or monstrous way, in every case bar one, as we have already suggested, it is the underdog who wreaks vengeance against the powerful, the victim who turns the tables on his or her victimizer, in short, the oppressed who turn on their oppressors. Thus the boys attack the teacher, Casey attacks her father *and* Holman himself, the bank clerk attacks his manager, and so on. The farmer is even attacked by his cows, and the pigeon fancier by his pigeons.

The exception is Mavis, the jilted lesbian, who, though she has passed through the fog, does not return to wreak her vengeance, but is instead trampled to death by the suicidal hoards of Bournemouth while she is trying to save the life of a child. There is evidence enough in this text of homophobia – the end reserved for the homosexual schoolmaster is far and away the most graphically awful – and thus, though Mavis is a victim, and all the rules of *The Fog* would indicate that she should kill her unfaithful lover, preferably caught *in flagrante delicto*, Mavis is instead herself killed, one is tempted to suggest, simply because she is a lesbian. Such a death would be in line with the over-arching sexism of the text but out of line with the general ideological push of the sub-plot episodes.

The text, then, presents us with a number of ideological contradictions. In the first place the framing of the story and the reliance upon individual male action are undermined by the utopian thrust of that action, which is set precisely against the institutions of the corporate state. In the second place, the fog itself, despite its 'evil' status, releases actions which reverse the power relations between the individual characters in the sub-plots. Is it for this reason that some readers experience a certain relish, a certain glee even, as one after the other various characters meet their grisly ends? Young readers who come to *The Fog* are presented with an overall ideological formulation that certainly supports the status quo. But it is clear that the status quo within the book is in uneasy and constant defence against individual utopian forays that cannot be contained, and that there is a constant danger that the tables will be turned.

Within the predominant institutions of socialization, the family and the school, it is the young, I would argue, who are disadvantaged. Adults have the power and the knowledge, and the young have to seek their own autonomy within a frame that is not of their making. However, despite the fact that the struggle for that autonomy is long, hard and sometimes bitter, the young, in my experience, are far from defeatist. In fact they experience a continual interplay of achievement and setback, of autonomy and powerlessness, of angry resentment and sweet victory. Even those at the bottom of the pile, as Paul Willis has shown in *Learning to Labour*, succeed in generating positive self-images by standing against the dominant forces in the school, by devaluing that which the school holds sacred and valuing that which the school condemns.

There are contradictory elements within *The Fog* which allow of contradictory readings. It is possible for young readers to take a positive path through the text, one that puts a positive gloss on the shaping of those futures. However, as we have seen, there is one exception to the general rule, and that is the death of Mavis *the lesbian*. The three top-stream boys criticize the inclusion of the lesbian scene, even though, paradoxically, it is a scene they like. They compare it with the boys' boarding school scene:

Peter: At least the, at least that um, the boys one had something to do with the
           fog and that ...

CS: Yes.

Peter: but the lesbian one, I mean, it just could have said the woman got trampled by all the people, going out to sea from Bournemouth – – – go through all the details – – – there wasn't much point.

Kenneth: Yeh, it could have done without it * * * But he could have just carried on just saying this woman was upset and that but he didn't have to go in to describing it with her other, with the other lesbian.

The ground for their criticism is that the lesbian scene is unrelated to the fog, in contradistinction to all the other sub-plot episodes:

Peter: they've all got something sort of to do with the fog, like pigeons they....

Kenneth: Yeh.

Peter: must have flown through the fog and that.

CS: Yes.

Peter: But she really hasn't, all she's doing is getting trampled by the people.

In fact Mavis does pass through the fog on her drive down to Bournemouth (p. 117) but, as we have seen, the episode is the only episode where the fog does not intervene in the relationship, dramatize the conflict, and resolve it by enabling the underdog, in this case the jilted lover, to gain revenge on her oppressor. I would argue that the boys' criticism that the lesbian scene was unnecessary, and that Mavis has nothing to do with the fog, must surely therefore be to do with the fact the relationship is not resolved by the fog, but that instead the fog intervenes in another way, in the form of the population of Bournemouth, to prevent the relationship from being resolved. Thus a positive reading of this particular episode is denied them and both in ideological terms and in purely aesthetic terms it constitutes a break in the pattern of the book.

Conclusions

In this chapter I have looked at the way in which fiction allows these boys and girls to 'play the understanding game', both in terms of immediate prediction into the text, and in terms of building up more comprehensive understandings of the world of the book. That much of the evidence comes from the younger pupils suggests that it may be crucial for them to play at understanding in a way that is no longer the case when they are older, though there is no clear evidence of this.

When they are older the opportunity of what I have called a positive path through the text seems to be important. It would not be difficult to link the boys' reading of The Fog in this respect, with the readings of First Blood offered by the bottom-stream boys, or even the readings of the girls of Carrie or Stranger with My Face. I shall attempt to draw such threads together in the final chapter.

9 Common threads: culture and response

Introductory

In this chapter I try to draw together some of the themes of this book, and to answer possible questions that may be raised. Since we are concerned with response and young people, it would be legitimate to ask what effect such factors as age or ability have. Since we are concerned with pupils in school it would be legitimate to raise issues of curriculum content and pedagogy. Since we are concerned with culture, then issues of adolescence, and of race, gender and class must be considered. Some of these I shall deal with briefly, some at greater length. I shall also be considering 'response' itself, and suggesting that we need to broaden our definition of what we mean by it and what is to be included in it.

Age

Though the research was designed to bring out the differences in response between younger and older secondary pupils, as I indicated in Chapter 2, this was not what in the event actually happened. Instead I found that the wealth of material from the older pupils warranted the sort of thematic exploration that I have embarked upon. However one or two general comments can be made.

Year 7 chose children's books, books that had children as their main characters, and children as their implied readers. We know from Ariès in 1962 that the concept of 'child' is a social construct, the product of history. Here the distinction that I am assuming is between the pre-pubertal and the post-pubertal. With the possible exception of *Iggie's House*, both the child characters and the implied child readers are constructed, as Rose suggests in 1984, as innocent, acultural and asexual. *John Diamond*, and *Grange Hill Home and Away* chosen by year 10 pupils, are also marketed as children's books. *John Diamond* is, among other things, about the loss of childhood innocence and the inappropriateness of childhood stories of treasure trove. But it does not remove the veil very far – the book ends with an encomium to the true treasure of friendship, and sexually the main 12-year-old characters remain remarkably innocent. Only *Grange Hill Home and Away*, never actually read by anybody in the study, is at all knowing. Otherwise the older pupils selected books from among adolescent fiction, that is, fiction marketed as such, with adolescent characters, and with, I would argue, an implied adolescent readership, or they chose books from among popular adult literature.

Walsh in 1983 suggests that the main distinction between older and younger readers is that of experience, and I hint at a similar distinction when I comment that Wayne's reading of *Super Gran* stems from his experiences of being bullied, an activity that takes a particular form, I would suggest, in child culture, and which is viewed by adult society at large as an inevitable part of growing up, no matter that it is to a greater or lesser extent disapproved of. A specific example such as that just quoted is suggestive rather than conclusive. Otherwise I have suggested that the understanding games that readers play with *Super Gran*, and the *Narnia* series, may also have more relevance to the younger readers in the study than to the older ones. But again such a suggestion is far from conclusive.

A brief glance at the books chosen by the younger readers offers scope for further speculation. *The BFG* and *Super Gran* both feature characters who are initially powerless, but gain in power in the course of the story. *Iggie's House* and *Cathy Away* contain a good deal of realistic detail from the lives of children, even if in the latter case the children are hardly typical. But themes of power are writ large in the reading of the older pupils, and realism of detail also occurs with them and is a source of appeal, as we have seen with *Stranger with My Face*.

All that can be suggested is that younger secondary school pupils like to read about characters of their own age in books that construct an implied reader that is a child. Older secondary pupils like to read about characters of their own age in books that construct their implied reader as an adolescent, but also like to read adult books with adult characters. In the specific placing of the adolescent in current social life – expected to behave like an adult without actually being an adult – this duality of taste is again suggestive. But I have offered no clear evidence of differences in response between year 7 and year 10 readers and there is clearly room here for further work.

Ability and academic achievement

In many ways much the same can be said of 'ability'. In the first place the only measure I had of academic achievement was the streaming and setting structure of the school, that is to say, the actual, or in the case of year 7, predicted achievement of the pupils. There was a surprising dearth of test results in the individual files to which I was able to gain access. Quite how useful such information would have been to me is not clear. We already know from Clark in 1976 and from Whitehead and his colleagues in 1977 that high-ability pupils read more than low-ability pupils. This was certainly true of the present study. The year 10 top-stream pupils read more than the middle-stream pupils, and the bottom-stream pupils only read the texts they had chosen and no others. Furthermore, only the top-stream pupils would read books they didn't like. I was thus particularly grateful to the group of top-stream girls who ploughed through *The Pearl* and who thus contributed much of the evidence of Chapter 7. With year 7 my only indication of ability was the prediction the teacher made about which sets the pupils were going to go into in the following year, but the pattern there was much the same.

Otherwise the evidence of the research would suggest that academic achievement and response bear little direct relationship. It may well be objected that my definition of response is too wide, that to include stories about the boyfriend–girlfriend entanglement of mates does not constitute 'response' to *Stranger with My Face*, that to include stories of fighting in school and on the streets of Bigton does not constitute 'response' to *First Blood*, or that to include stories of being bullied does not constitute 'response' to *Super Gran*. The answer to such an objection would be that those stories are indicative of knowledges of the world, of cultural presuppositions, and of shared value systems that are essential prerequisites to the sorts of comment that the pupils made about the actual texts themselves. If 'response' itself must always be directed to the text then the sort of evidence I am offering could perhaps be called evidence of *pre-response*. I would call it culture.

Class/the politics of school

The question of class is related to that of academic achievement. Again my only measure of class was whether the pupils came from a council house or from a private house, a coarse enough measure in all conscience, and I only gleaned that information by asking the health visitor resident in the school about the addresses of the pupils. I certainly had no systematic measure of social class. However, within the politics of school there are some suggestive findings.

In the first place, I need to redress a certain imbalance in the study. I have concentrated on popular fiction, I have concentrated on fiction chosen by the pupils themselves. I have devoted a whole chapter to the rejection of texts being studied in class. It is necessary to point out that there was plenty of evidence of pupils *enjoying* the fiction that they studied in class. Mary, Tracey, Rosie and Deborah, the year 10 middle-stream girls we have seen so much of, had enjoyed *A Taste of Honey*, and spoke in glowing terms of *Romeo and Juliet* which they had studied in the previous year. All the top-stream pupils had enjoyed *To Kill a Mockingbird* and some of them had enjoyed *Cider with Rosie*. And I have indicated that *The Weathermonger* was proving popular with the girls who had so hated *The Last Battle*, and Victoria, for one, had certainly enjoyed the latter book when it was read in class.

Another impression that may be gained from the book is that the teachers are the baddies and the pupils the goodies in a never to be resolved battle. Here there *is* a distinction to be made. It seemed pretty clear to me that the bottom-stream pupils, the boys in particular, had a pretty jaundiced view of all teachers. The top-stream pupils, by contrast were very different in their attitude, and even when critical, were much more positive. Perhaps the most telling piece of evidence of this comes from Roland's view of his English teacher, and his English teacher's view of Roland. Paul Whitemarsh, the top-stream English teacher in question, rated Roland very highly. Roland listened, understood, and had come on well, particularly in his appreciation of poetry. Roland, in his turn, liked English, found the lessons interesting, and felt that he had learned a lot, particularly about poetry. By and large the middle-stream pupils fell between these two extremes.

In Chapter 5 I suggest that the top-stream boys, two of them future school prefects, respond to the social disorder of *The Fog* by lining themselves up on the side of order, while bottom-stream John aligns himself with Rambo's attack upon the state. Such indications, and they are no more than that, are supported to a certain extent by the book choice of the groups. The top-stream pupils chose *John Diamond* by Leon Garfield, a children's author already canonized by Fred Inglis in *The Promise of Happiness* and Margery Fisher in *Classics for Children and Young People*. They also chose *Stranger with My Face* by Lois Duncan, an author being promoted by the local schools library service as a good writer. By contrast, the popular horror, violence, and romance was chosen by the middle- and bottom-stream pupils.

These are only indications, projects for further research, rather than definitive conclusions, but it seems to me probable that there are differences in response that can be attributed to class difference, particularly if class is redefined in terms of the body politic of the school itself.

Ethnicity

I have no evidence to offer under this heading. However, John Lee's work in 1984 is highly suggestive, and the sorts of approach that I have used in the present study would seem to have application to questions of race, racism and ethnicity. In particular, the notion that texts are open to a plurality of readings, and the suggestions that I make in Chapter 4 that girls and boys read the same text differently, suggests that black pupils, or Asian pupils, or pupils from other ethnic minority backgrounds may well bring cultural presuppositions to bear upon their readings in ways that will distinguish them from the readings of white middle- or working-class pupils.

Gender

In Chapter 4 I suggest that differences in gender account both for book choice, and for different *readings* by boys and by girls. I would suggest that this becomes more marked with older pupils, though surveys suggest that gender-differentiated choice occurs at earlier ages, too.

Let me just illustrate the question of book choice with the example of Lena Kennedy's *Maggie*. *Maggie* was chosen by the year 10 bottom-stream girls. Unfortunately timing problems meant that few other groups had the opportunity of reading it. All the middle- and bottom-stream boys' groups refused to read it, and the top-stream boy's group never got the opportunity. The book tells the story of a woman's life, from childhood to grandmotherhood. It is about being a mother and about being a wife, it is about faithfulness and faithlessness to a drunken and somewhat violent husband. It is about bringing up children, whether you are sister, mother, cousin, or simply there. It has a fairytale rags-to-riches structure: it is about finding and keeping the right man who will rescue you from drudgery and the East End and set you up for happy ever after life in a cottage in the country. In that sense it is, without doubt, popular romantic fiction. It is about how, as a woman, you pay your dues to your family and at the same time insist on a personal life that is independent of them. It is about how, as a woman, you square your responsibility to your family with your need for autonomy.

That I have not discussed the book in detail stems from the fact the girls who chose it were not very forthcoming. Whether this was because they were not used to talking about what they read or saw, or whether they found it difficult to talk to a strange male interviewer, or whether they were just silent girls, or whether it was a combination of all three, is not clear. All the boys' groups who turned it down did so after very cursory inspection. The presentational symbolism of the cover, gold with an oval black and white photograph of the head and shoulders of a young woman in 1930s hairstyle and a fur-collared coat, was enough for most of them. Those that glanced through it soon picked up enough flavour of the content to confirm them in their view. It was, apart from anything else, going to be 'old-fashioned'.

From the description that I have offered of the content of the book it is difficult to resist the notion that its *implied* reader is female. A male reader must at the very least empathize with the concerns that I have outlined. From what we have seen so far of adolescent male culture, and from the theoretical perspectives offered by Rowbotham in 1973 and others, such empathy would be a very foreign experience. And to read across the the ideology of the text, that is, to regard Maggie as a 'silly cow', to use an obnoxious but pertinent expression, would, I suggest be very difficult.

Maggie is a useful example, since it points an extreme. There are plenty of texts, and we saw that *Carrie* was one, that are plural in the requisite ways to allow of both male and female adolescent readings.

Otherwise I have, I hope, demonstrated that female adolescent culture and male adolescent culture bring different frameworks to texts, and that different readings of those texts ensue. There is, I would suggest, more work to be done with younger boys and girls here.

Youth/power

At this point I would like to suggest that there is one factor that unites, though only loosely, much of the evidence that I have presented. That factor is the somewhat conventional notion of the search for identity that is supposed to take place during adolescence.

Ariès in *Centuries of Childhood* traces the development of 'childhood' in Western culture, and has suggested that it is a comparatively modern phenomenon. One of the aspects of this development has been the systematic raising of the school leaving age if I may so express it. He suggests that over the years older and older people have been removed from the working population and categorized as children. In Britain the successive raising of the school leaving age can be seen in that light, I would argue, and the removal of all those under 18 years of age from the unemployment register by the use of compulsory training schemes and so on would seem to fit into such a pattern, too.

John Schostak, in work already noted, has suggested that as that process of 'enchildization', to coin an ugly word, has continued, so society's methods of coercion and persuasion have become more subtle, and adolescents find themselves, as Stevi Jackson in 1982 suggests, half-way in between, expected to behave as adults without actually being adults. Schostak has traced the violation that many adolescents experience in school, and we have noted one or two cases in the present study. Let me at this stage present a further piece of evidence. It comes from the middle-stream girls' response to *Carrie*.

Adolescent revolt is one of the themes that informs the book. It is played out in terms of the conflict between the mother and the daughter, and the metaphysical elements allow King to dramatize that conflict, the mother's religious repression emphasizing the parental control, and the daughter's paranormal powers dramatizing her rebellion. Here is Mary making a spontaneous comment on the theme:

> *Mary:* What I find good about Carrie is that she's trying to fight her mother from having, drawing her into what her mother is.

In the book Carrie is both drawn to her mother, and in revolt from her. We noted in Chapter 4 Tracey's suggestion that Mrs White has Carrie's best interests at heart and it is in the context of this discussion that Tracey says:

> *Tracey:* But in her way I think her mum's protecting her as well.

Such protection, and Carrie's own recognition that her mother loves her, emphasizes the conflict inherent in Carrie's own rebellion. None the less, in order to 'become herself' she has to rebel. I ask:

> *CS:* Do you feel for Carrie in the book, do you feel sympathy for her, do you feel with her when she's getting back at her mum and so on?
> *Mary:* Yes. I do because I think well she needs, she, she's getting back at her mum, I mean she's not, I know she's been a bit divided about it, but I

> mean I feel really sorry for her because she wants to be a natural person,
> she wants to be taught, erm erm treated like a natural person ...

Mary's slip of the tongue there offers a hint that teachers as well as parents prevent you from being yourself, and I would suggest that at the heart of the discussion is the notion that others, parents, teachers, the adult world in general, want you to be other than what you 'really' are – in Mary's terms, a 'natural person'.

These girls are in the middle-stream group. There is no sense of the deep and destructive bitterness that we saw with the bottom-stream boys who had been in the bottom set all their life. None the less, they do feel as if they have limited control over their options. On one tape they talk at some length about their experience of frustration. One of them has had the same English teacher all her school career, she would have preferred a change. They all suggest that more than one teacher would have shown them different sides of a subject. Furthermore, if they don't get on with one teacher then a change is necessary. Over and beyond that, Rosie, for instance, feels that she should have been in the top set for language but her literature is not good enough.

> *Rosie:* There's no way she's going to put me up so I'm just going to end up doing
> CSE on both of them, that's no good, because I want to be a teacher, and
> that means if she don't put me up for O level language now I'm going to
> have to take O level in um sixth form and that's, that's just wasting my
> time ...

At the heart of Rosie's complaint is the fact of someone else passing judgement on her:

> *Rosie:* She thinks she knows me, but she don't. If anyone knows me, I, you know,
> I do, and I know I'm capable of doing that O level language.

Rosie is not alone. Tracey, too, has experience of getting grade 1's, but of being unable to move up. Gavin, one of the middle-stream boys talks, too, of being angry with school, of feelings that the world is against him, and of how nice it would be at such a time to possess Carrie's powers.

What I would suggest is that Carrie's somewhat violent strategies for fighting her extraordinarily repressive parent dramatize for these girls in particular the conflict they feel themselves to be in when others make decisions on their behalf. It is a response which echoes that of the bottom-stream boys to *First Blood*, that echoes, too, the response of the top-stream boys to *The Fog* when they are denied what I called a positive path through the text, and that is echoed elsewhere in the study. Central to such responses are books about power. I would suggest that such a theme unites *Super Gran*, *The BFG*, *Carrie*, *First Blood* and *The Fog*.

For the younger pupils reading *Super Gran*, the theme is felt in terms of their physical powers:

CS: Is like being a kid and having, and being, you said ...

Wayne: Having an old lady's looks.

CS: No. Oh, go on, go on.

Wayne: You kind of, it's like me dressing up you know like an old lady, and then going out and playing football, and you know it would, everybody, you'd be able to tackle them easy 'cause they'd just be going ... you know, open, mouths dropped about a mile and they're just looking at you.

CS: Yes.

A little detail, about the grannies being scared of being made super (p. 120), sets them off on stories of their being scared, and screwing up their courage to do things. For Wayne it is going over a jump on his BMX and Dave talks about jumping off the high board. Paul puts it in a familial context and tells of his dad bringing home chips:

Paul: I felt a bit sleepy so I went to bed and I had to, and I goes to my mum, 'If dad does bring some chips home for me, could, could you wake me up,' and that certain look in her eye sort of thing said 'She isn't going to wake me up. I can't trust her', and I just had to stay awake.

Within the theoretical frameworks that I have outlined, the young are in a continuous process of negotiation of power and autonomy. In their desire to predict and control their future they take an active role in the cognitive process of learning, both in school and out of it, and both from the adult culture and within youth culture. Politically, within the family, within the school and within the peer group, they must jockey for power and battle for autonomy. The fact that many of these popular books contain the negotiation of power as a major theme is thus perhaps no accident. And the fact that they so violently or strikingly dramatize that negotiation perhaps accounts for the enthusiasm, the emotional involvement, that they educe in their young readers.

Conflict and contradiction

I devoted the whole of Chapter 1 to the notion that in the entry into social life we enter into the contradictions of the culture in which we find ourselves. For teachers as teachers, it is schools that provide the conflictual context, for children and young people it is their life both in and out of school, and for researchers it is the impetus and conditions of the research itself.

This notion of a conflictual and divided society has a close bearing upon the nature of the cultural artefacts that are available and of interest to young people in that society, and upon their response to them. I hope that I have shown that in books like *The Fog, Carrie* and *First Blood* the conflict is between the utopian thrust of their narrative and the ideological closure of their endings. The same would be true of *The BFG* (Dahl 1982), not a text I have discussed, but one that was chosen by a group of year 7 pupils. There the heroine, orphan Sophie, is an independent no-nonsense character who acts as the main driving force behind the whole story, only to settle into the arms of surrogate father and mother and within the security of their palace home at the end. And even the knockabout of *Super Gran* falls into the same category.

I further hope that I have shown how those conflicts reflect similar conflicts in the lives of the young people who read them. The bottom-stream boys are at one and the same time highly critical of the social order in which they find themselves, yet resort to counterproductive measures to respond to their feelings. The middle-stream girls are at one and the same time battling for independence within patriarchal society, and recognizing that one of their aims is to be treated decently by a boy.

Let me sum up by making six points.

1 We live in a corporate capitalist state that is riven with conflicts and divisions.
2 Those conflicts and divisions will penetrate both the institutions and the cultural artefacts of that state, and they will be demonstrated in the lives of the individuals who live in it.
3 I have argued that the teachers I talked to demonstrated some of those divisions. In particular, I suggested that they were at one and the same time emancipatory in their motivations, and yet constrained to be less so by the circumstances, both physical and ideological, within which they found themselves.
4 I have argued that I as the researcher and writer of this book was and am similarly riven by the unresolved conflicts of the research itself, and by my liberal tendencies fighting against my Marxist analysis.
5 I also hope that I have demonstrated how the children and young people in school that I talked with are also beset by conflict and unresolved contradiction: conflict and unresolved contradiction that emerged most clearly in their discussion of class, violence and gender.
6 I am further arguing that much of the literature – and, by extension, film and video – that children and young people growing up in this plural and conflictual culture are so enthusiastic about *also* expresses the conflicts and divisions of their lives, and, by extension, of the corporate capitalist state itself.

I won't spell out the detail of this any further for I hope it has been adequately explored in earlier chapters. I now want to move on to the second half of my concern in this chapter, to consider the whole notion of response itself.

'Response'?

It has been a basic assumption of the research that if we want to look for the roots of response, then they will be found equally in the text and in the reader. There is a long tradition of studying text, and a short one of studying readers. Most previous studies of readers have been predicated upon views of 'correct' and 'incorrect' response, of 'good' and 'poor' response. These were, in their turn, predicated upon particular readings of the texts themselves. I have attempted to avoid such evaluative approaches. Furthermore, in the suspension of a search for a developmental model I have been able to lay to one side questions of the 'relevance' or 'irrelevance' of response and that has allowed me to bring a much wider swathe of evidence into consideration. I would argue that to see response as an aspect of culture is a fruitful way of looking at things. I have, in other words, investigated what it is that readers have that makes them capable of the sorts of response that they produce, and what it is in texts that relates to that. It has been, in Iser's term, an investigation of the cultural *repertoire* of readers and of texts.

Nevertheless, there is a common-sense usage of the word 'response' which suggests that we read a book and respond to it, so what I want to do here is to redefine 'response' in such a way as to encompass the wider interactive and cultural perspectives that would seem to be required. Given the general conservatism of the world in general and the National Curriculum in England and Wales in particular, which still sees the interrelation between reader and text as a one-way process of communication from author to reader, I think it will be more fruitful to proceed in this way. Some of the theoretical ground of such a reconsideration has already been implied in the way that I have written about texts and readers in earlier chapters, and is spelt out in the Appendix.

At this point it is instructive to return to I. A. Richard's *Practical Criticism*, written way back in 1929, for he drew a map of the field whose contours have been followed by much subsequent work. I want to turn him on his head, because, in doing so, I can draw attention to precisely those areas in which the debate has been relocated. Richards suggested that there were a number of features that impaired a 'correct' reading of text, and he actually investigated what they were:

1 readers have a stock of images in their own minds that inform their reading,
2 readers bring their personal associations to bear upon their reading,
3 readers bring a set of stock responses to bear upon their reading,
4 readers bring their own ideological framings to bear upon their reading,
5 readers bring critical frameworks to bear upon their reading.

Richards, of course, sees these as negative factors, but I hope that the reader will recognize many of these features in the responses of the young people in this book, and will realize that I do not consider them to be negative.

Although Richards's study was concerned with poetry, it also served as a model for much of the work that was subsequently done on prose fiction, most notably that of James Squire in 1964. Squire studied the response of adolescents to four short stories. In his conclusions he starts to fill in some of the detail within the categories that Richards had outlined for us. Particularly useful to me, in my contrary mode of reading against the intention of the researcher, is the exploration of some of the details of the stock response. He indicates five stock responses to the stories:

1 Adolescent readers think that adolescent characters are not responsible for their own actions – it is the fault of their upbringing, the situation, etc.
2 A boy or girl in trouble does not have a healthy home life.
3 Wealth and happiness are incompatible.
4 In adult–adolescent conflict adults are always wrong.
5 Punishment of adolescents for wrongdoing is wrong.

Squire wants to insist that such responses are 'inappropriate':

> Whether one approves or disapproves of the basic concepts expressed by these pat, somewhat aphoristic statements of behaviour, the reliance of readers on such trite and commonplace ideas as a substitute for their own thinking must be deplored.
>
> (p. 41)

For me, a spotty adolescent at precisely the same time as Squire must have been doing his research, his findings present a fascinating insight into the way I, as a middle-class, utopian, liberal Christian, thought at the time, and I can assure him that those ideas, trite and commonplace as they may have been, were arrived at after a good deal of thought and sometimes after bitter argument.

I have emphasized one aspect of Squire's work. It is important, in recompense, to note that he established a whole strand of inquiry into the detail of response that has been pursued up until the present day: recently, for example, in the work of Robert Protherough in 1983(a), by Mike Benton and Geof Fox in 1985, and by Jack Thomson in 1987. It is clear from such work that young readers have a whole repertoire of response which includes, in no particular order:

retelling;
judgement of quality;
empathy with character and situation;
identification with character as well as more detached observation in the spectator role;
analogizing from and into their own experience of life;
generalization about theme; and
involvement with the plot.

It is not part of my purpose here to deny any of those findings. I will just comment, however, on the question of the judgement of quality. We have been used, indeed we still are used, to the notion that we wish to determine the quality of texts. In the past we have been tempted to assign quality in some absolute and transcendent sense. Recent developments in literary criticism have put such certainties behind us. Nevertheless, the very popularity of some authors among the young must depend upon an underground of information about quality – 'Hey, you must read the latest Virginia Andrews/Stephen King/James Herbert, it's really great!' – and we ourselves, I don't doubt, do the same. I certainly save up until the summer holiday my latest unread Dickens or Hardy in the sure knowledge of enjoyment from an experience of 'real quality' – and indeed the voice of my past still admonishes me – Hardy??, Dickens?? surely not authors of the *very first* quality! But the truth is that I now recognize the inevitable relativism of such a term, and perhaps my enjoyment is the more wholesome for that. It is instead much more useful, it seems to me, to suggest that we all wish to create canons, but the canon will depend upon which social group we wish to join. One of the ways in which we elect ourselves into that social group is to become *au fait* with the cultural artefacts that are of dominant importance for that group. For 10-year-olds in the late 1980s it may well have been the crucial distinctions between Bros and Kylie Minogue, for us as English teachers, the relative merits of William Golding or Graham Greene.

That said, and given that I am not disputing any of the other elements of response mentioned in that list, what I want to do now is to approach it from a different angle altogether, in an effort to illuminate what there might be in readers and texts that promotes all those activities.

More recent work, particularly that of David Jackson and Donald Fry, has started to emphasize the importance of what readers bring to texts. They leave us with a clear picture that reading does indeed involve bringing a developing and changing experience of the world to bear upon the text. And I respond particularly positively to Fry's insistence that the emotional satisfactions of reading are not restricted to the reading of 'great literature'.

There are other studies, such as that of Reinstein in 1983, which shows how contrasting ethnic background and the experience, or lack of it, of life in the inner-city can affect response, and that of Marriott in 1985, which shows how the response of children in Northern Ireland to a contemporary book with a Northern Irish setting is affected by their cultural and religious affiliations.

This more recent work is indicative of the way in which the whole social process of meaning making, that is, *culture*, has a bearing on response. Such a view is supported by Shirley Brice Heath's study of the relation between culture and literacy itself, reported in *Ways with Words* in 1983. Her descriptions of how all interactions with written text are intimately bound up with the wider social and cultural life of the community are highly suggestive of the sorts of factor that may well influence response to specific texts. She shows how such interactions are affected by a whole variety of factors. Truthfulness, authority, invention, exaggeration, social and private habits of reading and storytelling, dependence upon characters from popular culture, appeal to biblical authority, and the function of proverbial and epigrammatical forms – all these are important cultural factors which suggest a whole new area of investigation that may well illuminate response itself. Shirley Brice Heath's work makes it clear that books themselves have specific and differing places and roles in different communities, and this is before anyone has opened them at all. And if, in the late 1980s, we needed any further proof of that, the Salman Rushdie affair, in which an author has had to go into hiding because his book has so offended a community as to provoke death threats, has surely provided it.

The evidence I have collected in the course of my research adds a further strand to this consideration of culture, and to discuss it I need to consider the role of narrative and the nature of 'stock'.

The role of narrative

Harold Rosen in his excellent paper on narrative, in 1984, draws attention to the ways in which we use narratives to appraise our life experience, and John Schostak, in a 1988 paper, has argued that we learn our whole social identity through a series of narratives.

> A narrative displays the *dramatis personae* of a given event, social situation and life sequence of events in ways which generalise for the listener beyond any one particular occurrence. A listener of an anecdote may say to his or herself, 'yes, that's just like teachers, that's how they treat me too.' In finding such a resonance in the listener the story becomes explanatory for that listener.
>
> (p. 9, original emphasis)

Schostak has been forced to such an analysis by his attempts to explain how the teachers and children and young people with whom he is concerned come to understand their situation and find an identity for themselves in it. He identifies some of the dramatis personae: 'mythical beings such as Them, Us, The Rich, The Poor, The Rulers, the People', and so on.

Such narratives and such dramatis personae are of crucial importance in the creation of culture, and they have featured in earlier chapters. I will not repeat that evidence here, but I shall be drawing heavily upon the discussion of *First Blood* by the bottom-stream boys in Chapter 3 and the discussions of *Stranger with My Face* in Chapter 6. In the course of those two chapters we saw how the boys, in the first instance, and the girls, in the second, were engaged in the social construction of meaning in which they sought to understand and evaluate their experience of life. Time and again they resorted to stories about their friends, about their life on the estate, about more general concerns – the police, teachers, school, and so on. However, though they continuously used narrative, they did not confine themselves to it. Instead, and more richly, I would argue, they combined narrative with argument, anecdote with precept. I will just draw attention to some of the features of their accounts to illustrate what I mean.

In the discussions of their life in school and on the estate, and in their discussions of *First Blood*, the bottom-stream boys resorted to a number of generalizations, 'stock' or 'mythic' places and characters – 'America'; 'American policemen'; 'last year's fifth-years'; the school as a 'nuthole'; 'gang warfare' – plus a number of 'mythic' incidents – 'they put this kid's head through a window', and so on. These generalizations feed into and are fed by direct observation of their life in school. Generalizations are made about teachers and kids, about black kids and white kids. Stereotypes, both racial and other, will inevitably be found here.

These boys were engaged in what we might call, along with James Britton, talk in the spectator role. In it they are trying to understand and categorize their experience, to evaluate their attitudes to that experience and recognize how they might feel about it. Back in 1970 Britton drew our attention to the link between gossip and literature:

> It seems to me that for the spoken form of language in the role of spectator we must use, as the nearest we can get, the term 'gossip'; and for the written form of language in the role of spectator, the word 'literature'.
>
> *(Language and Learning*, p. 107)

Britton emphasizes the cognitive and affective functions of gossip: we use it to explore how the world works and how we feel about it. In their discussions of boyfriends and girlfriends, of the morality of possessiveness and jealousy, the girls in their 'gossip' in Chapter 6 did much the same as the boys. They stuck closely to the narrative mode, offering two specific stories about the possessiveness of the boyfriend of one of their friends. Both stories were designed to make the same point, that such possessiveness was unreasonable. The girls used the narrative form both to encapsulate observation and to explain and evaluate and generalize from their experience in exactly the way that Schostak describes above. Mary even managed to condense the whole narrative into a little moral precept:

> *Mary:* The fact is that I don't think that any boyfriend should take you away from your friends and not let you go out with them.

Stock

In her seminal study of popular literature, Q. D. Leavis, in 1932, talks of popular authors being able 'to depend on stock responses which enable them by a few clumsy strokes to evoke a composite picture that is already stowed away in their readers minds'. And James Squire in the study I quoted above, complains of books that 'deliberately exploit such automatic reader reactions'. Again, by turning such comments on their head, we can agree with both authors but suggest that is how all texts work. In other words, popular texts, whether popular children's books or popular adult fiction, are constructed in such a way that the widest number of readers can use elements of shared cultural experience to construct meaning.

James Squire showed us some examples of 'stock'. What I am endeavouring to do here is to offer further evidence of the form that 'stock' will take. I want to suggest, after Schostak, that there will be events, anecdotes, descriptions of social situations, all of which will be shared in a generalized form by a particular social group. These events will be peopled by dramatis personae who, like the characters in folk tale and popular literature, are cast in their social role – teacher, policeman – or generalized in a wider social context – us, them, the rich, the poor, nutcases, gangs. There will also be precepts, cases argued, generalizations about the world – America is violent, boys shouldn't take you away from your friends. Furthermore, there will be some issues which are salient for children and young people. Adolescents may well be interested in sex, violence, relationships, and in order to learn about such things they need to generalize, classify and order – such, as I have already implied, is the learning process, and the sorts of cultural generalizations that we have noted are essential to such a process.

In the model of response that follows I have tried to incorporate what we already know with the further perspectives I have discussed. Not so much a redefinition, perhaps, as a wider definition than we have hitherto accepted.

A model of response

1 Reponse is an active process of meaning making that occurs when a reader reads a text.

2 Reponse is an experience whose content is emotional.

3 Response is the product of the reader's cognitive framework.

4 The cognitive framework of the reader will consist of his or her:
   (a) literal and inferential knowledge of the language;
   (b) knowledge of larger linguistic convention and cliché;
   (c) knowledge of narrative structure and process;
   (d) personal stock of images and associations;
   (e) knowledge of other texts;
   (f) personal psychological make-up;
   (g) knowledges of the world.

5 The cognitive framework of the reader will be penetrated by his or her ideology and culture.

6 The culture of the reader will take the form of the socially constructed and shared narratives, anecdotes, descriptions of events and social situations, precepts and argued cases, all of which will have a meaning beyond the individual instance, a relevance for the larger social group.

7 The culture of the reader will take the form of precepts, generalizations about and classifications of the world, generalized characterizations, classifications of relationships, identifications of social role.

8 The response of the reader will be dependent upon what issues are salient for the reader given his or her individual history and psychology, and biological and social position in society as a whole.

9 The response of the reader will be the product of the text.

10 The meanings that are generated by the text will depend upon the relationships between the linguistic, narratological, cultural, experiential, ideological and cultural elements of the text and those of the reader.

11 The reading of the reader will be an active process in the spectator role,

involving identification or somewhat more detached empathy with character, situation and implied reader, or a flexible interchange between the three.

12 The reading of the reader will involve detached evaluation and judgement both of the characters and the action of the book.

13 The reading of the reader will involve evaluation of the worth of the book within the reader's particular framework of quality and value.

14 The actions of response will be various, ranging from the retelling of a 4-year-old, to *S/Z*, or *Northanger Abbey*, and in every mode, musical, pictorial, dramatic, filmic, literary, oral.

Access to response will be via the text, using all the modern tools of critical analysis.

Access to response will be via an exploration of the socially mediated meaning making of the reader, that is, his or her culture.

Access to the culture of the reader will, *inter alia*, be via the text, and access to the meanings of the text will, *inter alia*, be via the culture of the reader.

This model of response is neither exhaustive, nor definitive.

An individual's response to a text may incorporate any or all of the above, or other factors yet to be discovered.

Note

You will see, perhaps, that what I am engaged in here is a sort of gathering in of a whole range of evidence to see if it is possible to make some sort of statement about what sorts of thing we might find contributing to, and forming part of response. To this end I need just to draw your attention very briefly to some further strands that may be very familiar to you, and which I have incorporated above.

The psychoanalytic approaches of Norman Holland in *Five Readers Reading*, and Bruno Bettleheim and Karen Zelan in *Learning to Read* tend to ignore, or even deny, the importance of culture in the generation of meaning. But there have been attempts to reconcile Freudian and Marxist approaches, and the psychoanalysts do at least draw our attention to the importance both of personal history and of the unconscious in the reactions of readers. The work of the Crago's in *Prelude to Literacy*, in their study of their daughter's early reading, has brought together the social, experiential, cognitive and psychological aspects of response that tend to be isolated into separate and unrelated areas by other researchers.

Otherwise, in earlier chapters, I have drawn attention to the idea that fiction for young people may be a creation for them of virtual futures: here is Margaret Meek, for instance, in 1987. Texts can 'offer the reader the chance to discover fiction as the focus of the contemplation of *possibilities*: what life might be like' (p. 111, original emphasis).

I have emphasized, too, in earlier chapters, the cognitive and affective function of fiction, seen as an extension of play, and thus as a way of knowing the world, of appraising our experience, and of predicting and ordering our future. And I would add that the role of reader as flexible, evaluative, empathizing spectator, a role familiar to us from the work of D. W. Harding, and a role that has been empirically investigated by Geoff Fox and Robert Protherough, among others, such a role fits in perfectly with the functions that we are attributing to narrative in general, and to fictional narrative in particular.

To this we need to add the insights of the reception theorists and the semiologists who have shown us, first, that reading is an *active* process of meaning making, and second, that readers and texts both have had ideological and cultural *repertoires*.

It is time to move towards some sort of conclusion.

Polemical pedagogical conclusion

I have examined the response of pupils to the books that they have chosen. As a result the texts tend not to be those of the approved exam syllabuses, nor yet those often promoted as the 'best' of children's literature.

It is part of my argument that at the ages of 14 and 15 the study of such texts requires analytic skills that are just as demanding as would be required by the study of the approved canon. In particular, I would suggest that it is the restriction of texts to the narrow canon of the old O level and CSE, or some of the exam options at GCSE, which excludes pupils who take one look at such texts and decide that they have nothing to offer them. When it comes to all coursework GCSE, as Sweetman suggests (1987b), 'It is necessary to say that books studied for GCSE may be contentious'. He further argues:

> It is as well to state that the new GCSE examination encourages children to reflect upon their independent reading and that the purpose of this self examination is to widen the scope of what is read and develop a more critical attitude towards it.

We may be alerted by that 'more critical'. Lurking behind such a wording is the old evaluative judgement in a new guise.

In preparation for the writing of these few concluding paragraphs I talked to two English teachers responsible for teaching GCSE. From different schools, they were both teaching 100 per cent coursework. They had met and talked to officials from the exam boards at moderating meetings, and they felt, as a result, that, though inevitably work on popular horror and romance was going to be submitted, if pupils want to get the higher grades then 'substantial' literature needed to be studied. They have also been told that 'close attention to language and imagery' is necessary for the pupil to do well. Such evidence supports my fear that beneath Sweetman's apparent openness, and it should be said that he was himself an examiner, many of the old discriminations persist.

If the first issue that comes to mind is the choice of texts, then the second must surely be the class study of one text. Whether this takes the form of reading a book to a whole class, as often happens with younger secondary pupils, or whether it is class study of one text for examination purposes, it seems very clear that some pupils will absolutely hate the process. Some teachers feel that class study of one work is beneficial. They argue that such study brings pupils to enjoy books that they would not otherwise have come into contact with. There is evidence in the study that this, too, is the case. The challenge, then, it seems to me, is how to do the one without doing the other. The only evidence that I have come across that suggests how the dilemma might be handled is contained in Peter Medway's book, *Finding a Language*, in which he gives an account of an experiment in autonomy of learning and a pupil-controlled curriculum. In the present time of the National Curriculum, it is difficult to know how such an initiative might succeed now, particularly in view of its curtailment in the mid-1970s.

A third issue that arises is teachers' unease at handling controversial texts in the classroom. Behind such unease lurks a very real fear of nervous head teachers, vigilante parents, and, worst of all, Fleet Street getting hold of it. Sweetman (1987a) suggests that such material has to be located within a range of books that are likely to be studied, and that teachers need to alert parents to their possible controversial content. I would tend to agree, but I would also want to suggest that many pupils read such material whether we like it or not. I would want to argue that, as the popular arts should be proper subjects for study in any well-balanced English course, then such material is bound to be included somewhere along the line. Furthermore, if pupils are going to study such texts then we need to develop the analytical tools that will help them to understand what they are dealing with.

Fourth, it is clear that popular video needs to be given similar attention. Teachers report copyright problems in this field, and these clearly need to be surmounted at national level. That said, I would wish to emphasize that by popular video I do not mean the standard 'film of the book' approaches of some English departments. Ken Loach's *Kes* and Joseph Losey's *The Go-Between* are not the issue. Neither *First Blood* nor *Carrie* fall into that category.

A fifth issue is the concern of teachers about the promotion and negotiation of value. They feel that books like *The Fog* or videos such as *First Blood* promote values with which they disagree, and that to consider such material in school is to lend credence to the values they feel are enshrined in it. It should be clear by now that I would wish to argue that our Leavisite inheritance has almost inextricably confused moral and aesthetic value. Thus, when we are led to condemn the morality of a text we are often led to disguise that condemnation as an aesthetic critique. And thus also, many pupils, told that the language of the book is 'inferior', have an inchoate but none the less very real sense that it is the morality of the book that is being got at, and even more insidiously, their own morality as appreciative readers. If we want to promote values with our pupils in school, and there is no doubt that is what some governments think we should be doing, then let us do it directly. Even if we wish to raise issues of value and morality without promoting them – as most teachers that I have talked to would much rather do, then still let us do it directly. Popular fiction like *The Fog* could be very useful as the starting point for such discussion, simply because it is so good at *showing* the value systems of current culture. To attack the text itself is to kill the messenger because we don't like the message.

Let me make one or two final comments about the use of popular fiction and video. The evidence I have presented suggests, I would argue, that, given the requisite encouragement, pupils can be remarkably perceptive about the texts that they enjoy. At various stages we have seen that they understand the workings of narrative, and appreciate the ebb and flow of narrative suspense and release and the cognitive games of narrative structuring. Furthermore, popular material lends itself to the study of character as role rather than as psychology. We have also seen that cliché and colloquial language repay study just as much as do more highly regarded imagery and circumlocution. We have, further, seen plenty of evidence of pupils' awareness of intertextuality, an awareness that can be used to relate texts to context and as a basis for exploring the uses and meaning of formulae in current cultural products.

At the level of content, I have suggested that popular material is particularly useful because of its dramatization of salient concerns of young people, and because it offers a window on to current cultural concerns. Furthermore, because pupils have no problem in understanding what they are reading or seeing, then at least one major stumbling block to its analysis is removed. However, if such material is going to be used for the discussion of issues, an activity familiar to many English teachers, let me repeat that to use the discussion of issues to attack the books or the videos will, in my view, be self-defeating – the pupils will instantly recognize it as the same old game: that that the ostensible subject matter of the discussion is being used as a covert attack upon them as appreciative readers.

If we are not to run away from popular material we have to take it, and the pupils who enjoy it, seriously. We have to handle their views with the same respect as we accord to the views of our colleagues or our critical mentors. In my experience, if we do that, we may discover that the pupils themselves are just as likely to become our critical mentors. Adolescents are avaricious learners, even if they don't always learn what we want them to learn, and as a result they know a great deal about their own culture. Perhaps, as English teachers, we should see our role not as telling them what they should know and what they shouldn't know, but instead as helping them to understand what they do know and enabling them to learn what they want to know.

Suggestions for
further reading

In the book so far I have made scant reference to some of the more theoretical work that has served to radically redefine the very process of reading fiction itself. In this appendix I want to redress the balance. I shall try, as far as possible, to avoid a long theoretical discussion of the 'Eagleton on the one hand, Scruton on the other' variety. I shall instead offer an annotated bibliography. The aim of such an exercise is to direct that convenient notion, 'the interested reader', to work that I have not discussed in any detail in the main body of the text, but which none the less has been crucial either in informing my discussions of the fiction that was chosen by the pupils or in informing my writing of the book as a whole.

Ariès, P. 1962. *Centuries of Childhood*. Harmondsworth: Penguin.

Ariès' historical work is invaluable in that it demonstrates so clearly that childhood is not a naturally occurring state but a culturally defined category. Any discussion of what constitutes literature that is suitable for children and young people needs to be seen in such a perspective. Particularly disturbing, seen in this light, is the continuous predilection for those short novels with nihilistic story lines like *The Pearl*, *The Red Pony* and *Kes* as suitable for 'less able' teenagers.

Aristotle 1965. 'On the Art of Poetry' in Aristotle, Horace, Longinus, *Classical Literary Criticism* (trans. T. S. Dorsch). Harmondsworth: Penguin.

Aristotle is well enough known for his theory that the representation of emotion on stage serves to purge the emotions of the viewer in a process of catharsis. We may wish nowadays to suggest that it is a little more complicated than that, but he also suggests that 'Fear and pity can also take their rise from the very structure of the action' (p. 49).

The idea that the very structure of the work is an emotional shaping is one that Susanne Langer takes up, and I discuss the idea more fully in discussing her work below. Artistotle extends his argument to make another point. He suggests that the action of tragedy is more important than the characters – indeed, that it would be possible to do without character altogether: 'for tragedy is a representation, not of men, but of action and life, of happiness and unhappiness – and happiness and unhappiness are bound up with action' (p. 39).

This notion that character is product of the action rather than vice versa is taken up by Propp (1968), and the modern structuralists like Todorov, and is crucial for the understanding of the way that character works in popular fiction. Holman, in Herbert's *The Fog*, for example, does not act in the way that he does because of complex psychological motivation provided by the author. On the contrary, his only motivation is entirely, and circularly, dependent on his role as hero within the action of the book.

Barthes, R. 1974. *S/Z*. New York: Hill & Wang.

Major semiological work in which Roland Barthes explores the ways in which texts use a series of codes to generate their meanings. His ideas have been expounded at length elsewhere, not least by Terence Hawkes in *Structuralism and Semiotics* (1977), which I recommend in its own right, but I will mention a couple of things that affect the present work.

Crucial for me is Barthes' announcement that texts are plural, having more than one meaning. This notion is particularly useful when we are considering young people reading. Indeed, my whole approach in the present study is predicated upon such possibilities. Popular horror and romance, for instance, are read with such enthusiasm by many young people and with such distaste by many teachers, that an explanation is required. The idea, then, that it may be possible to have more than one reading of the same text – and, furthermore, that no single reading has any particular claim of superiority – is obviously a very fruitful one. Children's literature is often even more problematic, and even though much criticism attempts to take into account the child as reader, here, too, the notion of a plurality of possible readings proves useful. It would never have occurred to me, an adult and one time teacher, that *Super Gran*, for instance, could have provoked such an interesting response as we have seen from those year 7 boys who were so enthusiastic about it.

The plurality of the text, what Barthes calls its 'polysemous' nature, is to be found in the five codes that interweave through it. I shall draw attention to two. First, there is the *hermeneutic* code. Questions are raised, explanations proffered, or postponed, suspense is generated. You will have seen how important this was in my analysis, in Chapter 8, of how *Super Gran* worked for the three boys, and of how the *Narnia* series worked for Victoria.

Second, there is the *proairetic* code. The text consists of a series of actions. 'The proairetic sequence is never more than the result of an artifice of reading' (p. 19). The sequences of actions 'imply a logic of human behaviour' (p. 18). Problems arise when the action of the book does not comply with the reader's experience of the logic of human behaviour. I would suggest that the enthusiasm of the girls in Chapter 6 for *Stranger with My Face* depends upon a match between the action of the book and the girls' experience of the logic of human behaviour, and I would also suggest that the rejection of *The Pearl* in Chapter 7 stems, among other things, from an equivalent mismatch.

Belsey, C. 1980. *Critical Practice*. London: Methuen.

A tremendously useful book. No one has better explained for me the recent history of criticism or more clearly 'placed' our Leavisite tradition. She draws on the ideas of Althusser, Lacan and Derrida to make an argument which I shall not do justice to in my attempt to summarize it here.

In brief, she attacks the dominant view that we have of literature as 'expressive realism': reality, as experienced by a single gifted individual writer, expressed in such a way that the rest of us spontaneously perceive it as 'true'. Meaning is then seen either as the intention of the author or as residing in the text itself. In both cases the reader has access to *the* meaning by the exercise of a sort of historically informed common sense. But, she argues, literature operates in conjunction with a particular social formation. It is historically determined, suffused with ideology, part of the ideological superstructure. Ideology, she suggests, is 'the very condition of our experience of the world' (p. 5) working in conjunction with political and economic practice to constitute our social formation. And as with literature, so, too, with 'common sense' itself.

Capitalism, Belsey argues, requires, calls forth – *interpellates* is Althusser's word – a subject who is a non-contradictory and therefore fundamentally unalterable individual whose unfettered consciousness is the origin of meaning, knowledge and action. Such a subject of capitalism is a subject who works by himself or herself, and freely exchanges her or his labour power for wages. So far as literature is concerned, expressive realism performs an ideological function in the promotion of capitalism. Working within the liberal humanist framework, expressive realism interpellates an undivided reader, a unitary subject. Such an interpellation is reinforced by the very language of expressive realism, a language that hides its own role, in particular in the creation of characters that appear themselves to be unitary sources of meaning and action.

In fact the ideological superstructure is riven with contradiction and conflict, and so thus are the subjects constructed within it (an argument I was making in Chapter 1). By its interpellation of a single unitary individual, expressive realism denies the contradictions inherent in any subject who is part of the modern corporate capitalist state.

(It is necessary to add that the notion of the divided self is seen in other terms which are not necessarily in conflict with the above analysis, but which may be seen to be in contradistinction to it. Thus according to Belsey, Lacan sees the self as inevitably divided between the self that is known and that self that knows; and Derrida argues that in the entry into language the self is divided into the self that can be spoken of in the social construct of language and the self that is not accessible to that language.)

You will be aware that I have taken a more complex view of popular literature than Belsey does. She sees it simply as part of the expressive realist tradition. In particular, I have suggested, as far as characterization is concerned, that popular literature does not conform entirely to the description of classic realism that she proposes. It may be true on one level that action is seen as entirely the expression of the intention of the characters, but the characters themselves do not derive their meaning from a unitary subjectivity, but from a social and hence plot role that, as often as not, is riven with contradiction.

Let me illustrate all this with two examples taken from the research. The girls who so positively respond to *Stranger with My Face*, I would suggest, do fall into the category outlined by Belsey. In other words, they are, as readers, interpellated as autonomous unitary subjects with resolved conflicts, accepting the resolution of the drama of the book, a drama which posits at its heart a divided self that is to be reunited, and that is seen by the end to be whole, single, and more 'true to itself' than it was at the beginning. But these same girls have a positive reaction to *Carrie*, too, and there the readers and the character of Carrie herself precisely fail to resolve the conflicts inherent in the complexity of being adolescent girls in a patriarchal culture. In Belsey's terms, then, *Stranger with My Face* may well interpellate the individual reader 'as a free, unified, autonomous subjectivity', but in my view, *Carrie* appellates a reader who is divided, riven by the contradictions of gender role in a modern capitalist state.

Benjamin, W. 1970. *Illuminations*. Glasgow: Fontana.

This collection of Benjamin's work (dating from the 1930s) has two essays that are particularly pertinent for me. In the first, 'The Storyteller', he suggests that in the folk tale there is no psychology. This is provided by the reader: 'The psychological connection of the events is not forced upon the reader. It is left to him to interpret things the way he understands them' (p. 89). In the second, 'The Work of Art in the Age of Mechanical Reproduction' he suggests that film, photography, and other methods of mass repro-duction have for ever destroyed any notion of the unique work of art with unique and transcendent value. Such a perspective certainly supported my attempts to come to terms with the inevitable relativism of discussions of 'quality'. And as an example of the first suggestion that it is up to the reader to supply the missing psychology, I would suggest that the way in which Wayne empathizes with the character of Tub in *Super Gran* in Chapter 6 is very much a case in point.

Eagleton, T. 1976a. *Marxism and Literary Criticism.* London: Methuen.

Eagleton, T. 1976b. *Criticism and Ideology.* London: Verso.

Terry Eagleton, for some while the *enfant terrible* of the British critical establishment, builds on the ideas of Althusser and the work of Macherey. Literature, the argument goes – indeed art in general – is an ideological production. Art does not simply reflect reality, rather it takes elements from the real world and selects, transforms and changes them. Furthermore, though it is secondary – virtual, to use Langer's term – it is still a real object making its effects in the real world. Indeed, the distinction between artistic production and other forms of production is a false one. In *Criticism and Ideology* Eagleton suggests that the fictional text is the *production* of ideology, rather like the performance of a play is a production of the playscript. To change the metaphor, ideology inheres in text rather as wood inheres in a chair. The production of the text is an oper-ation of labour upon ideology rather as the production of the chair is an operation of labour upon wood.

Furthermore, since the world is riven by conflict and contradiction, then conflict and contradiction will inevitably occur in the artistic product, too. Some texts are particularly useful in this regard since they sit athwart the dominant ideology of the time in which they were written. As such they contain ideological rifts and contradictions that make them particularly fruitful for study.

Both these ideas seemed suggestive to me. In the first place, if children were rejecting texts, was it because they were rejecting the ideology inherent in them? You will have seen that this is a view that I took, particularly in Chapter 7. In the second place, as you will have gathered, I have taken the idea that texts may contain ideological rift and contradiction, and applied it to popular fiction. This is a notion taken up by Jack Zipes, whom I discuss below.

Eco, U. 1981. *The Role of the Reader.* London: Hutchinson.

This work by the semiologist, Umberto Eco, is the most thoroughgoing analysis of how texts generate meaning. His work is not in contradistinction to that of Iser (see below) or Barthes, but he fills in details that they barely touch upon.

In the first place he details those elements that the reader must share with the writer.

1 The reader must be able to understand the meaning of the words on the page.
2 The reader must accept that what the writer says is the case is the case. Thus, for example, when Tolkein writes, 'In a hole in the ground lived a Hobbit', it is not open to readers to say 'Oh no he didn't'.

3 The reader has to share knowledges of the world with the writer: has to know that holes occur in the ground, however questionable the nature of hobbits.

Within these three general categories, in the second place, Eco details some ten factors that contribute to the communication of meaning, two or three of which are particularly important for my purposes.

Among them is 'the encyclopedia of meaning': both writer and reader draw upon overlapping encyclopedias, which include not only basic dictionaries but properties, connotations and inferences. The writer may depend upon the reader's drawing a common inference in the simple portrayal of the action or in the assumptions that underlie irony, for instance.

The writer may use convention and cliché, what Eco calls rhetorical and stylistic overcoding, where the words carry more than their ostensible meaning. 'Once upon a time', for instance, does not mean simply 'in the past', it also means 'I am going to tell you a story'. In such cases the writer depends upon the reader's understanding the convention.

Further, there are 'intertextual references', references to other texts, or general assumptions about how texts work.

Readers read, Eco argues, by drawing on these common knowledges and assumptions that they share with the author, making inferences on the basis of them and reading on to find out if they are correct or not. If there is a sufficient mismatch then the reading simply will not occur. If there is a sufficient match then the reader takes inferential walks through the text constructing the *fabula*, the formalist term for the underlying story. Even in a long text the underlying story can often be reduced to a fairly small number of propositions. A deadly microplasma is manufactured; it is accidentally released; it infects people and sends them mad; it grows; it is attacked; it is destroyed. Such would be the *fabula* of The Fog, though the plot, the *sjuzet* is so constructed that readers have to read half the book before they can establish the first two of those propositions.

To all of these Eco adds ideological factors. All texts carry ideological assumptions, whether overt or covert. Readers have three options, according to Eco:

1 They can assume the ideology of the text and subsume it into their own reading.
2 They can miss or ignore the ideology of the text and import their own, thus producing 'aberrant' readings '(where "aberrant" means only different from the ones envisaged by the sender)' (p. 22).
3 They can question the text in order to reveal the underlying ideology.

In my view option (2) is crucial. Many young readers read against the ideological closure of the text, particularly in the case of popular forms. And in order to understand their readings it is necessary for us to take option (3) and interrogate the text in order to get it to reveal its underlying ideological contradictions.

Eco also makes a distinction between what he calls open and closed texts. In some texts, particularly modern ones, the reader has to make links, to draw inferences, to make connections that are not made in the text itself. Such texts, by their very structure, insist upon reader participation. In doing so, however, they offer us a model for the reading of all texts. Paradoxically, open texts lay down guidelines that offer readers a comparatively small number of choices about how they shall be read. The reader is forced into reading in a certain sort of way to make the links required.

At the other end of the spectrum, authors write for an audience that is assumed to share all their presuppositions, values and knowledge. When the texts that they produce are not read by such readers, when the real reader differs from the 'model reader' then anything may happen. Such texts 'are in fact open to any possible "aberrant" decoding. A text so immoderately "open" to every possible interpretation will be called a *closed* one' (p. 8).

Eco isolates closed and open texts at the opposite ends of a continuum. Most real texts will to some extent be open and to some extent closed. Many of the texts chosen by the pupils in the present study were to a greater or lesser extent closed, and it will be clear by now that my analysis of those texts has, in some cases, assumed that they are open to 'aberrant' readings.

Some examples from the discussion of *The Fog* by the top-stream boys: they comment on Herbert's use of everyday language (the shared encyclopedia of meaning); they comment on his use of cliché (stylistic overcoding); they comment upon what I called a narrative cliché, whereby they knew how the opening of the book was working because, among other things, of their *intertextual* knowledge about how other similar texts have worked.

Eco's discussion of open and closed texts, and his various versions of reading with or against the ideology of the text can also be illustrated with some examples. The response to *Stranger with My Face* is a good example of Eco's first option, where readers read along with the ideology of the text. As I have suggested, the book fulfils Belsey's description as classic realism. By the end of the book the central character is mistress of her own destiny, a unified subject who is the sole author of action. None of the readers I talked with showed any signs of diverging from this ideological closure. *First Blood* provides a contrast. It has all the appearance of a right-wing tract. This is even clearer with the benefit of hindsight after we have seen its sequel, *Rambo*. Rambo, the character, appears to represent all that liberal opinion finds most disturbing about American imperialism. He gains his way by the exercise of force. He never for a moment criticizes the role of America in Vietnam. Indeed, all his actions are predicated upon the belief that the Americans should have been in Vietnam and should have won. But Jack Zipes (see below) has alerted us to the idea that there may be a utopian foray lurking within this framing, as I also argue in Chapter 3. The bottom-stream boys who so enjoyed the video don't quite take Eco's second option – they are aware of the ideological closure, John even suggesting at one point, if you remember, that he would like to restart the Vietnam war. But, as I argue in the chapter, the utopian foray that Rambo makes against the state is more important for them. You will recognize that I made a similar case for *The Fog*.

Within a similar paradigm, *Carrie* is also open to two readings. In one reading the whole book is a product of the male chauvinist imagination: Carrie White representing the feared other of female sexuality at its most awesomely powerful. This reading is supported by the closure of both the book and the film: the character has to be killed off. De Palma, and/or his scriptwriter offer a little twist as Carrie's hand emerges from the grave, but that merely reinforces the same ideological closure. The feared other is literally other-worldly, it will reach up and grab you from beyond the grave. Yet we have seen that the girls who responded so positively ignore that closure. The book instead dramatizes their fears in a chauvinist society, and dramatizes their requirement precisely *not* to become victims of it. They clearly fit into Eco's second option, ignoring the dominant ideology, importing their own, and producing an 'aberrant' reading.

It may well be thought that the only options open to young people are to read with the ideology of the text or to ignore the ideology of the text in the ways that I have just outlined. I would want to suggest, however, that both the rejection of *The Pearl*, and, even more strikingly, given the age of the readers, the rejection of *The Last Battle*, are examples of school pupils managing to deconstruct a book, thereby exposing its ideology. The fact that that deconstruction is expressed in terms of an emotional response – 'it's boring' is an essentially emotional response – does not, in my view, alter the fact that a successful deconstruction has occurred. They have not so much taken up Eco's third option *per se* – questioning the book to get it to reveal its underlying ideology. They have, rather, more simply *recognized* the underlying ideology and therefore rejected the book. The 12-year-old girls have refused the reading altogether, while the older pupils have read the book but refused any *engagement* with it.

Griffin, S. 1981. *Pornography and Silence*. London: The Women's Press.

Susan Griffin's book is useful in that she draws attention to some of the features of what many would regard as pornographic material. It is distinguished, she argues, by the way in which women, along with racial minorities, and children, are seen as a threat by what she calls the chauvinist pornographic imagination. As such they have to be subdued, beaten into submission. The ideological form of pornography is, in other words, the suppression, punishment, or exploitation of the feared 'other'.

Griffin is idealist in her analysis, seeing pornography as a feature of the antagonism between nature, represented by the woman and the child, and culture, as represented by man. Love is the product of nature and violence the product of culture. The child in particular is radically decultured: 'when we love a child we love human nature before it has been reshaped by culture' (p. 253). I would wish to part company with her here, but she produces plenty of evidence to support her central findings, and her comments would seem to be relevant to some of the material chosen by the young people in my research.

Many people would see *The Fog* as a pornographic work. Indeed, Rosie, in Chapter 4, suggests just that, and many of the more notorious scenes in the book involve degradation of women and the young. And the feared other would seem to have particular application to Carrie White in *Carrie*. Carrie's awesome power is explicitly released with her first menstruation and it would be easy to cast her as the avenging angel of female sexuality, that which is to be most feared by the pornographic, male chauvinist imagination. But as I have shown, *Carrie* is a complex case, particularly when we take into account the response of the girls who so enjoyed the book.

Iser, W. 1978. *The Act of Reading*. London: Routledge and Kegan Paul.

Wolfgang Iser's book is another landmark in recent thinking about how readers and texts together generate meaning. His ideas have been covered elsewhere, I know, but let me offer this brief summary.

A most important idea for children's literature is the idea of the implied reader. This is a reader generated by the text, who is expected to share the standpoint of the author, and who is called into being by the structure of the plot, the nature of the characterization, the perspective of the narrator, and even the status of any fictional reader within the text. Within this text, for instance, there is a fictional reader whom I sometimes call 'you', and whom I occasionally try to pal up with by using the pronoun 'we'. The real reader, whose view, Iser suggests, is inevitably partial, may well not conform at all to the implied reader.

The text brings with it a *repertoire*, references to historical knowledge, previous texts, culture: the real reader, too, has a repertoire which may or may not match the repertoire of the text. This repertoire of the text is unwritten. It is a set of assumptions about culture, about general knowledge, about common sense, that underlies the text. The text has a series of 'blanks', the parameters of which determine the nature of these assumptions. In order to appreciate the text the real reader has to fit her or his repertoire to the blanks in the text. It is quite clear, for instance, that the readers in Chapter 7 who failed to appreciate *The Pearl* brought a different repertoire to the text from that apparently required by Steinbeck. And it is also quite clear, in the discussion of *Stranger with my Face*, that the repertoire of the readers almost perfectly matched that of the text.

Langer, S. K. 1942. *Philosophy in a New Key*. Cambridge, Mass.: Harvard University Press.

Langer, S. K. 1953. *Feeling and Form*. London: Routledge and Kegan Paul.

Susanne Langer is an aesthetic philosopher whose work I still find highly relevant, though I turn it to my own ends. There are two ideas that are particularly useful to me. First, she suggests that the novel presents readers with a virtual world, specifically a world in the form of a virtual past. When readers talk of being able or not being able to 'get into' a book it seems clear to me that what they can or cannot get into is this 'virtual world' of the story. We saw in Chapter 9 that Wayne actually uses Langer's term when he suggests that events in fiction have to be 'virtually' possible. But you will also be aware from that chapter that I have taken up Margaret Meek's suggestion that, for children in particular, fiction presents them not with virtual pasts but with virtual futures; and indeed psychologists like Kelly (1955) and Gregory (1977) suggest that our very thought processes themselves are explorations in the form of fiction of virtual futures. Such ideas were crucial in my analysis of what the three boys were doing with *Super Gran* and Victoria was doing with the *Narnia* series. But such ideas clearly have a wider reference, most clearly to the readings of *Stranger with My Face* and to the rejection of *The Pearl*.

Second, Langer claims that the form of a work of art is an emotional representation. Here I venture into one of my own contradictions. By and large I have taken the view that individuals are socially constructed subjects. Yet here I am talking about the emotional life of the individual. My problem is that I have not come across a thoroughgoing Marxist account of emotion. So I am left with the need to insist that the *engagement* with a work of fiction is, *inter alia*, an engagement in and of the emotions, and only Langer can offer me some account of this. In brief, she suggests that the structure of the work is the form of the structure of our emotions, and I would want to argue, along with Gordon Craig (1976, p. 15) that: 'Shifts of feeling, of energy, of absorption do not just accompany the act of reading: they are the form of that act for any given instance.'

My discussion of the rejection of texts in Chapter 7 is predicated on the assumption that those pupils never entered into that emotional engagement. And that chapter itself, I hope, demonstrates the cultural and ideological factors in that emotional non-engagement. And I would also argue that the enthusiasm that readers showed for *Carrie* or *Super Gran* or *Stranger with My Face*, to take three examples, demonstrated precisely that emotional engagement of which Craig talks. But by this time I am well adrift from Langer herself, for she has an elitist view of art, and would claim that only certain works have that necessary emotional form – and, indeed, that the degree to which they *do* have it is a measure of the degree to which they are true works of art. She would claim, I guess, that emotional life takes a universal inherent human form, whereas my own somewhat unthought-out notion would be that it is a product of the meetings between biology and meaning/culture.

Leavis, F. R. 1943. *Education and the University*. Cambridge: Cambridge University Press.

The Marxist attack upon Leavis, and the liberal humanist tradition, has been well rehearsed elsewhere. I do just want to draw attention here to one aspect of Leavis's work that has a particular *educational* implication, and that is in the specific hiding of questions of value, and in the deliberate conflation of those questions with aesthetic questions. It is in *Education and the University*, interestingly enough, rather than in his more direct literary criticism, that F. R. Leavis is most overt about his aims and purposes. He writes: 'Schools and colleges are, or should be, society trying to preserve and develop a continuity of consciousness and a mature directing sense of value – a sense of value informed by a traditional wisdom' (p. 15). For Leavis the very heart of that enterprise was to be found in the English school, with its avowed aim of the education of 'intelligence and sensibility' (p. 7), and the central focus was the study of 'the best that has been thought and said in the world', to quote Arnold (1932), as it was to be found in English Literature. Thus: 'The more advanced the work the more unmistakably is the judgment that is concerned inseparable from that profoundest sense of relative value which determines, or should determine, the important choices of actual life' (Leavis 1943, p. 35). If, however, we ask what those values actually are he is surprisingly coy:

> we can, in attempting at an ancient university an experiment in liberal education, count on a sufficient measure of agreement, overt and implicitly, about essential values to make it unnecessary to discuss ultimate sanctions, or provide a philosophy, before starting to work. This I assume; and I believe further that what is unnecessary is best avoided.

(p. 18)

The point I would wish to make is that central to the practice of English teaching has been the notion of the promotion of values through the use of carefully selected texts, and the development of sensitive and intelligent readings of those texts. This was confirmed by the teachers I talked with in the course of the study, as I hope I have already demonstrated in Chapter 1. It is confirmed by the teachers that I talk with when I am discussing my findings. As I argued in Chapter 9, I think it is high time we disentangled questions of value from aesthetic questions, and stopped disguising one as the other.

Other elements of the Leavisite tradition, the emphasis upon language and style, the rejection of cliché and 'slickness', and the emphasis upon character as the source of meaning and action – all this is and was of no use to me in my attempts to analyse the bulk of the material chosen by the young people in this study.

Leeson, R. 1985. *Reading and Righting*. London: Collins.

In a series of articles and papers Robert Leeson has sustained a Marxist perspective of the children's book scene which is unique in the field. He has drawn attention to the sexism and class bias of much children's fiction, and he has consistently inveighed against what he calls 'lit-crit'. He has, in particular, argued that enthusiasm for psychological characterization is a bourgeois trait. The old tales didn't need psychology, they had action and moral. The claims made by traditional 'lit-crit' for such characterization are elitist, and have little application for the general reader. His work has culminated in this history of children's literature. He draws on Harvey Darton's excellent earlier work, *Children's Books in England* (1958), but pays more attention than Darton did to the actual subject matter of the work, thus providing a critical and political perspective. In particular, he draws attention to the roots of popular fiction in folk tale, and suggests that the political content, albeit somewhat subdued, survived in the written forms. He also traces the conflict between respectable middle-class literature and popular 'trash' which survives to the present day.

Lévi-Strauss, C. 1963. 'The Structural Study of Myth' in C. Lévi-Strauss, *Structural Anthropology*. Harmondsworth: Penguin.

It was Saussure in this century who showed us that language was a symbolic system of *meaning*, abiding by certain rules, and imbued with regular structures. It took anthropologists like Lévi-Strauss to take up his ideas and look for structures of meanings in the myths that he observed in the course of his investigations. So here he looks for elements that can be related paradigmatically, a sort of structural *semantics* in which he is able to relate structures of ideas and relationships that occur within myths to similar structures of ideas and relationships both in other myths and in the real world. He finds that myths are built up of *bundles* of *relations*. In each relation an action is linked with a character. When they are 'bundled' then different characters performing different actions are found to have something in common. This 'something in common' is the basic constituent unit of the myth. In my discussions of *The Fog* I draw the idea of 'bundling' character–action relations to discover links between them in order to describe the structural principles underlying all the sub-plot episodes in the book.

Propp, V. 1968. *Morphology of the Folk Tale*. Austin: Texas University Press.

Despite its publication date in the West, this book was actually written in 1928. In it Propp attempts to provide a scientific description of the structures of the Russian folk tale. In his analysis of 100 tales he discovers that character can be defined in terms of role in the plot, and that, thus viewed, there are only seven different roles to be identified. General terms such as 'hero', 'villain' and 'helper' are used, and the purely individual aspects of character in any particular tale do not materially affect their role. Furthermore: 'One may observe in general that the feelings and intentions of the dramatis personae do not have an effect on the course of the action in any instances at all' (p. 78).

In his analysis, Propp offers a syntagmatic description of character and action, showing how textual variation is describable in terms of a sort of *syntax* of the folk tale. He suggests that the tale can be described in some 31 acts, or *functions*, and that these can be combined in some variations, but not in others. Furthermore, these functions often occur in answering pairs – a test is set, a test is performed, for example. We find this pairing sort of relationship very clearly in *The Fog* in those sub-plot episodes where conflicts are set up and then resolved by the intervention of the fog itself.

Rose, J. 1984. *The Case of Peter Pan or the Impossibility of Children's Fiction*. London: Macmillan.

Jacqueline Rose applies some modern critical perspectives to children's literature. She is concerned particularly with how the child is constructed in and by children's books, both as character and as reader. At every turn, she suggests, the literature constructs the child as innocent. It does so by denying the sexuality of the child. It does so by positing a 'pre-cultural' child, a child that is an innocent and primary being untainted by culture, and that as such has a privileged perception and knowledge. Such a child is apolitical, having no politics within the group of other children within which he or she is set, nor yet a politics in relation to the wider social milieu.

Rose is defining an extreme, and it is not difficult to think of children's books in which most of the above is not so clear-cut. None the less, Robert Leeson's *Grange Hill Home and Away*, chosen by a group of year 10 boys who never read it, was the only children's book chosen in the study where the characters were to any degree knowing, and where the reader was expected to be similarly so. In all the children's books chosen by year 7, Rose's analysis would certainly be correct.

Rosen, H. 1984. *Stories and Meanings*. Sheffield: NATE.

Harold Rosen, as I indicated at the beginning of this book, has been influential, even inspirational, in his consistent and radical critique on the English teaching scene. He has taken a consistent political stance and I have come across nothing by him that is not worth reading. This paper is mentioned here since, as well as being part and parcel of his determination to recognize the voices of ordinary kids and ordinary teachers, it is also an extremely useful summary of the importance of narrative in the cognitive process. Virtually all my evidence in this book was collected in narrative form, and my analysis of my material is the more confident in the light of Rosen's work.

Todorov, T. 1977. *The Poetics of Prose*. New York: Cornell University Press.

First published in French in 1971, *The Poetics of Prose* is a collection of articles written during the 1960s. Two or three were particularly useful to me. He built on the ideas of the Russian formalists like Propp, and was one of the first structuralists to turn his attention to popular forms. In particular, he develops ideas about characterization in action in what he calls 'a-psychological narrative'. In such cases, 'All character traits are immediately causal; as soon as they appear they provoke an action' (p. 68). He also draws our attention to a further distinction made by the Russian formalists between *fabula* (story) and *sjuzet* (plot): 'the story is what has happened in life, the plot is the way the author presents it to us' (p. 45). So, in *Carrie* for instance, King uses a number of different narrative devices to tell a fairly simple story, and we saw how successful these were with one reader in Chapter 6. And the top-stream boys who discussed *The Fog* with me were well aware of the ways in which Herbert manipulated the underlying story, deferring information in order to build up suspense.

Zipes, J. 1979. *Breaking the Magic Spell, Radical Theories of Folk and Fairy Tales*. London: Heinemann.

Zipes, J. 1983. *Fairy Tales and the Art of Subversion*. London: Heinemann.

Jack Zipes's work has been particularly influential on my analysis. He is unique, in my experience, in addressing popular literature, folk tale, and children's literature itself, and to all of these he brings a penetrating ideological analysis. In particular, he introduces the idea that popular texts contain contradiction and are thus open to, in Eco's term, 'aberrant' readings, readings that ignore or even run against the ideological closure of the narrative. He links popular literature and film with their precursors in folk tale and romance, and suggests, after Bloch, that it offers the hope of autonomy and self-determination, in admittedly utopian forms, while at the same time affirming dominant capitalist ideology. In other words, he denies the implications of Eagleton's work that only texts that sit athwart the prevailing ideology can be open to countervailing readings, and he denies, too, the implications of Belsey's work that popular forms sit within the classic expressive realist tradition, and as such demand readings that are congruent with the dominant ideology.

The protagonists of *Carrie, First Blood, The BFG, Super Gran* and *The Fog* all operate by making individual utopian forays against the prevailing order. The closure, where it occurs, is a formulaic gesture. At the end of *First Blood* (the book), for instance, Rambo is simply killed, an ending which in the movie is partially transformed as he emerges invincible to be led away to the state penitentiary by the colonel who trained him. In *The Fog*, Holman closes the door of his flat behind him and his girlfriend, but essentially lives to fight another day. In *The BFG*, the folk tale form is even stronger as Sophie moves from orphan to ersatz princess with a little cottage in the grounds of Windsor Great Park, a very compliant giant as her father and a somewhat less compliant but none the less very tractable Queen as her mother.

Zipes (1979, p. 170), talking of folk and fairy tale, concludes with an injunction that could apply almost perfectly to the present study:

> What is obviously necessary in working with the impact of the tales on children is a method which takes into consideration the aesthetics of reception. Such a method would have to investigate the possibilities for comprehension by children in the light of the dialectic relationship of a specific audience to the tale at a given moment in history.

The present study is a – doubtless somewhat inadequate – move in that direction.

Bibliography

Primary literature

Blume, J. (1981). *Iggie's House*. London: Pan.
Dahl, R. (1982). *The BFG*. London: Jonathan Cape.
Duncan, L. (1983). *Stranger with My Face*. London: Hamish Hamilton.
Garfield, L. (1980). *John Diamond*. Harmondsworth: Penguin.
Herbert, J. (1975). *The Fog*. London: New English Library.
Hines, B. (1968). *Kes*. Harmondsworth: Penguin.
Hinton, S. E. (1970). *The Outsiders*. London: Fontana Lions.
Kennedy, L. (1979). *Maggie*. London: Futura.
King, S. (1974). *Carrie*. London: New English Library.
Lee, H. (1960). *To Kill a Mockingbird*. London: Pan.
Leeson, R. (1982). *Grange Hill Home and Away*. London: Fontana Lions.
Lewis, C.S. (1950). *The Lion, the Witch and the Wardrobe*. London: Fontana Lions.
Lewis, C.S. (1951). *Prince Caspian*. London: Fontana Lions.
Lewis, C.S. (1952). *The Voyage of the Dawn Treader*. London: Fontana Lions.
Lewis, C.S. (1953). *The Silver Chair*. London: Fontana Lions.
Lewis, C.S. (1954). *The Horse and His Boy*. London: Fontana Lions.
Lewis, C.S. (1955). *The Magician's Nephew*. London: Fontana Lions.
Lewis, C.S. (1956). *The Last Battle*. London: Fontana Lions.
Mitchell, Y. (1964). *Cathy Away*. London: Heinemann Educational.
Morrell, D. (1972). *First Blood*. London: Pan.
Sampson, F. (1982). *Sus*. Durham: Dennis Dobson.
Smith, A. C. H. (1982). *The Dark Crystal*. London: Futura.
Steinbeck, J. (1937). *Of Mice and Men*. London: Pan.
Steinbeck, J. (1948). *The Pearl*. London: Pan.
Tolkein, J. R. R. (1937). *The Hobbit*. London: George Allen and Unwin.
Wilson, F. (1978). *Super Gran*. Harmondsworth: Puffin.

Secondary literature

Abbs, P. (1976). *Root and Blossom*. London: Heinemann.
Abbs, P. (1980). 'English within the Arts: The Arts within a Total Curriculum', *Use of English*, vol. 32, no. 1. Autumn.

Adams, A. (ed.) (1982). *New Directions in English Teaching*. Lewes: Falmer Press.

Adams, P. (1987). 'Writing from Reading – "Dependent Authorship" as a Response' in B. Corcoran, and E. Evans (eds), *Readers, Texts, Teachers*. Milton Keynes: Open University Press, pp. 119–52.

Aers, L. (1975). 'Mind Forged Manacles', *English in Education*, vol. 9, no. 1.

Aiken, J. (1982). *The Way to Write for Children*. London: Elm Tree Books.

Alberghene, J. M. (1985). 'Writing in *Charlotte's Web*', *Children's Literature in Education*, vol. 16, no. 1.

Althusser, L. (1971). 'Ideology and Ideological State Apparatuses' in L. Althusser, *Lenin and Philosophy and Other Essays*. London: New Left Books, pp. 121–76.

Applebee, A. N. (1978). *The Child's Concept of Story*. Chicago: University of Chicago Press.

Ardizzone, E. (1969). 'Creation of a Picture Book' in S. Egoff, E. T. Stubbs and L. F. Ashley (eds), *Only Connect*. Oxford: Oxford University Press, pp. 347–56.

Ariès, P. (1962). *Centuries of Childhood*. Harmondsworth: Penguin.

Aristotle (1965). 'On the Art of Poetry' in Aristotle, Horace and Longinus, *Classical Literary Criticism* (trans. T. S. Dorsch). Harmondsworth: Penguin.

Armstrong, J. (1982). 'In Defence of Adventure Stories', *Children's Literature in Education*, vol. 13, no. 3.

Arnold, M. (1932). *Culture and Anarchy*. Cambridge: Cambridge University Press.

Assessment of Performance Unit (1978). *Language Performance*. London: Department of Education and Science.

Atkinson, J. (1985). 'How Children Read Poems at Different Ages', *English in Education*, vol. 19, no. 1.

Austin, J. L. (1962). *How To Do Things with Words*. Oxford: Oxford University Press.

Bailey, J. and Hollindale, P. (1986). 'Children's Books in Teacher Education at York University', *Signal*, 51.

Bardgett, K. (1972). '*Skinhead* in the Classroom', *Children's Literature in Education*, 8.

Bardgett, K. (1977). 'The Nature of Reluctance' in J. L. Foster (ed.), *Reluctant to Read*. London: Ward Lock, pp. 1–16.

Barker, F., Coombes, J., Hulme, P., Musselwhite, D. and Osborne, R. (eds) (1977). *Literature, Society, and the Sociology of Literature*. Colchester: University of Essex.

Barker, M. (ed.) (1984). *The Video Nasties*. London: Pluto.

Barlow, G. and Hill, A. (eds) (1985). *Video Violence and Children*. London. Hodder and Stoughton.

Barnes, D., Barnes, D. and Clarke, S. (1984). *Versions of English*. London: Heinemann Educational.

Barnes, D., Churley, P. and Thompson, C. (1971). 'Group Talk and Literary Response', *English in Education*, vol. 5, no. 3.

Barnes, D. and Seed, J. (1984). 'Seals of Approval: An Analysis of English Examinations' in I. F. Goodson and S. J. Ball (eds), *Defining the Curriculum*. London: Falmer Press, pp. 263–98.

Barnes, D. and Todd, F. (1977). *Communication and Learning in Small Groups*. London: Routledge and Kegan Paul.

Barry, P. (1983). 'Battering the Verbal Icon: Some Comments on "Re- reading English"', *English in Education*, vol. 17, no. 3.

Barton, L. and Meighan, R. (eds) (1978). *Sociological Interpretations of Schooling and Classrooms: A Reappraisal*. Driffield: Nafferton Books.

Barthes, R. (1974). *S/Z*. New York: Hill and Wang.

Barthes, R. (1975). *The Pleasure of the Text*. New York: Hill and Wang.

Barthes, R. (1982). 'The Metaphor of the Eye' in G. Bataille, *The Story of the Eye*. Harmondsworth: Penguin.

Bataille, G. (1982). *The Story of the Eye*. Harmondsworth: Penguin.

Bawden, N. (1975). 'The Imprisoned Child' in E. Blishen (ed.), *The Thorny Paradise*. Harmondsworth: Kestrel, pp. 62–4.

Bawden, N. (1976). 'A Dead Pig and My Father' in G. Fox, G. Hammond, T. Jones, F. Smith and K. Sterk (eds), *Writers, Critics and Children*. London: Heinemann, pp. 3–14.

Bazer, D. (1979). 'Literature without Examination', *English in Education*, vol. 13, no. 3.

Belsey, C. (1980). *Critical Practice*. London: Methuen.

Belsey, C. (1984). '"Re-reading English" and the Uncommitted Reader', *English in Education*, vol. 18, no. 2.

Benjamin, W. (1970). *Illuminations*. Glasgow: Fontana.

Bennet, J. (1984). *Reading, How Parents can Help*. Sheffield: NATE.

Benton, M. (1977). *The First Two Rs*. Southampton: University of Southampton.

Benton, M. (1979). 'Children's Response to Stories', *Children's Literature in Education*, vol. 10, no. 2.

Benton, M. (ed.) (1980). *Approaches to Research in Children's Literature*. Southampton: University of Southampton, Department of Education.

Benton, M. and Fox, G. (1984). 'Good and Bad Books', *Times Education Supplement*, 2 November.

Benton, M. and Fox, G. (1985). *Teaching Literature Nine to Fourteen*. Oxford: Oxford University Press.

Bethel, A. (1984). 'Media Studies' in J. Miller (ed.), *Eccentric Propositions*. London. Routledge and Kegan Paul, pp. 219–30.

Bettleheim, B. (1976). *The Uses of Enchantment. The Meaning and Importance of Fairy Tales*. Harmondsworth: Penguin.

Bettleheim, B. and Zelan, K. (1981). *On Learning to Read*. London: Thames and Hudson.

Beynon, J., Doyle, B., Goulden, H. and Hartley, J. (1983). 'The Teaching about Television Debate', *English in Education*, vol. 17, no. 3.

Billman, C. (1984). 'The Child Reader as Sleuth', *Children's Literature in Education*, vol. 15, no. 1.

Bixler, P. and Agosta, L. (1984). 'Formula Fiction and Children's Literature: Thornton Waldo Burgess and Franciss Hodgson Burnett', *Children's Literature in Education*, vol. 15, no. 2.

Blackie, P. (1970). 'Approaching Prose Literature', *English in Education*, vol. 4, no. 1.

Blackie, P. (1971). 'Asking Questions', *English in Education*, vol. 5, no. 3.

Blishen, E. (ed.) (1975). *The Thorny Paradise*. Harmondsworth: Kestrel.

Blunt, J. (1977). 'Response to Reading: How Some Young Readers Describe the Process', *English in Education*, vol. 11, no. 3.

Bolt, S. (1969). 'The Novel', *English in Education*, vol. 3, no. 2.

Bourdieu, P. (1971). 'Intellectual Field and Creative Project' in M. Young (ed.), *Knowledge and Control*. London: Collier-Macmillan.

Bourdieu, P. (1973). 'Cultural Reproduction and Social Reproduction' in R. Brown (ed.), *Knowledge, Education and Cultural Change*. London: Tavistock Publications.

Bown, R. (1983). 'Comic Culture – The Significance of Children's Unofficial Literature', *Links*, vol. 8, no. 2.

Brake, M. (1980). *The Sociology of Youth Culture and Youth Subcultures*. London: Routledge and Kegan Paul.

Bratton, J. S. (1981). *The Impact of Victorian Children's Fiction*. London: Croom Helm.

Britton, J. (1970). *Language and Learning*. Harmondsworth: Penguin.

Britton, J. (1977). 'The Role of Fantasy' in M. Meek, A. Warlow and G. Barton (eds), *The Cool Web*. London: Bodley Head, pp. 40–47.

Britton, J. (1981). 'English Teaching: Prospect and Retrospect', *English in Education*, vol. 15, no. 2.

Brown, B. (1984a). 'Exactly What We Wanted' in M. Barker (ed.), *The Video Nasties*. London: Pluto.

Brown, B. (1984b). 'Video Victory', *Times Educational Supplement*, 12 October, p. 37.

Brown, M. (1976). 'Reading Together: Eight to Ten Year Olds as Critics', *Children's Literature in Education*, 21.

Bruner, J. S. (1971). *Relevance of Education*. Harmondsworth: Penguin.

Burke, S. J. and Brumfitt, C. (1974). 'Is Literature Language? OR Is Language Literature?', *English in Education*, vol. 8, no. 2.

Burns, E. and Burns, T. (eds) (1973). *Sociology of Literature and Drama*. Harmondsworth: Penguin.

Buss, R. (1984). 'Guides to the Celulloid Jungle', *Times Educational Supplement*, 12 October.

Butler, D. (1975). *Cushla and Her Books*. Sevenoaks: Hodder and Stoughton.

Butler, D. (1980). *Babies Need Books*. Harmondsworth: Penguin.

Carter, R. (1981). 'Studying Language: An Integrated Approach to Lexis in Literature', *English in Education*, vol. 15, no. 3.

Cervantes, M. de (1950). *Don Quixote* (trans. J. M. Cohen). Harmondsworth: Penguin.

Chambers, A. (1973). *Introducing Books to Children*. London: Heinemann (2nd revised and expanded edn 1983).

Chambers, A. (1980a). 'The Reader in the Book' in N. Chambers (ed.), *The Signal Approach to Children's Books*. Harmondsworth: Kestrel, pp. 250–75.

Chambers, A. (1980b). 'An Interview with Alan Garner' in N. Chambers (ed.), *The Signal Approach to Children's Books*. Harmondsworth: Kestrel, pp. 276–328.

Chambers, A. (1983). 'The Child's Changing Story', *Signal*, 40.

Chambers, A. (1985). *Booktalk*. London: Bodley Head.

Chambers, A. (1986). 'All of a Tremble to See His Danger', *Signal*, 51, pp. 193–212.

Chambers, N. (ed.) (1980). *The Signal Approach to Children's Books*. Harmondsworth: Kestrel.

Chapman, J. (1983). *Reading Development and Cohesion*. London: Heinemann.

Chukovsky, K. (1963). *From Two to Five*. Berkeley, Calif.: University of California Press.

Clark, M. (1976). *Young Fluent Readers*. London: Heinemann.

Clarke, S. (1984). 'An Area of Neglect. Teaching the Reading of Argument', *English in Education*, vol. 18, no. 2.

Cooper, C. (ed.) (1985). *Researching Response to Literature and the Teaching of Literature*. Norwood, New Jersey: Ablex.

Corcoran, B. (1987). 'Teachers Creating Readers' in B. Corcoran and E. Evans (eds), *Readers, Texts, Teachers*. Milton Keynes: Open University Press, pp. 41–74.

Corcoran, B. and Evans, E. (eds) (1987). *Readers, Texts, Teachers*. Milton Keynes: Open University Press.

Coveney, P. (1957). *The Image of Childhood*. Harmondsworth: Penguin.

Crago, H. (1982). 'The Readers in the Reader', *Signal*, 39.

Crago, H. (1986). 'A Signal Conversation', *Signal*, 50.

Crago, H. (1987). 'Easy Connections: Emotional Truth and Fictional Gratification', *Signal*, 52.

Crago, H. and Crago, M. (1976). 'The Untrained Eye? The Pre-school Child Explores Felix Hoffman's *Rapunzel*', *Children's Literature in Education*, 22.

Crago, M. and Crago, H. (1983). *Prelude to Literacy*. Edwardsville: Southern Illinois University Press.

Craig, D. (ed.) (1975). *Marxists on Literature*. Harmondsworth: Penguin.

Craig, D. (1983). 'A Reply to Peter Barry', *English in Education*, vol. 17, no. 3.

Craig, G. (1976). 'Who is Doing What to Whom' in G. Josipovici (ed.), *The Modern English Novel*. London: Open Books, pp. 15–36.

Crisp, F. M. (1978). 'Questioning Children's Reading – An Application of Barret's Taxonomy', *Reading*, vol. 12, no. 1.

Crouch, M. (1972). *The Nesbit Tradition*. London: Ernest Benn.

Crowther, S. (1986). 'Is It Goodbye to 1984 and All That …?', *English in Education*, vol. 20, no. 1.

Curry, J. (1970). 'On the Elvish Craft', *Signal*, 2.

Dale, S., Gerrard, S. and Hoffman, M. (1982). *Finding Out About Children's Books: An Information Guide for Teachers*, Open University Inset. Milton Keynes: Open University Press.

D'Arcy, P. (1973). *Reading for Meaning*. Vol. 2. London: Hutchinson.

Darton, E. J. H. (1958). *Children's Books in England* (2nd edn). Cambridge: Cambridge University Press.

Davies, F. (1982). 'Quiver Full of Darts', *Times Educational Supplement*, 9 July.

Davies, P. (ed.) (1982) *Multicultural Literature in the Classroom*. Wolverhampton: Wolverhampton Education Authority.

Davies, T. and Peart, R. (1987). 'The Man Who Thought He Was Rambo', *Sunday Telegraph*, 23 August.

DES (1975). *A Language For Life* (The Bullock Report). London: HMSO.

DES (1983). *Popular TV & Schoolchildren* London: HMSO.

Dickinson, P. (1976). 'In Defence of Rubbish' in G. Fox, G. Hammond, T. Jones, F. Smith and K. Sterk (eds), *Writers, Critics and Children*. London: Heinemann, pp. 73–6.

Dixon, B. (1974). 'The Nice, The Naughty and The Nasty: The Tiny World of Enid Blyton', *Children's Literature in Education*, 15.

Dixon, B. (1977). *Catching Them Young* (2 vols). London: Pluto Press.

Dixon, B. (1982). *Now Read On*. London: Pluto Press.

Dixon, J. (1967). *Growth through English*. Oxford: Oxford University Press.

Dixon, J. and Brown, J. (1984). *Responses to Literature – What is Being Assessed?* Vol. 1. London: School Curriculum Development Committee.

Dixon, J. and Brown, J. (1985). *Responses to Literature – What is Being Assessed?* Vol. 2. London: School Curriculum Development Committee.

Docherty, M. (1984). 'That's Not Right. Look! There's No Daddy in This Book' in J. Miller (ed.), *Eccentric Propositions*. London: Routledge and Kegan Paul, pp. 14–26.

Donaldson, M. (1978). *Children's Minds*. Glasgow: Fontana.

Dollimore, J. (1983). 'Politics, Teaching, Literature', *Journal of Literature Teaching Politics*, 2, pp. 108–19.

Dombey, H. (1983). 'Learning the Language of Books' in M. Meek (ed.), *Opening Moves*, Bedford Way Paper 17. London: University of London Institute of Education, pp. 26–43.

Doughty, P. (1972). 'Pupils Also Use Language to Live: A Defense of a Linguistic Approach to Language Study in the Classroom', *English in Education*, vol. 6, no. 1.

Doughty, P., Pearce, J. and Thornton, G. (1971). *Language in Use*. London: Arnold.

Duane, M. (1970). 'Speech and Reading', *English in Education*, vol. 4, no. 3.

Dunning, J. (1985). 'Reluctant and Willing Story Tellers in the Classroom', *English in Education*, vol. 19, no. 1.

Durkin, D. (1981). 'Reading Comprehension', *Language Arts*, vol. 58, no. 1.

Eagleton, T. (1976a). *Marxism and Literary Criticism*. London: Methuen.

Eagleton, T. (1976b). *Criticism and Ideology*. London: Verso.

Eagleton, T. (1982). 'The End of Criticism', *English in Education*, vol. 16, no. 2.

Eagleton, T. (1985). 'The Subject of Literature', *The English Magazine*, 15.

Earnshaw, B. (1982). 'Planets of Awful Dread', *Children's Literature in Education*, vol. 14, no. 4.

Eaton, T. (1984). 'Philosophy and English A Level', *Times Educational Supplement*, 4 May.

Eco, U. (1981). *The Role of the Reader*. London: Hutchinson.

Egan, K. (1983). 'Children's Path to Reality from Fantasy: Contrary Thoughts about Curriculum Foundations', *Journal of Curriculum Studies*, vol. 15, no. 4.

Egoff, S., Stubbs, E. T. and Ashley, L. F. (eds) (1969). *Only Connect*. Oxford: Oxford University Press.

Eliot, T. S. (1948). *Notes towards the Definition of Culture*. London: Faber and Faber.

Eliot, T. S. (1969). '*Huckleberry Finn*: A Critical Essay' in S. Egoff, E. T. Stubbs and L. F. Ashley (eds), *Only Connect*. Oxford: Oxford University Press, pp. 299–309.

Ella, C. (1982). 'Teenage Literature – Drawing That Line', *Children's Literature in Education*, vol. 13, no. 1.

Ellis, J. (1969). 'A Reading Survey by Warwickshire NATE', *English in Education*, vol. 3, no. 1.

Empson, W. (1935). *Some Versions of Pastoral*. London: Chatto and Windus.

Evans, E. (1981). '*The Act of Reading* and the English Teacher', *English in Education*, vol. 15, no. 3.

Evans, E. (1987). ' "Quality" and "Non-Quality": Some New Criteria', *English in Education*, vol. 21, no. 3, pp. 36–43.

Eyre, F. (1971). *British Children's Books in the Twentieth Century*. London: Longman.

Fader, D. (1970). 'Getting Them to Use Their Reading', *English in Education*, vol. 4, no. 3.

Fawcus, W. (1971). 'Reading Without Primers', *English in Education*, vol. 5, no. 3.

Fisher, M. (1964). *Intent upon Reading*. Leicester: Brockhampton.

Fisher, M. (1986). *Classics for Children and Young People*. Stroud: Thimble Press.

Foreman-Peck, L. (1985). 'Evaluating Children's Talk about Literature: A Theoretical Perspective', *Children's Literature in Education*, vol. 16, no. 4.

Foster, J. L. (ed.) (1977). *Reluctant to Read*. London: Ward Lock.

Foucault, M. (1978). *The History of Sexuality. Volume 1: An Introduction*. Harmondsworth: Penguin.

Fox, C. (1983). 'Talking Like a Book' in M. Meek (ed.), *Opening Moves*, Bedford Way Paper 17. London: University of London Institute of Education, pp. 12–25.

Fox. G. (1977). 'Reading Fiction, Starting where the Kids are' in J. L. Foster (ed.), *Reluctant to Read*. London: Ward Lock, pp. 17–28.

Fox, G. (1979). 'Dark Watchers: Young Readers and Their Fiction', *English in Education*, vol. 13, no. 1.

Fox, G., Hammond, G., Jones, T., Smith, F. and Sterk, K. (eds) (1976). *Writers, Critics and Children*. London: Heinemann.

Francis, H. (1982). *Learning to Read*. Hemel Hempstead: Allen and Unwin.

Freire, P. (1972). *Pedagogy of the Oppressed*. Harmondsworth: Penguin.

Freud, S. (1975). 'The Uncanny' in A. Dickson (ed.), *The Pelican Freud Library, Vol. 14. Art and Literature*. Harmondsworth: Penguin, pp. 335–76.

Frith, G. (1979). 'Reading and Response, Some Questions, No Answers', *English in Education*, vol. 13, no. 1.

Frith, S. (1978). 'Best Sellers', *English in Education*, vol. 12, no. 3.

Fry, D. (1985). *Children Talk about Books: Seeing Themselves as Readers*. Milton Keynes: Open University Press.

Frye, N. (1957). *Anatomy of Criticism*. Princeton, New Jersey: Princeton University Press.

Frye, N. (1970). *The Stubborn Structure*. London: Methuen.

Gertz, C. (1976). 'Deep Play' in J. Bruner, A. Jolly and K. Sylva (eds), *Play*. Harmondsworth: Penguin.

Gibson, R. (1981). 'Educational Theory and Literary Theory', *Higher Education Review*, vol. 14, no. 1.

Gilliland, J. (1972). *Readability*. London: Hodder and Stoughton.

Gintis, H. and Bowles, S. (1980). 'Contradiction and Reproduction in Educational Theory' in L. Barton, R. Meighan and S. Walker (eds), *Schooling, Ideology and The Curriculum*. London: Falmer Press.

Giroux, H. A. (1981). *Ideology, Culture, and The Process of Schooling*. London: Falmer Press.

Glasgow University Media Group (1982). *Really Bad News*. London: Writers and Readers.

Goddard, R. (1985). 'Beyond the Literary Heritage: Meeting the Needs in English at 16–19', *English in Education*, vol. 19, no. 2.

Goelman, H., Oberg, A. and Smith, F. (eds) (1984). *Awakening to Literacy*. London: Heinemann.

Goldthwaite, J. (1985a). 'The Black Rabbit Part I', *Signal*, 47.

Goldthwaite, J. (1985b). 'The Black Rabbit Part II', *Signal*, 48.

Goodman, K. (1982). *Language and Literacy, Vol. 1. Process, Theory, Research*. London: Routledge and Kegan Paul.

Gramsci, A. (1971). *Selections from Prison Notebooks* (edited by G. N. Smith and Q. Hoare). London: Lawrence and Wishart.

Green, P. (1982). 'The Rentier's Rural Dream', *Times Literary Supplement*, 26 November.

Greenwell, B. (1982). *Alternatives at English A Level. A Survey of Current 'Alternative' Syllabuses*, NATE Examinations Booklet No. 4. Sheffield: NATE.

Gregory, E. (1984). 'A Story ... A Story ...', *English in Education*, vol. 18, no. 2.

Gregory, R. L. (1977). 'Psychology: Towards a Science of Fiction' in M. Meek, A. Warlow and G. Barton (eds), *The Cool Web*. London: Bodley Head.

Griffin, S. (1981). *Pornography and Silence*. London: The Women's Press.

Grixti, J. (1982). 'Horror and Helplessness: The Case of James Herbert', *Use of English*, vol. 34, no. 1, pp. 43–51.

Grugeon, E. (1971). 'Help with Reading', *English in Education*, vol. 5, no. 3.

Grugeon, E. and Walden, P. (eds) (1978). *Literature and Learning*. London: Ward Lock.

Gurney, R. (1982). 'Aspects of Discourse in the Story Reading and Reading Development of Young Children', unpublished Ph.D. thesis. London: University of London Institute of Education.

Gurney, R. (1983). 'Reading: The Invitation to Collaborate', unpublished seminar paper. Cambridge: Cambridge Institute of Education.

Hadley, E. (1982). 'I Have Therefore an Axe to Grind' in A. Adams (ed.), *New Directions in English Teaching*. Lewes: Falmer Press, pp. 163–76.

Haigh, G. (1982). 'For Non Squiffletrotters Only', *Times Educational Supplement*, 19 November.

Hall, L. (1983). '*A Taste for Greatness*', *Times Educational Supplement*, 29 April.

Halliday, M. A. K. (1973). *Explorations in the Functions of Language*. London: Arnold.

Halliday, M. A. K. (1978). *Language as Social Semiotic*. London: Edward Arnold.

Hamilton, L. (1983). 'Blume's Adolescents: Coming of Age in Limbo', *Signal*, 41.

Hardcastle, J. (1985). 'Classrooms as Sites for Cultural Making', *English in Education*, vol. 19, no. 3.

Harding, D. W. (1967). 'Considered Experience: The Invitation of the Novel', *English in Education*, vol. 1, no. 2.

Harding, D. W. (1977a). 'Psychological Processes in the Reading of Fiction' in M. Meek, A. Warlow and G. Barton (eds), *The Cool Web*. London: Bodley Head, pp. 58–72.

Harding, D. W. (1977b). 'The Bond with the Author' in M. Meek, A. Warlow and G. Barton (eds), *The Cool Web*. London: Bodley Head pp. 201–215.

Hardy, B. (1968). 'The Teaching of English. Life, Literature and Literary Criticism', *English in Education*, vol. 2, no. 2.

Hardy, B. (1975). *Tellers and Listeners*. London: Athlone.

Hardy, B. (1977). 'Towards a Poetics of Fiction: An Approach through Narrative' in M. Meek, A. Warlow and G. Barton (eds), *The Cool Web*. London: Bodley Head, pp. 12–23.

Harpin, W. S. (1966). 'The Appreciation of Prose', *Educational Review*, 19, pp. 13–22.

Harri-Augstein, S., Smith, M. and Thomas, L. (1982). *Reading to Learn*. London: Methuen.

Hawkes, T. (1977). *Structuralism and Semiotics*. London: Methuen.

Hawkins, J. (1986). '"It's how the story is really": Response to Two Types of Narrative in Some Primary Children', *English in Education*, vol. 20, no. 3.

Hayhoe, M. (1980). '*CSE Literature Texts*', unpublished survey. Norwich: University of East Anglia.

Hayhoe, M. and Parker, S. (1984). *Working with Fiction*. London: Edward Arnold.

Heath, S. B. (1982). 'Protean Shapes in Literacy Events: Ever Shifting Oral and Literate Traditions' in D. Tannen (ed.), *Spoken and Written Language*. Norwood, NJ: Ablex.

Heath, S. B. (1983). *Ways with Words: Language, Life, and Work in Communities and Classrooms*. Cambridge: Cambridge University Press.

Heather, P. (1981). *Young People's Reading: A Study of the Leisure Reading of 13–15 Year Olds*. Sheffield: University of Sheffield.

Hentof, N. (1969). 'Fiction for Teenagers' in S. Egoff, E. T. Stubbs and L. F. Ashley (eds), *Only Connect*. Oxford. Oxford University Press, pp. 399–407.

Her Majesty's Inspectorate (1983). *Bullock Revisited: A Discussion Paper*. Available Through Local Education Authorities.

Her Majesty's Inspectorate (1984). *English from 5 to 16*. London: Her Majesty's Stationary Office.

Her Majesty's Inspectorate (1986). *English from 5 to 16. Second Edition (incorporating responses)*. London: Her Majesty's Stationary Office.

Hildick, W. (1970). *Children and Fiction*. London: Evans.

Hodgeon, J. (1980). 'Topsy & Tim Rule – OK?', *English in Education*, vol. 14, no. 1.

Hoffman, M. (1983). 'Parent Partners', *Times Educational Supplement*, 1 July.

Hoffman, M., Jeffcoate, R., Maybin, J. and Mercer, N. (1982). *Children, Language and Literature*, OU Inset Publication. Milton Keynes: Open University Press.

Hoggart, R. (1957). *The Uses of Literacy*. Harmondsworth: Penguin.

Holbrook, D. (1970). 'The English Teacher, The Avant Garde and The Revolution in Philosophical Anthropology', *English in Education*, vol. 4, no. 1.

Holbrook, D. (1973). 'The Problem of C. S. Lewis', *Children's Literature in Education*, 10.

Holbrook, D. (1984). 'Cutting Out the Frills, Cutting Out the Thrills,' *Times Educational Supplement*, 2 November.

Holland, N. (1976). *Five Readers Reading*. New Haven, Conn.: Yale University Press.

Hollindale, P. (1981). 'Children's Books or Children's Literature', *Use of English*, vol. 32, no. 2.

Hollingworth, B. (1974). 'Marshall Macluhan and the Apocalypse', *English in Education*, vol. 8, no. 1.

Hughes, T. (1976). 'Myth and Education' in G. Fox, G. Hammond, T. Jones, F. Smith and K. Sterk (eds), *Writers, Critics and Children*. London: Heinemann, pp. 77–94.

Hunt, P. (1978). 'The Cliché Count: A Practical Aid for the Selection of Books for Children', *Children's Literature in Education*, vol. 9, no. 3.

Hunt, P. (1980). 'Children's Books, Children's Literature, Criticism and Research' in M. Benton (ed.), *Approaches to Research in Children's Literature*. Southampton: University of Southampton, Department of Education, pp. 13–26.

Hunt, P. (1981). 'Criticism and Pseudo Criticism', *Signal*, 34, pp. 14–21.

IBBY (1982). *Story in a Child's Changing World*, papers and proceedings of the 18th Congress of the International Board on Books For Young People.

Ingham, J. (1981). *Books and Reading Development*. London: Heinemann.

Ingham, J. (1982a). 'Middle School Children's Responses to Enid Blyton in the Bradford Book Flood Experiment', *Journal of Research in Reading*, vol. 5, no. 1.

Ingham, J. (1982b). 'Television Viewing and Reading Habits', *Reading*, 16.

Inglis, F. (1971a). 'How to Do Things with Words: A Critique of Language Studies', *English in Education*, vol. 5, no. 2.

Inglis, F. (1971b) 'Reading Children's Novels', *Children's Literature in Education*, 5.

Inglis, F. (1974). 'The Awkward Ages, or What Shall We Tell the Children', *Children's Literature in Education*, 13.

Inglis, F. (1975). 'Against Proportional Representation: The Ambitious Heart of English Teaching', *English in Education*, vol. 9, no. 1.

Inglis, F. (1981). *The Promise of Happiness*. Cambridge: Cambridge University Press.

Iser, W. (1978). *The Act of Reading*. London: Routledge and Kegan Paul.

Jackson, D. (1978). 'Using *The Midnight Fox* with a Group of Secondary School First Formers', *English in Education*, vol. 12, no. 1.

Jackson, D. (1980). 'First Encounters: The Importance of Initial Response to Literature', *Children's Literature in Education*, vol. 11, no. 4.

Jackson, D. (1982). *Continuity in Secondary English*. London: Methuen.

Jackson, D. (1983a). *Encounters with Books*. London: Methuen.

Jackson, D. (1983b). 'Dignifying Anecdote', *English in Education*, vol. 17, no. 1.

Jackson, R. (1981). *Fantasy, the Literature of Subversion*. London: Methuen.

Jackson, S. (1982). *Childhood and Sexuality*. Oxford: Blackwell.

Jameson, F. (1981). *The Political Unconscious*. New York: Cornell University Press.

Jenkins, S. (1984). 'Love, Loss and Seeking: Maternal Deprivation and the Quest', *Children's Literature in Education*, vol. 15, no. 2.

Jenkinson, A. J. (1940). *What do Boys and Girls Read*. London: Methuen.

Johnson, G. A. (1984). 'Historicity, Narratives, and an Understanding of Human Life', *Journal of the British Society for Phenomenology*, vol. 15, no. 3.

Jones, A. and Buttrey, J. (1970). *Children and Stories*. Oxford: Blackwell.

Katz, W. R. (1980). 'Some Uses of Food in Children's Literature', *Children's Literature in Education*, vol. 11, no. 4.

Kelly, G. A. (1955). *The Psychology of Personal Constructs*. New York: W. W. Norton.

Kermode, F. (1979). *The Genesis of Secrecy*. Cambridge, Mass.: Harvard University Press.

Kertzer, A. E. (1984). 'Inventing the Child Reader: How We Read Children's Books', *Children's Literature in Education*, vol. 15, no. 1.

King, R. (1978). 'Story Worlds as Multiple Realities', *English in Education*, vol. 12, no. 3.

Knight, R. (1982). 'Understanding "Discrimination": The Case against Television Studies', *English in Education*, vol. 16, no. 3.

Knight, R. (1984). 'Denying the Imagination', *Times Educational Supplement*, 2 November.

Labov, W. (1972). *Language in the Inner City*. Philadelphia: University of Pennsylvania Press.

Langer, S. K. (1942). *Philosophy in a New Key*. Cambridge, Mass.: Harvard University Press.

Langer, S. K. (1953). *Feeling and Form*. London: Routledge and Kegan Paul.

LATE (1980). *English Exams at 16*. London: London Association for the Teaching of English.

Leavis, F. R. (1943). *Education and the University*. Cambridge: Cambridge University Press.

Leavis, F. R. (1948). *The Great Tradition*. Harmondsworth: Penguin.

Leavis, F. R. (1955). *D.H. Lawrence: Novelist*. Harmondsworth: Penguin.

Leavis, Q. D. (1932). *Fiction and the Reading Public*. Harmondsworth: Penguin.

Lee, J. (1984). 'For their Own Purposes – Reading African and Caribbean Literature with Young Black People' in J. Miller (ed.), *Eccentric Propositions. Essays on Literature and the Curriculum*. London: Routledge and Kegan Paul, pp. 231–42.

Leeson, R. (1977a). *Children's Books and Class Society*. London: Writers and Readers.

Leeson, R. (1977b). 'A Reluctant Literature' in J. L. Foster (ed.), *Reluctant to Read*. London: Ward Lock, pp. 29–45.

Leeson, R. (1980). 'To the Toyland Frontier' in N. Chambers (ed.), *The Signal Approach to Children's Books*. Harmondsworth: Kestrel, pp. 208–216.

Leeson, R. (1982). 'Not in Front of the Children', *English in Education*, vol. 16, no. 2.

Leeson, R. (1983). 'Authentic Accents', *Times Educational Supplement*, 3 June.

Leeson, R. (1985). *Reading and Righting*. London: Collins.

Lévi-Strauss, C. (1963). 'The Structural Study of Myth' in C. Lévi-Strauss, *Structural Anthropology*. Harmondsworth: Penguin, pp. 206–231.

Lewis, C. S. (1969). 'On Three Ways of Writing for Children' in S. Egoff, E. T. Stubbs and L. F. Ashley (eds), *Only Connect*. Oxford: Oxford University Press, pp. 207–220.

Light, D. (1983). 'Culture and Civilisation: The Politics of English Teaching', *English in Education*, vol. 17, no. 1.

Loeff, A. R. van de (1976). 'A Sense of Audience 1' in G. Fox, G. Hammond, T. Jones, F. Smith and K. Sterk (eds), *Writers, Critics and Children*. London: Heinemann, pp. 27–30.

Logan, T. (1984). 'Learning Through Interviewing' in J. Schostack and T. Logan (eds), *Pupil Experience*. London: Croom Helm, pp. 17–28.

London Borough of Camden Libraries and Arts Department (1982a). *Bibliography of Books for Teenagers*. London: London Borough of Camden Libraries and Arts Department.

London Borough of Camden Libraries and Arts Department (1982b). *Survey of Periodicals for Teenagers*. London: London Borough of Camden Libraries and Arts Department.

London Borough of Camden Libraries and Arts Department (1983). *Report of the Working Group on Library Provision for Teenagers*. London: London Borough of Camden Libraries and Arts Department.

Lukács, G. (1975), 'Tolstoy and the Development of Realism' in D. Craig (ed.), *Marxists on Literature*. Harmondsworth: Penguin.

Lunzer, E. and Gardener, K. (1979). *The Effective Use of Reading*. London: Heinemann.

Lynn, J. L. (1985). 'Runes to Ward off Sorrow: Rhetoric of the English Nursery Rhyme', *Children's Literature in Education*, vol. 16, no. 1.

Macdonald, M. (1980). 'Schooling and the Reproduction of Class and Gender Relations' in L. Barton, R. Meighar and S. Walker (eds), *Schooling, Ideology, and the Curriculum*. Lewes: Falmer Press.

Mackay, D., Thompson, B. and Schaub, P. (1970). *Breakthrough to Literacy*. London: Longman.

Macleod, A. S. (1984). 'Secret in the Trash Bin: On the Perenial Popularity of Juvenile Series Books', *Children's Literature in Education*, vol. 15, no. 3.

Macherey, P. (1977). 'Problems of Reflection' in F. Barker, J. Coombes, P. Hulme, D. Musselwhite and R. Osborne (eds), *Literature, Society, and the Sociology of Literature*. Colchester: University of Essex.

Mallett, M. (1983). 'The Ballad of Charlotte Dymond', *English in Education*, vol. 17, no. 2.

Manning, R. (1970). 'A Book is a Book is a Book', *Signal*, 3.

Marcuse, H. (1978). *The Aesthetic Dimension*. London: Macmillan.

Marks, E. and Courtivron, I. de (eds) (1980). *New French Feminisms*. Amherst: University of Massachusetts Press.

Marriott, S. (1985). '"Me mum, she says it's bigotry". Children's Response to *The Twelfth Day of July*', *Children's Literature in Education*, vol. 16, no. 1.

Martin, N. (1976). 'Encounters with Models', *English in Education*, vol. 10, no. 1.

Marx, K. and Engels, F. (1971). *Historical Materialism*. London: Pluto Press.

Masterman, L. (1980). *Teaching about Television*. London: Macmillan.

Masterman, L. (1982a). 'Television and the English Teacher' in A. Adams (ed.), *New Directions in English Teaching*, Lewes: Falmer Press, pp. 43–78.

Masterman, L. (1982b). 'A Response to Roger Knight', *English in Education*, vol. 16, no. 3.

Mathieson, M. (1975). *The Preachers of Culture*. London: George Allen and Unwin.

Mathieson, M. (1985). *Teaching Practical Criticism*. Dover, New Hampshire: Croom Helm.

McDowell, M. (1973). 'Fiction for Children and Adults: Some Essential Differences', *Children's Literature in Education*, 10.

McGillis, R. (1984). 'Calling a Voice out of Silence: Hearing what We Read', *Children's Literature in Education*, vol. 15, no. 1.

Medway, P. (1980). *Finding a Language. Autonomy and Learning in School*. London: Writers and Readers.

Meek, M. (1980). 'Prolegomena for a Study of Childrens Literature' in M. Benton (ed.), *Approaches to Research in Childrens Literature*. Southampton: University of Southampton, Department of Education, pp. 27–39.

Meek, M. (1981). *Response – Begin Again*. London: London University Institute of Education.

Meek, M. (1982). *Learning to Read*. London: Bodley Head.

Meek, M. (1984). 'Speaking of Shifters' in M. Meek and J. Miller (eds), *Changing English*. London: Heinemann Educational Books, pp. 204–19.

Meek, M. (1987). 'Symbolic Outlining: The Academic Study of Children's Literature', *Signal*, 53.

Meek, M. (1988). *How Texts Teach What Readers Learn*. Stroud: Thimble Press.

Meek, M. with Armstrong, S., Austerfield, V., Graham, J. and Plackett, E. (1983). *Achieving Literacy*. London: Routledge and Kegan Paul.

Meek, M. and Miller, J. (eds) (1984). *Changing English*. London: Heinemann Educational Books.

Meek, M., Warlow, A. and Barton, G. (eds) (1977). *The Cool Web*. London: Bodley Head.

Midland Examining Group (1987). *English. English Literature. Syllabuses for Joint GCE O Level/CSE Examination*. Nottingham.

Millar, D. (1969). 'Towards an Improvement in Literature Teaching', *English in Education*, vol. 5, no. 3.

Miller, J. (ed.) (1984). *Eccentric Propositions. Essays on Literature and the Curriculum*. London: Routledge and Kegan Paul.

Millet, J. (1969). *Sexual Politics*. London: Hart Davis.

Mitchell, D. C. (1982). *The Process of Reading*. Chichester: Wiley.

Moffett, J. (1968). *Teaching the Universe of Discourse*. Boston: Houghton Mifflin.

Moon, C. and Raban, B. (1975). *A Question of Reading*. London: Ward Lock.

Morris, R. (1963). *Success and Failure in Learning to Read*. London: Oldbourne.

Morris, R. (1971). 'What Children Learn in Learning to Read', *English in Education*, vol. 5, no. 3.

Morse, B. (1971). 'Poetry, Children and Ted Hughes', *Signal*, 6.

Moss, E. (1977). 'The "Peppermint" Lesson' in M. Meek, A. Warlow and G. Barton (eds), *The Cool Web*. London: Bodley Head, pp. 140–2.

Moy, B. and Raleigh, M. (1984). 'Comprehension. Bringing it Back Alive' in J. Miller (ed.), *Eccentric Propositions. Essays on Literature and the Curriculum*. London: Routledge and Kegan Paul, pp. 148–92.

NATE (n.d.). *Children Reading to Their Teachers*. Sheffield: NATE.

NATE Language and Gender Working Party (1985). *Alice in Genderland*. Sheffield: NATE.

Nodelman, P. (1986). 'Teaching Children's Literature: An Intellectual Snob Confronts Some Generalisers', *Children's Literature in Education*, vol. 17, no. 4.

O'Neill, M. (1983). 'More Thoughts about Learning to Read', *Signal*, 41.

Outhwaite, W. (1975). *Understanding Social Life: The Method Called Verstehen*. London: George Allen and Unwin.

Pawling, C. (ed.) (1984). *Popular Fiction and Social Change*. London: Macmillan.

Peacock, C. (1980). *English and a General Education*. Stirling: University of Stirling Seminar Paper no. 7.

Peel, E. A. (1971). *The Nature of Adolescent Judgement*. London: Staples Press.

Philip, N. (1984a). 'This Way Confusion', *Signal*, 43.

Philip, N. (1984b). 'What Makes a Children's Classic', *Times Educational Supplement*, 13 January.

Phillips, T. (1971). 'Poetry in the Junior School', *English in Education*, vol. 5, no. 3.

Piaget, J. (1951). *Play, Dreams and Imitation in Childhood*. London: Routledge and Kegan Paul.

Pickard, P. M. (1961). *I Could a Tale Unfold*. London: Tavistock.

Pickering, S. (1982). 'The Function of Criticism in Children's Literature', *Children's Literature in Education*, vol. 13, no. 1.

Plekhanov, G. V. (1957). *Art and Social Life*. Moscow: Progress Publishers.

Probst, R. E. (1984). *Adolescent Literature: Response and Analysis*. Columbus, Ohio: Charles E. Merrill.

Propp, V. (1968). *Morphology of the Folk Tale*. Austin: Texas University Press.

Protherough, R. (1983a). *Developing Response to Fiction*. Milton Keynes: Open University Press.

Protherough, R. (1983b). 'How Children Judge Stories', *Children's Literature in Education*, vol. 14, no. 1.

Protherough, R. (1987). 'The Stories that Readers Tell' in B. Corcoran and E. Evans (eds), *Readers, Texts, Teachers*. Milton Keynes: Open University Press.

Purves, A. C. (1973). *Literature Education in Ten Countries*. New York: Halstead Press.

Raban, B. and Moon, C. (1978). *Books and Learning to Read*. London: School Library Association.

Ray, S. (1982). *The Blyton Phenomenon*. London: Deutsch.

Reinstein, P. G. (1983). 'Aesop and Grimm: Contrast in Ethical Codes and Contemporary Values', *Children's Literature in Education*, vol. 14, no. 1.

Richards, I. A. (1929). *Practical Criticism*. London: Routledge and Kegan Paul.

Rose, J. (1984). *The Case of Peter Pan or The Impossibility of Children's Fiction*. London: Macmillan.

Rosen, H. (1975). 'Out There Where the Masons Went', *English in Education*, vol. 9, no. 1.

Rosen, H. (1982). *The Language Monitors*, Bedford Way Paper no. 11. London: University of London Institute of Education.

Rosen, H. (1984). *Stories and Meanings*. Sheffield: NATE.

Rosenblatt, L. M. (1968). *Literature as Exploration*. London: Heinemann.

Rosenblatt, L. M. (1971). 'Pattern and Process. A Polemic', *Use of English*, vol. 22, no. 3.

Rosenblatt, L. M. (1978). *The Reader, The Text, The Poem*. Carbondale: Southern Illinois University Press.

Rosenheim, E. W. Jr (1969). 'Children's Reading and Adults' Values' in S. Egoff, E. T. Stubbs and L. F. Ashley (eds), *Only Connect*. Oxford: Oxford University Press, pp. 17–32.

Rowbotham, S. (1973). *Woman's Consciousness, Man's World*. Harmondsworth: Penguin.

Rowe, P. (1987). 'Metaphors of the Imagination', unpublished paper given at the 3rd British Research Seminar on Children's Literature, at Bulmershe College of Higher Education, Reading, 3–5 July.

Salter, D. (1972). 'The Hard Core of Children's Fiction', *Children's Literature in Education*, 8.

Salter, D. (1986). 'Birth Strangled Babe?', *English in Education*, vol. 20, no. 3.

Sarland, C. (1982a). 'The Child and the Book: A Critical Exploration with Cultural Implications', unpublished MA thesis. London: University of London Institute of Education.

Sarland, C. (1982b). 'The Premise of Happiness', *Signal*, 37, pp. 11–20.

Sarland, C. (1983). 'The Secret Seven versus The Twits: Cultural Clash or Cosy Combination?', *Signal*, vol. 42, pp. 155–71.

Sarland, C. (1985). 'Piaget, Blyton and Story: Children's Play and the Reading Process', *Children's Literature in Education*, vol. 16, no. 2, pp. 102–9.

Saussure, F. de (1959). *Course in General Linguistics*. London: Fontana.

Schlager, N. (1978). 'Predicting Children's Choices in Literature: A Developmental Approach', *Children's Literature in Education*, vol. 9, no. 3.

Schostak, J. (1983). *Maladjusted Schooling. Deviance, Social Control and Individuality in Secondary Schooling*. Lewes: Falmer Press.

Schostak, J. (1986). *Schooling the Violent Imagination*. London: Routledge and Kegan Paul.

Schostak, J. (1988). 'The Nature of Structural Violation', unpublished paper. Norwich: University of East Anglia.

Schostak, J. and Logan, T. (eds) (1984). *Pupil Experience*. London: Croom Helm.

Sendak, M. (1969). 'Interview with Nat Hentof: Among the Wild Things' in S. Egoff, E. T. Stubbs and L. F. Ashley (eds), *Only Connect*. Oxford: Oxford University Press, pp. 323–46.

Sims, A. and Melville-Thomas, G. (1985). 'Psychiatrists' Survey' in G. Barlow and A. Hill (eds), *Video Violence and Children*. London: Hodder and Stoughton, pp. 86–106.

Sinfield, A. (1983). 'Four Ways with a Reactionary Text', *Journal of Literature Teaching Politics*, 2, pp. 81–95.

Smith, F. (1971). *Understanding Reading*. New York: Holt, Rinehart and Winston.

Smith, F. (1973). *Psycholinguistics and Reading*. New York: Holt, Rinehart and Winston.

Smith, F. (1978). *Reading*. Cambridge: Cambridge University Press.

Sontag, S. (1982). 'The Pornographic Imagination' in G. Bataille (ed.), *The Story of the Eye*. Harmondsworth: Penguin, pp. 83–118.

Southgate, V., Arnold, H. and Johnson, S. (1981). *Extending Beginning Reading*. London: Heinemann.

Speier, M. (1982). 'The Everyday World of the Child' in C. Jenks (ed.), *The Sociology of Childhood*. London: Batsford.

Spencer, M. (1976). 'Stories are for Telling', *English in Education*, vol. 10, no. 1.

Squire, J. R. (1964). *The Responses of Adolescents while Reading Four Short Stories*. Champaign, Ill.: National Council of Teachers of English.

Stanton, M. (1980). 'Art Exists to Make the Stone Stoney', *English in Education*, vol. 14, no. 3.

Stanton, M. (1982). 'Language and Power in the Secondary English Classroom', *English in Education*, vol. 16, no. 2.

Steedman, C. (1982). *The Tidy House*. London: Virago.

Steiner, G. (1971). *In Bluebeard's Castle*. London: Faber and Faber.

Stibbs, A. (1980a). 'For Realism in Children's Fiction', *Use of English*, vol. 32, no. 1.

Stibbs, A. (1980b). 'Honour Be Blowed', *English in Education*, vol. 14, no. 3.

Stierer, B. (1983). 'A Researcher Reading Teachers' Reading Children Reading' in M. Meek (ed.), *Opening Moves*, Bedford Way Paper no. 17. London: University of London Institute of Education, pp. 56–71.

Storr, A. (1969). 'The Child and the Book' in S. Egoff, E. T. Stubbs and L. F. Ashley (eds), *Only Connect*. Oxford: Oxford University Press, pp. 91–6.

Street, B. (1983). 'Theory and Practice in Literacy Teaching in the U.K.', *Journal of Literature Teaching Politics*, no. 2, pp. 16–33.

Stubbs, M. and Delamont, S. (1976). *Explorations in Classroom Observation*. London: Wiley.

Sweetman, J. (1987a). 'Examining Literature through the Creative Response', *English in Education*, vol. 21, no. 1.

Sweetman, J. (1987b). 'Dirty Stories', *Times Educational Supplement*, 30 October, p. 40.

Tabbert, R. (1979). 'The Impact of Children's Books, Cases and Concepts', *Children's Literature in Education*, vol. 10, nos 2–3.

Tarleton, R. (1983). 'Children's Thinking and Poetry', *English in Education*, vol. 17, no. 3.

Thomson, J. (1979). 'Response to Reading: The Process as Described by one Fourteen Year Old', *English in Education*, vol. 13, no. 3.

Thomson, J. (1987). *Understanding Teenagers' Reading*. New York: Nichols Pub. Co.

Todorov, T. (1973). *The Fantastic*. New York: Cornell University Press.

Todorov, T. (1977). *The Poetics of Prose*. New York: Cornell University Press.

Tolkien, J. R. R. (1964). *Tree and Leaf*. London: George Allen and Unwin.

Torbe, M. (1974). 'Modes of Response: Some Interactions Between Reader and Literature', *English in Education*, vol. 8, no. 2.

Torbe, M. (1976). 'What Reading does to Readers', *English in Education*, vol. 10, no. 3.

Torbe, M. and Medway, P. (1981). *The Climate for Learning*, Core Book 1 of *Language, Teaching and Learning*. London: Ward Lock.

Townsend, J. R. (1974). *Written for Children*. Harmondsworth: Kestrel.

Townsend, J. R. (1980). 'Standards of Criticism for Children's Literature' in N. Chambers (ed.), *The Signal Approach to Children's Books*. Harmondsworth: Kestrel, pp. 193–207.

Travers, P. L. (1969). 'Only Connect' in S. Egoff, E. T. Stubbs and L. F. Ashley (eds), *Only Connect*. Oxford: Oxford University Press, pp. 183–206.

Trease, G. (1964). *Tales Out of School*. London: Heinemann.

Trotsky, L. (1974). *Class and Art*. London: New Park Publications.

Truffaut, F. (1978). *Hitchcock*. St Albans: Paladin.

Tucker, N. (1972). 'How Children Respond to Fiction', *Children's Literature in Education*, 9.

Tucker, N. (1975). 'The Blyton Enigma', *Children's Literature in Education*, 19.

Tucker, N. (1980). 'Can We Ever Know the Reader's Response' in M. Benton (ed.), *Approaches to Research on Children's Literature*. Southampton: University of Southampton, Department of Education, pp. 1–132.

Tucker, N. (1981). *The Child and the Book*. Cambridge: Cambridge University Press.
Tucker, N. (1982). 'Animal Magic', *Times Educational Supplement*, 18 February.
Tucker, N. (1984). 'Dr. Bettleheim and Enchantment', *Signal*, 43.
Wade, B. (n.d.). *Story at Home and School*. Educational Review, Occasional Publication no. 10. Birmingham: University of Birmingham.
Wade, B. (1982). 'That's Not A Book', *Children's Literature in Education*, vol. 13, no. 1.
Wade, B. (1984). 'A Literature Losing Touch', *Times Educational Supplement*, 4 May.
Walker, C. (1974). *Reading Development and Extension*. London: Ward Lock.
Walker, L. (1979). 'Models of Literature in the Secondary School', *Language for Learning*, vol. 1, no. 3.
Walkerdine, V. (1981). 'Sex, Power and Pedagogy', *Screen Education*, no. 1, Spring, pp. 14–24.
Walsh, J. P. (1975). 'Seeing Green' in E. Blishen (ed.), *The Thorny Paradise*. Harmondsworth: Kestrel, pp. 58–61.
Walsh, J. P. (1983). 'The Writers in the Writer', *Signal*, 40.
Walter, C. (1983). 'The Practice of Teaching Children Poetry in Schools: Form or Formula' in M. Meek (ed.), *Opening Moves*. London: University of London Institute of Education, pp. 56–71.
Waterland, L. (1985). *Read With Me. An Apprenticeship Approach to Reading*. Stroud: Thimble Press.
Warlow, A. (1972). *Associateship Report*. London: University of London Institute of Education.
Wells, G. (1976). 'Comprehension: What It Means to Understand', *English in Education*, vol. 10, no. 2.
Wells, G. (ed.) (1981). *Learning through Interaction*. Cambridge: Cambridge University Press.
Wells, G. (1986). *The Meaning Makers*. London: Hodder and Stoughton.
Welsh, C. (1958). 'Dear Little Noddy', *Encounter*, vol. 10, no. 1.
Westal, R. (1979). 'How Real Do You Want Your Realism', *Signal*, 28.
White, A. (1983). 'The Dismal Sacred Word, Academic Language and the Social Reproduction of Seriousness', *Journal of Literature Teaching Politics*, no. 2, pp. 4–15.
White, D. (1954). *Books before Five*. Oxford: Oxford University Press.
Whitehead, F. (1956). 'The Attitude of Grammar School Pupils to Novels Commonly Read in School', *British Journal of Educational Psychology*, vol. 26, pp. 104–11.
Whitehead, F., Capey, A. C., Maddren, W. and Wellings, A. (eds) (1977). *Children and Their Books*. London: Macmillan.
Whitehead, M. (1980). 'Once Upon A Time', *English in Education*, vol. 14, no. 1.
Whitehead, M. (1983). 'Proto-narrative Moves in Early Conversations between Infants and Caregivers' in M. Meek (ed.), *Opening Moves*. London: University of London Institute of Education, pp. 44–55.
Widdowson, H. G. (1975). *Stylistics and the Teaching of Literature*. London: Longman.
Wigglesworth, C. and Daniel, S. (1973). 'Children as Readers', *Dialogue*, 15.
Wiley, G. (1977). 'Teaching a Short Story', *English in Education*, vol. 11, no. 3.
Williams, G. (1985). 'Texts and Training: Some Notes on the Metaphor of Reading as a Military Operation', *Signal*, 48, pp. 182–8.
Williams, J. (1970). 'Children's Books and the Humanities', *Signal*, 1.
Willis, P. (1977). *Learning to Labour*. Farnborough: Gower.

Wilson A., Cockroft, R. and Urch, C. (1981). *Fiction as a Starting Point for Learning*, 3 booklets. Leeds: Bretton Hall.

Wilson A. (1983). *Magical Thought in Creative Writing*. Stroud: Thimble Press.

Wilson, J. (1982). 'Choosing Information Books', *Signal*, 39.

Winnicott, D. W. (1971). *Playing and Reality*. Harmondsworth: Penguin.

Wolff, J. (1983). *Aesthetics and the Sociology of Art*. London: George Allen and Unwin.

Wollen, P. (1969). *Signs and Meaning in the Cinema*. London: Secker and Warburg.

Wood, R. (1968). *Howard Hawks*. London: Secker and Warburg.

Worpole, K. (1976). 'The Gates: Writing Within the Community' in G. Fox, G. Hammond, T. Jones, F. Smith and K. Sterk (eds), *Writers, Critics and Children*. London: Heinemann, pp. 228–41.

Worpole, K. (1984). *Reading by Numbers: Contemporary Publishing and Popular Fiction*. London: Comedia.

Worsdale, M. (1982). 'Literature in the Fourth and Fifth Year of the Secondary School', *English in Education*, vol. 16, no. 1.

Wright, P. (1980). 'Five Run Away Together – Should We Let Them Back?', *English in Education*, vol. 14, no. 1.

Writers and Readers Publishing Cooperative (1979). *Racism and Sexism in Children's Books*. London: Writers and Readers.

Yates, J. (1983). 'Cannibalism is Taboo', *Times Educational Supplement*, 3 June.

Yates, J. (1984). 'Controversial Teenage Fiction', *The School Librarian*, vol. 32, no. 3.

Yorke, J. M. (1977). 'An Examination of Teachers' Objectives in Teaching Literature to the 9–13 Age Group', unpublished Ph.D. thesis. Sheffield: Sheffield University.

Yorke, M. (1979). 'Purely for Pleasure', *English in Education*, vol. 13, no. 1.

Young, M. F. D. (ed.) (1971). *Knowledge and Control*. London. Collier-Macmillan.

Zanger, J. (1977). 'Goblins, Morlocks and Weasels: Classic Fantasy and the Industrial Revolution', *Children's Literature in Education*, vol. 8, no. 4.

Zimet, S. G. (1976). *Print and Prejudice*. Sevenoaks: Hodder and Stoughton.

Zipes, J. (1979). *Breaking the Magic Spell. Radical Theories of Folk and Fairy Tales*. London: Heinemann.

Zipes, J. (1983). *Fairy Tales and the Art of Subversion*. London: Heinemann.

Index